Literary Autobiography and Arab National Struggles

Tahia Abdel Nasser

EDINBURGH
University Press

For my grandfather,
Gamal Abdel Nasser,
and my father,
Khaled Gamal Abdel Nasser

Edinburgh University Press is one of the leading university presses in the UK. We publish academic books and journals in our selected subject areas across the humanities and social sciences, combining cutting-edge scholarship with high editorial and production values to produce academic works of lasting importance. For more information visit our website: edinburghuniversitypress.com

Edinburgh University Press Ltd
The Tun – Holyrood Road
12 (2f) Jackson's Entry
Edinburgh EH8 8PJ

First published in hardback by Edinburgh University Press 2017

Typeset in 11/15 Adobe Garamond by
Servis Filmsetting Ltd, Stockport, Cheshire,
and printed and bound in Great Britain by
CPI Group (UK) Ltd, Croydon CR0 4YY

A CIP record for this book is available from the British Library

ISBN 978 1 4744 2022 8 (hardback)
ISBN 978 1 4744 4409 5 (paperback)
ISBN 978 1 4744 2023 5 (webready PDF)
ISBN 978 1 4744 2024 2 (epub)

Literary Autobiography and Arab National Struggles

Edinburgh Studies in Modern Arabic Literature
Series Editor: Rasheed El-Enany

Writing Beirut: Mappings of the City in the Modern Arabic Novel
Samira Aghacy

Autobiographical Identities in Contemporary Arab Literature
Valerie Anishchenkova

The Iraqi Novel: Key Writers, Key Texts
Fabio Caiani and Catherine Cobham

Sufism in the Contemporary Arabic Novel
Ziad Elmarsafy

Gender, Nation, and the Arabic Novel: Egypt 1892–2008
Hoda Elsadda

The Unmaking of the Arab Intellectual: Prophecy, Exile and the Nation
Zeina G. Halabi

Post-War Anglophone Lebanese Fiction: Home Matters in the Diaspora
Syrine Hout

Nasser in the Egyptian Imaginary
Omar Khalifah

War and Occupation in Iraqi Fiction
Ikram Masmoudi

Literary Autobiography and Arab National Struggles
Tahia Abdel Nasser

The Arab Nahḍah*: The Making of the Intellectual and Humanist Movement*
Abdulrazzak Patel

Sonallah Ibrahim: Rebel with a Pen
Paul Starkey

www.edinburghuniversitypress.com/series/smal

Contents

Series Editor's Foreword

The Edinburgh Studies in Modern Arabic Literature is a new and unique series that will, it is hoped, fill in a glaring gap in scholarship in the field of modern Arabic literature. Its dedication to Arabic literature in the modern period, that is, from the nineteenth century onwards, is what makes it unique among series undertaken by academic publishers in the English-speaking world. Individual books on modern Arabic literature in general or aspects of it have been and continue to be published sporadically. Series on Islamic studies and Arab/Islamic thought and civilisation are not in short supply either in the academic world, but these are far removed from the study of Arabic literature qua literature, that is, imaginative, creative literature as we understand the term when, for instance, we speak of English literature or French literature. Even series labelled 'Arabic/Middle Eastern Literature' make no period distinction, extending their purview from the sixth century to the present, and often including non-Arabic literatures of the region. This series aims to redress the situation by focusing on the Arabic literature and criticism of today, stretching its interest to the earliest beginnings of Arab modernity in the nineteenth century.

The need for such a dedicated series, and generally for the redoubling of scholarly endeavour in researching and introducing modern Arabic literature to the Western reader, has never been stronger. Among activities and events heightening public, let alone academic, interest in all things Arab, and not least Arabic literature, are the significant growth in the last decades of the translation of contemporary Arab authors from all genres, especially fiction, into English; the higher profile of Arabic literature internationally since the award of the Nobel Prize for Literature to Naguib Mahfouz in 1988; the growing number of Arab authors living in the Western diaspora and writing both in

English and Arabic; the adoption of such authors and others by mainstream, high-circulation publishers, as opposed to the academic publishers of the past; the establishment of prestigious prizes, such as the International Prize for Arabic Fiction (the Arabic Booker), run by the Man Booker Foundation, which brings huge publicity to the shortlist and winner every year, as well as translation contracts into English and other languages; and very recently the events of the Arab Spring. It is therefore part of the ambition of this series that it will increasingly address a wider reading public beyond its natural territory of students and researchers in Arabic and world literature. Nor indeed is the academic readership of the series expected to be confined to specialists in literature in the light of the growing trend for interdisciplinarity, which increasingly sees scholars crossing field boundaries in their research tools and coming up with findings that equally cross discipline borders in their appeal.

Critical examinations of autobiography, memoirs, and other forms of self-writing in Arabic literature are few and far between, leaving scholarship lagging behind a steadily growing genre in Arabic literature, not only in Arabic but also in Francophone and Anglophone literature penned by Arab writers. This series has already contributed to the redress of this imbalance with Valerie Anishchenkova's title, *Autobiographical Identities in Contemporary Arab Culture* (2014). The title in hand extends the subject further in at least two ways: by focusing the study within the context of a post-colonial, anti-imperialist approach, bringing in a multiplicity of new authors and texts, and going beyond texts written in Arabic to include also Anglophone and Francophone texts authored by Arab writers, during the colonial period and post-independence up to the twenty-first century. The scope of the book is broad, not only in the period it covers, nearly a hundred years, with a full spectrum of changing social and political conditions, but also in the geographic spread of the authors and texts investigated that extend across the Middle East and North Africa (MENA) region with its different cultures, different ethnicities, and different colonial and post-colonial experiences, and indeed the experience of Arab writers in the diaspora, too (for example, Edward Said). The breadth of coverage is further strengthened by the author not limiting herself to narrative prose, the natural medium of autobiography and memoirs, but extending her interest across genres to include poetry (for example, Mahmoud Darwish and Mourid Barghouti), especially relevant to the postcolonial framework of her approach. This strategy enhances the representative quality of the study and underscores the cross-genre uniformity of the literary response to the changing historical conditions and the socio-political scene. Particularly original too in the author's theoretical context is her movement away from the traditional Eurocentric approach that juxtaposes East and West, opting rather to place the Arab experience in the 'global South' or a 'South–South' perspective where the Arab literature is examined comparatively in relation to other national experiences of colonisation and independence.

Professor Rasheed El-Enany, Series Editor,
Emeritus Professor, University of Exeter;
Professor of Arabic and Comparative Literature,
Dean of Social Sciences and Humanities,
Doha Institute for Graduate Studies

Acknowledgments

Any scholarly study comes to fruition over years of research and exchange. Many friends and interlocutors offered fruitful comments and guidance. I am deeply grateful to Ferial Ghazoul for her generous comments and support. I am also grateful to Samia Mehrez for her support and comments. I wish to thank my supervisor, the late Malak Hashem, for her supervision and support, and Hoda Gindi for her support and interest in the project.

I am grateful to Rasheed El-Enany for his helpful comments and guidance through the stages of the completion of the book. Many thanks also to Nicola Ramsey at Edinburgh University Press for her enthusiasm and support. The anonymous reviewers offered fruitful and generous comments. I thank Rebecca Mackenzie for her advice and patience and Ellie Bush for her help with the preparation of the manuscript. I would also like to thank Ersev Ersoy and Eddie Clark who took the book through its final stages. I thank Laura Booth for her copyediting. Any errors and infelicities are my own.

I am grateful to Samah Selim for her invaluable comments on the manuscript. Many friends and colleagues kindly shared knowledge and advice: Randa Aboubakr, Reem Abou-El-Fadl, Mona Baker, Mahmoud El Lozy, Sharif Elmusa, Hoda Elsadda, AbdelAziz Ezzelarab, Nadia Gindi, Nathalie Handal, Salah D. Hassan, Yasmine Khayyat, Munira Khayyat, Hanan Kholoussy, Elias Khoury, Suha Kudsieh, Hisham Matar, Khaled Mattawa, Stephen Sheehi, Bahia Shehab, Mounira Soliman, Mona Tolba, Daniel Vitkus, Abdo Wazen, and Marina Warner. I especially want to thank Elizabeth Holt and Shaden Tageldin for comments and conversations that contributed to chapters in this book. Many thanks to Rola Khayyat who kindly granted me permission to use her beautiful artwork for the book cover.

Many writers generously shared recollections, anecdotes, and materials. I am grateful for conversations with the late Radwa Ashour, Mourid Barghouti, Jean Said Makdisi, Mariam Said, and Ahdaf Soueif. I was fortunate to meet Edward Said and Mahmoud Darwish whose memoirs are included in this book. Najla Said graciously provided me with material. Haifa Zangana and Mona Prince generously answered questions and shared important material. I am grateful for conversations and communication with Héctor Abad Faciolince and Lina Meruane whose work is the subject of another project. This book is also a testament to the rich local literary scene in Egypt that has helped shape many of the readings.

My colleagues in the Department of English and Comparative Literature at the American University in Cairo (AUC) offered me support while completing the manuscript. I thank Ferial Ghazoul, William Melaney, and Stephen Nimis. My undergraduate and graduate students in seminars in the Department of English and Comparative Literature inspired me to revisit many of these writers in new ways. I thank Randa Ali for her interest and dedication to literature. I am thankful to Wafaa Fahmy at the library of the American University in Cairo who has long offered generous assistance. An AUC pretenure leave made possible the completion of my manuscript. Faculty grants generously offered me the opportunity to share my research with scholars and colleagues at international conferences and meetings.

In the United States, I thank Asaad Al-Saleh, Hosam Aboul-Ela, Nathaniel Greenberg, Gretchen Head, Suha Kudsieh, Christopher Mickelthwaite, Kamran Rastegar, Rania Said, Ken Seigneurie, and Stephen Sheehi for opportunities to present my research at conferences.

In Berlin, while working on another project, I enjoyed the support and hospitality of friends and scholars. I would like to thank Ottmar Ette, Georges Khalil, Susanne Klengel, Elias Khoury, Alexandra Ortiz Wallner, and Friedericke Pannewicke who were generous interlocutors.

Early drafts of chapters were presented at the Modern Language Association, Columbia University in the City of New York, the University of Oxford, the University of London, Università degli Studi di Napoli 'L'Orientale', the American University in Cairo, and Cairo University. Many colleagues shared feedback on portions of the manuscript at meetings and conferences. I am grateful to the generous audiences, scholars, and interlocutors at the Modern Language Association, the American Comparative

Literature Association, Columbia University, and the European Association for Modern Arabic Literature. Early versions of some of the arguments in Chapter 3 appeared in *Journal of Arabic Literature* 45 (2014): 244–64. I am grateful for permission to reprint material here.

I am deeply grateful to my parents, Khaled Gamal Abdel Nasser and Dahlia Fahmy, who continually supported all my literary endeavours. I remember my father's love, kindness, generosity, and appreciation of literature. This book is dedicated to him with love and gratitude. My husband, Ahmed Fahmy, has long offered love, support, and encouragement. My daughter, Nadine Fahmy, was a joy throughout my work on the book. I dedicate the book to her with love.

A Note on Transliteration and Translation

I adopt the standard system of transliteration from Arabic to English used by IJMES (*International Journal of Middle East Studies*). Personal names with spellings that have become standard in English are rendered in the forms known to an Anglophone audience (for example, Gamal Abdel Nasser). The names of authors whose works have been translated into English are transliterated upon first mention, and appear thenceforth in the conventional English spellings (for example, Taha Hussein). The names of Arab authors writing in English and French are rendered in the most common and preferred spelling.

All references to Arabic memoirs and novels are to the original. I use existing translations of works that have been translated from Arabic or French to English. Parenthetical citations refer to the Arabic or French original, followed by the English translation. Unless otherwise noted, all translations are my own. A list of abbreviations for all literary works cited is included.

Abbreviations

A1, A2, A3	*al-Ayyām*
Aa	*al-Ajnabīyah*
Ab	*Aṭyāf*
AD	*Fī Arwiqat al-Dhākirah*
AF	*L'Amour, la fantasia*
BM	*al-Bāb al-Maftūḥ*
C	*Children of the New World*
DB	*Dreaming of Baghdad*
DN	*Dhākirah li-l Nisyān*
EC	*An Egyptian Childhood*
F	*Fantasia: An Algerian Cavalcade*
HT	*Ḥamlat Taftīsh: Awrāq Shakhṣīyyah*
IW	*I Was Born There, I Was Born Here*
J	*Jidārīyya*
JO	*Journal of an Ordinary Grief*
LP	*Looking for Palestine*
M	*Mural*
MF	*Memory for Forgetfulness*
N	*Notes from the Oases Prison*
NP	*Nulle part dans la maison de mon père*
OD	*The Open Door*
OP	*Out of Place*
PF	*A Passage to France*
R	*al-Riḥlah*
RR	*Ra'aytu Rāmallāh*
Ṣ	*al-Ṣarkhah*

Sc	*The Scream*
Sa	*Specters*
Sb	*Stealth*
SD	*The Stream of Days*
SP	*The Search: Personal Papers*
SR	*I Saw Ramallah*
SS	*State of Siege*
T	*al-Talaṣṣuṣ*
TR	*Tilka al-Rā'iḥa*
TS	*That Smell*
W	*Wulidtu Hunākah, Wulidtu Hunā*
Y	*Yawmiyyāt al-Ḥuzn al-'Ādī*

Introduction
Literary Solitude: Autobiography, Modernity, and Independence

> Life is not what one lived, but what one remembers and how one remembers it in order to recount it.
>
> Gabriel García Márquez, *Living to Tell the Tale*

In 1926, the Egyptian reformer Taha Hussein (Ṭāhā Ḥusayn) (1889–1973) wrote the first volume of his autobiography, *al-Ayyām* (*The Days*), in France.[1] The evocation of the journey of the young blind boy from the village to the Azhar showed very little of the effects of the controversy of the publication of his book *Fī al-Shiʿr al-Jāhilī* (*On Pre-Islamic Poetry*, 1926).[2] However, the story of his boyhood – and, over the three volumes, the narration of his rise from poverty to the pinnacle of the Egyptian literary community – was written in response to the controversy. The story of the completion of his three-volume autobiography from 1926 to 1967– two volumes are separated by another controversy – is a chronicle of the journey of the Egyptian reformer. Years later, when he was discharged from his post at the modern Egyptian University (renamed Fu'ad I and now Cairo University) in 1932 for his political writings (Cachia 2012), he wrote the second volume *The Stream of Days: A Student at the Azhar* (1939). The history of his autobiographical project enacts the deep public involvement and solitude of the writer.

In the second half of the twentieth century, Arab autobiography flourished in different forms, including memoirs, the autobiographical novel, journals, diaries, and poetry. With roots in medieval Arabic chronicles, treatises, and travelogues, the nineteenth-century novel, and the foundational autobiography by Taha Hussein, Arab writers developed new autobiographical forms.[3] At the same time, they created new conceptions of subjectivity, the role of the writer, and political agency in response to colonialism, nationalism, and independence. The colonial encounter produced new Anglophone and Francophone autobiography that further enriched Arab cultural production and simultaneously contributed to global literary networks. In many ways, the trajectories of writers in the twentieth century opened up the form to a constellation of local and global influences. From 1926, autobiographical writing evoked the experiences of the solitary writer, the embattled critic, the revolutionary, the prisoner, the exile, and the émigré.

Arab autobiography in the mid-twentieth century responded to the enduring effects of colonialism, national movements, and independence. Important political junctures in the Arab world such as the founding of Israel in 1948, the Arab–Israeli 1967 War (Six-Day War), the Lebanese civil war (1975–90), the 1982 Israeli invasion of Lebanon, and the 2003 US invasion of Iraq had a profound effect on the production and directions of the genre. For Arab writers, whose formation and careers spanned these major historical moments, their autobiographical production is fraught with the representation of subjectivity vis-à-vis anticolonial and anti-imperialist movements. They explored the tension between the communal and the individual in a form that was broadly conceived as the writer's expression of subjectivity within collective struggles in the Arab world.

The rise of Arabic autobiography dovetailed the private and the public, the individual and the national. Jean Franco observes that memoirs increasingly and directly address 'unity, association, community, bonding' and 'solitude, fragmentation, entropy' (Franco 2002: 78). In her reading of Pablo Neruda's poetry and memoirs, she draws attention to autobiographical strands in his early poems 'interwoven with accounts of solitude' (79). Neruda's *Confieso que he vivido: Memorias* (*Memoirs*, 1974) is framed with an epigraph: 'In these memoirs or recollections there are gaps here and there, and sometimes they are also forgetful, because life is like that . . . Many of the things I remember have blurred as I recalled them, they have crumbled to dust, like irreparably shattered glass' (Neruda 2001). Franco further notes that Neruda (1904–73) produced an oblique memoir, with 'episodes that needed explanation yet could not be fully revealed' and that the events he recounts are more of 'publicly acceptable material' and 'represent the public and authorized narrative that reveal little that is not already known' (2002: 82–3). While Neruda offers a more public story, Gabriel García Márquez (1927–2014) recounts a comparatively solitary life in his memoir. In *Vivir para contarla* (*Living to Tell the Tale*), his 2002 memoir, García Márquez recounts his commitment to a literary life in his youth, telling his story the way he remembers his literary vocation. He writes in the epigraph: '*Life is not what one lived, but what one remembers and how one remembers it in order to recount it*' (García Márquez 2003; italics in original). García Márquez revisits the explosive world of 'La Violencia' in Colombia during the late 1940s and 1950s, embedding events that are 'erased from historical memory' (283) such as the Banana Massacre in his story.[4] In chronicling his literary life, he looks at national and continental history, but recounts the story of the youthful solitary writer.

The stature of writers and, in the words of Franco, the status of the writer as 'hero' (2002: 3) is central to the production of autobiography. Franco alludes to a Latin American culture where 'writers pronounced on politics, revolution, and literature' (5). Edward Said observes that the veneration of writers in all cultures endows them with a separate, special role. Importantly, Said notes 'the special symbolic role of writers' as defenders or chroniclers of the communal struggles of 'emblematized regions' (2004: 127). As Franco writes, in Latin America poets and novelists inspired how 'literature was read, history understood, and language valued', 'created canons', and evaluated contemporary culture (2002: 4). Arab writers chronicled life and experience within vast networks of cultural–historical relations; they explicitly or obliquely revisited the national landscape that shaped them. These writers influenced national culture and crossed cultural borders: Taha Hussein through his reforms for a modern, secular nation-state and his influence by European culture; Edward Said (1935–2003) through his foundation of postcolonial studies in the US; and Assia Djebar (1936–2015) through her Francophone North African literature in France.

The purpose of this book is to explore the autobiographical production of revolutionary Arab writers with prominent roles in national cultures and anticolonial movements and new writers as well as the reinvention of Arab autobiography through encounters with other cultures and languages. At the same time, it examines Anglophone, Francophone, and Arabic autobiography not only as the appropriation of a Western form but also as a form that draws on indigenous sources and responds to historical moments such as colonialism, national movements, and independence. The book explores Arab autobiography, tracing its adaptation of local forms, Western canon, and affiliations with other literatures of the global South.

Autobiography enabled Arab writers to further explore the writer's role in national culture in the twentieth-century contexts of colonialism, dispossession, and postcolonialism and to depart from the forms prevailing in Western and premodern Arabic literature. The rise of autobiography is connected to modernity, national movements, and independence and its contemporary reworkings show these complex intertwinings in a new light. By focusing on anticolonial movements and the development of literary forms such as autobiography, this book examines the literary imagination of the cultural, national, and transnational roles of Arab writers during colonialism and independence.

Autobiography developed and endured as a literary form throughout the twentieth century. Novelists, poets, and critics – nationalist, Western-educated, leftist, and secular – produced Arabic, Anglophone, and Francophone autobiography in colonial, revolutionary, and postcolonial cultures. Autobiography has bridged genres and cultures from Arab medieval treatises to European autobiography to Neruda's *Memorial de Isla Negra* (*Isla Negra: A Notebook*, 1964), a collection of autobiographical poems. In modern Arab culture, the form has persisted and evolved from the autobiography of Taha Hussein to Assia Djebar's Francophone autobiographical novels and Mahmoud Darwish's prose memoirs.

Throughout the twentieth century, Arab writers produced autobiography during colonialism, revolution, and independence. Autobiography, a form deeply influenced by these contexts, traced developments in the Arab world from colonialism to independence through the national landscapes of the writer's life. Moreover, the cultural role and transnational encounters of the writers further infused the form. In Egypt and Lebanon, writers such as Taha Hussein and Mikhail Nu'aymah (Mikhaīl Nu'aymah) (1889–1988) explored the encounter with the West throughout the colonial period. Arab writers revisited national movements that played an important role in their literary formation.

The importance of these Arab memoirs and autobiographical works rests in the transnational status of some of these writers. Some of these writers enjoyed pre-eminence on account of the translation of their autobiographical works or their Anglophone and Francophone writing. Edward Said inaugurated the field of postcolonial studies, which reformulated the study of comparative literature, and Assia Djebar was elected to the Académie Française. *Literary Autobiography and Arab National Struggles* explores a growing body of autobiographical literature that has rethought the relationship of writers to national cultures and languages, adapted the form, and explored colonialism.

A study of twentieth- and twenty-first century Arab autobiography helps illuminate the role of the writer in the national and literary imagination. By rethinking the form within colonial encounters and national movements, Arab writers rethought the role of the writer in national culture. While reading autobiography in particular contexts embeds it in broader cultural, literary, and political landscapes, the form also stages the desire to write a life story that can be appreciated for its particularity. Autobiographical writing produced within national movements and postcolonial situations highlights the role of national culture and colonial encounters. In this context, Arab writers reworked the form to challenge autobiographical conventions and offer more indigenous reworkings of the genre in response to local historical and cultural change.

There is no book-length study in any language that has employed a comparative framework across three languages to examine Arab autobiography over the last half-century. Contemporary Arab memoirs written in anticolonial and anti-imperialist movements have yet to be more fully explored. *Literary Autobiography and Arab National Struggles* examines Arab autobiography in Arabic, English, and French, primarily from the second half of the twentieth century to the twenty-first century. It examines different aspects of the contemporary autobiography as it has evolved in the Arab world for more than half a century with a focus on more recent autobiographical production. By focusing on autobiography from Egypt, Algeria, Iraq, and Palestine, in Arabic, English, and French, the book examines the effects of anticolonial movements on autobiographical production. In this way, it explores the rise of contemporary Arab autobiography and the role of the Arab writer in national cultures and global networks, extending the study to writers who have been influential not only in Arab culture but also in Anglophone and Francophone transnational literary circuits.

The autobiographical works considered here are landmarks in contemporary Arab autobiography that problematise conventional autobiographical forms. Many of the writers have enjoyed a transnational status or crossed cultural borders through translation. In these autobiographical works, the writers work through introspection at important historical junctures. The study is far from exhaustive. Instead, it offers an examination of prominent and new writers, canonical and contemporary memoirs, focusing on the effects of revolutionary movements, the writer's cultural status, and encounters with other cultures.

The trajectories of *Literary Autobiography and Arab National Struggles* cross national, cultural, and linguistic borders. They encompass the rural village, the Azhar seminary, the prison cell, the mountains of the Algerian rebels, the Parisian apartment, the besieged apartment in Beirut, the Palestinian ancestral village, colonial Cairo, New York, the hospital room, and the square.

Critics have focused on the difference between autobiography (*sīra dhātīyya*), a form that focuses on the development of the author's personality, and memoir (*mudhakkirāt*), written at a late moment in the author's life.[5] Memoirs chronicle the context more explicitly than autobiography and examine the role of the writer in the events.[6] Other Arabic terms have different associations such as '*tarjama*' (literally, 'translation'), '*yawmiyyāt*' ('diary') (Rooke 1997: 66), and '*sīra*' (biography of the prophet Muhammad or *sīra nabawiyya*). The word 'autobiography' encompasses broadly the autobiographical production of writers from the Arab world. For works in which the authors describe the genre, I distinguish between memoir and autobiography. Moreover, I examine paratexts and the ways in which works focus on the development of the author's life or external events.[7] Although the terms 'autobiography' and 'Arab' do not accurately capture the complexity of cultures and ethnicities in the works under consideration here because not all the works are 'autobiography' and not all the writers are Arab (Assia Djebar is Amazigh and Haifa Zangana is Kurdish), I employ the term 'Arab' to encompass writers from the Arab world and examine these complex belongings in each chapter. Autobiography spans memoirs, autobiographical novels, journals, notebooks, and diaries whose poetics and aesthetics each chapter examines. The autobiographical works examined here were produced between the early twentieth century and the twenty-first and encompass a series of stages of colonisation and neocolonialism.

Autobiography and the Modern Nation

Arab writers promoted literary modernity in the nineteenth century by creating new literary forms. It was in the wake of the cultural movement of the Nahda (Renaissance), the Arab literary revival in the nineteenth and twentieth centuries, with such luminaries as Taha Hussein, that autobiography became a feature of modernity. Like the novel, autobiography served to explore the central topoi of tradition and modernity and East and West.[8]

The history of the rise of autobiography in the West has been the subject of much scholarly attention.[9] Moreover, critics have amply noted that the prevalence of autobiography in Arabic literature is not a modern phenomenon.[10] Modern Arab autobiography has drawn on Arab premodern forms such as biography (*sīra*), travelogues (*riḥla*), religious tracts (Rooke 1997: 75–83; Anishchenkova 2014: 17), anecdotes (*akhbār*), chronicles, travelogues, and biographical dictionaries (Ostle 1998: 19). Arab writers who elaborated the form in the early and mid-twentieth century were most likely aware of a long autobiographical tradition, especially the medieval origins of the genre in Arabic. These writers would have perhaps known such classics as the spiritual and secular autobiographies of al-Ghazālī and Usāma b. Munqidh, including the travelogues of Ibn Faḍlān on the lands of Rūs and the nomadic Turks, Andalusian traveller Ibn Jubayr (540/1145–614/1217), who writes about the East, and Jerusalemite geographer al-Mukaddasī who surveys both the extreme West and the extreme East of the Islamic world.[11]

Taha Hussein is widely acknowledged as the 'father of modern Arabic autobiography'.[12] The appearance of Taha Hussein's autobiography was central to the rise of modern Arabic autobiography, not only in the way in which it produced a generation of authors who fused the genre with the conventions of the European novel (Reynolds 2001: 10), but also because of its foundation of a form that staged the encounters between European colonialism and Arab nationalism.[13] Although two volumes (1929 and 1939) are set during colonial rule, volume III (serialised in 1955 and published in 1967) was written and published after independence. Early in *The Days*, the reformer who chronicles his passage from the Egyptian village to the Sorbonne introduces the narrative of the Western-educated Arab intellectual bridging cultures, epochs, and worlds.

In the second half of the twentieth century, Arab writers adapted an inherently colonial genre to re-envision subjectivity in colonial and postcolonial worlds.[14] The moment of the burgeoning of the autobiographical form or *sīra dhātiyya* was also a context of British and French imperial domination in the Arab world. Modern Arab autobiography was concerned with the formation of modern nation-states and national history (Enderwitz 1998: 81). In this context, writers reworked existing literary forms and rethought the genre from the perspective of the colonised. Arab writers reworked a tradition of autobiographical production – *sīra*, chronicle, travelogue, and lyric poetry – and blurred the borders of autobiography and fiction, and problematised notions of subjectivity, creating hybrid literary genres and inventing new autobiographical forms. They further revitalised the form by elaborating postcolonial subjectivity.

As a form that flourished in anticolonial movements and postcolonial cultures, autobiography was typically read as a communal form within which Arab writers framed the story of the individual at particular national and cultural moments. Postcolonial critics have focused on the enduring importance of the nation as a category in the cultural production of former colonies. Benedict Anderson argues that the nation acquired its form through print culture.[15] Partha Chatterjee refutes the notion of the West supplying the forms for anticolonial nationalism to the postcolonial world and that national culture is a site of sovereignty from colonialism.[16] The formation of the modern nation was central to Arab autobiographical production in the twentieth century. In many ways, anticolonial nationalisms deeply influenced Arab autobiography produced at important moments in national history. Writers involved in national movements drew on the rise of the modern nation in autobiographical writing and explored subjectivity in anticolonial movements. During colonialism and the prevalence of concerns with modernity, autobiography flourished on the Arab literary scene. It adapted to the imperatives of the context in which it was produced, particularly national movements and critical moments in the Arab world such as the loss of Palestine in 1948. While autobiography recounted the writer's life, it revisited important historical moments and framed the history of the writer within anticolonial and anti-imperialist struggles.[17]

Since the 1980s, writers have produced different autobiographical forms that foreground the solitude of the writer. Palestinian writer Fadwa Tuqan (Fadwa Ṭūqān) explores the effects of a patriarchal culture on her formation, especially her journey to become a poet in *Riḥlah Jabalīyah, Riḥlah Ṣaʻbah* (*Mountainous Journey, Difficult Journey*) (translated as *A Mountainous Journey: An Autobiography*), her 1985 autobiography. Palestinian-Iraqi writer Jabra Ibrahim Jabra (Jabrā Ibrahīm Jabrā) wrote two memoirs on his youth in British Mandate Palestine and his life in post-World War II Iraq: *al-Biʼr al-Ūlā: Fuṣūl min Sīra Dhātiyya* (*The First Well: A Bethlehem Boyhood*, 1987) and *Shāriʻ al-Amīrāt: Fuṣūl min Sīra Dhātiyya* (*Princesses' Street: Baghdad Memories*, 1994). Egyptian writer Latifa al-Zayyat (Latīfa al-Zayyāt) (1923–96) began her memoir in the women's prison. Palestinian poet Mahmoud Darwish (Mahmūd Darwīsh) (1941–2008) wrote *Dhākirah li-l Nisyān* (*Memory for Forgetfulness*, 1986), a prose memoir about the 1982 Israeli invasion of Lebanon, in exile in France.

The writer's solitude is connected in complex ways to the narrative of the modern nation. In modern Arab autobiography, subjectivity and solitude are explored in ways that focus on the relationship of the writers to the anticolonial and anti-imperialist movements in which they were involved. The word 'solitude' evokes seclusion, isolation, separation, or exclusion.[18] The writers examined here place a greater premium on solitude by focusing on the solitary writer or self-imposed solitude. While towering writers were prominent in national culture and the public sphere, they focused on solitude at moments of deep public involvement in their autobiographical works. Taha Hussein, Sonallah Ibrahim (Ṣunʻ Allāh Ibrahīm), Latifa al-Zayyat, Assia Djebar, Mahmoud Darwish, Mourid Barghouti (Murīd Barghūtī), Edward Said, Haifa Zangana (Haifāʼ Zangana), and Radwa Ashour (Raḍwā ʻAshūr) all use the word 'solitude' or the state in complex ways as a form of isolation and freedom that does not preclude political commitment.

The book offers an examination of the development of Arab autobiography through anticolonial nationalism and postcolonialism. Colonialism, culture, and language provide important frameworks for the examination and comparison of Arab autobiography in Arabic, English, and French over the last half-century. These frameworks trace the influence of anticolonial movements on the development of the genre from modernity to independence by examining the role of the writers and the forms of solitude in which they wrote, re-reading Arab autobiography through a state of revolutionary solitude, the contemplation of commitment, and independence from the state.

The rise of autobiography in postcolonial cultures responded to the effects of colonialism and subverted colonial domination throughout the twentieth century. Arab autobiography produced in colonial and postcolonial cultures is characterised by cultural and historical particularity. Reworkings of the genre show networks of affiliations with other literatures, the legacy of colonialism, the centrality of nationalism, and the autonomy of the writer.

Postcolonial Autobiography

Literary Autobiography and Arab National Struggles explores Anglophone, Francophone, and Arabic autobiographical production by influential Arab writers whose isolation or self-imposed solitude followed a period of deep involvement in national movements at major historical moments. By examining contemporary autobiographical production through anticolonial nationalism and independence, it looks at ways in which the writers reexamine conceptions of subjectivity and the role of the writer from national movements in the twentieth and the twenty-first centuries, focusing on the particularity of the genre written in different languages but pertaining to one overarching Arab culture. The book examines canonical and new Arab memoirs that have not been the subject of critical attention, tracing the range of autobiographical forms produced over the last half-century during national movements and independence.

The study explores the ways in which the genre offers new perspectives on subjectivity from the second half of the twentieth century. It serves to examine the influence of anticolonial movements on the production of contemporary Arab autobiography, and to make a contribution to comparative scholarship by examining Arab adaptations of the genre, as well as the influences of a long Arab tradition and other networks of the global South. It problematises assumptions that Arab writers produced what critics have described as 'collective autobiography' and explores ways in which Arab autobiography has offered uniquely different readings of the legacy of colonialism and postcolonial nation-states. Focusing on autobiography from Egypt, Algeria, Palestine, and Iraq, it examines reworkings of the genre by exploring the effects of anticolonial movements on autobiographical production and the role of the Arab writer in national cultures and global networks.

Postcolonial literatures developed along with national movements and apart from the 'imperial center' (Ashcroft el al 1989: 4). In the postindependence period, writers continued to challenge colonialism through cultural production (Ashcroft et al. 1989: 6). Postcolonial autobiography created new representations of subjectivity by examining the role of the writer vis-à-vis anticolonial movements and, in postcolonial cultures, adopted languages and local sources to overturn Western conventions of the form.

The work of Aimé Césaire, Frantz Fanon, Albert Memmi, and Edward Said, which renewed the study of the cultural production of the formerly colonised, has opened up the study of autobiographical production during anticolonial nationalism and independence.[19] The resurgence of autobiography in the era of decolonisation during the 1950s and 1960s offered responses to Western colonialism and forms of self-representation centred on the formation of the writer in colonial worlds. Arab writers produced forms of autobiography that challenged imperial cultural formations by chronicling the writers' self-formation and public involvement in independence struggles. As Aijaz Ahmad observes of cultural nationalism, writing within a culture or tradition of 'the Third World' is 'itself an act of anti-imperialist resistance' (1987: 9). Postcolonial autobiography draws on local traditions and hybridises colonial and indigenous languages (Moore-Gilbert 2009: xxiii). Further, Arab autobiography shares common features with autobiographical production in other postcolonial literatures such as African and Latin American autobiography.

Arab autobiography in the postindependence period revisited colonial experience and explored stages of the independent nation through its effects on the writer: for instance, Latifa al-Zayyat's *Ḥamlat Taftīsh: Awrāq Shakhṣiyyah* (*The Search: Personal Papers*, 1992), Sonallah Ibrahim's *al-Talaṣṣuṣ* (*Stealth*, 2007), and Radwa Ashour's *Aṭyāf* (*Specters*, 1999) revisit the life of the writer in major historical moments in the Arab world such as anticolonial struggles, the Palestine War, and postindependence periods.

While postcolonial autobiography dealt with the effects of colonialism in the Arab world and offered forms of self-representation to challenge colonial and Orientalist misrepresentations, Palestinian memoirs focused on the writer's relationship to Palestine. These memoirs dealt with the legacy of the *Nakba* (catastrophe), the Israeli occupation, and the segregation enforced on the Palestinian population since 1948. Writers revisited their youth in British Mandate Palestine or the effects of the loss of Palestine in 1948 and the 1967 War in memoirs such as Jabra's *The First Well,* Tuqan's *A Mountainous Journey: An Autobiography,* Darwish's *Memory for Forgetfulness* and *Jidārīyya* (*Mural,* 1999), and Mourid Barghouti's *Ra'aytu Rāmallah* (*I Saw Ramallah,* 1997) and *Wulidtu Hunākah, Wulidtu Hunā* (*I Was Born There, I Was Born Here,* 2009).[20] By chronicling a history of dispossession in autobiography, Arab writers re-envision subjectivity through memory and rework the form.

Postcolonial autobiography extends beyond monolingualism and poses the themes of language and translation. Francophone and Anglophone autobiography explores notions of hybridity, cultural translation, and postcoloniality. As Ashcroft et al. note, the 'appropriation of language' appeared as one of the most important features of postcolonial literatures (1989: 6). The contest between languages in the autobiographical production of the formerly colonised explores a history of colonial conquest. Kilito notes the hierarchy of languages: 'Bilingualism does not evoke an image of two gladiators advancing upon each other armed with nets and tridents; rather, it suggests that one of the two combatants is already sprawled in the dust awaiting the fatal blow' (2008: 108). Kilito outlines a contest between languages, a definition of bilingualism through violence (Hassan 2008: xvii).[21] Francophone and Anglophone autobiography contravenes the conventions of the genre by infusing it with the cultures and languages of the formerly colonised. Cultural hybridity enabled writers to adapt the genre in response to colonialism and employ the ensuing metaphors of conquest and hybridisation to represent postcolonial subjectivity.

Francophone and Anglophone autobiography opened up ways for the writer's story to migrate between languages and in turn to be enriched by this migration. Education, exchange, exile, migration, and translation inform much of the autobiographical production of the twentieth century. Taha Hussein learned French, Latin, and Greek and earned a doctorate from France; Sonallah Ibrahim avidly read Arabic translations of Hemingway and

Jorge Amado in prison and later went on cultural exchanges in Berlin and Moscow; Assia Djebar attended the French Lycée in Blida and then L'Ecole Supérieure in Sévres; and Darwish moved between the Arab world, Moscow, and Paris. Language informed the autobiographical production of writers who came into contact with other languages: French for Taha Hussein and Assia Djebar; English for Edward Said; Hebrew for Darwish;[22] and Kurdish for Haifa Zangana.

Francophone autobiography in the Maghreb offers a rich autobiographical corpus that developed in response to French colonial rule and North African national movements. Francophone autobiography adopted local forms drawn from Arab and Amazigh culture, such as oral testimony, song, rituals, and travelogues. Francophone literature in the Maghreb created a hybridised language to challenge colonial hegemony. Thus, writers from the Maghreb reworked the language of the former coloniser to serve anticolonial ends, creating a 'hybrid language' or 'linguistic métissage' (Lionnet 1995: 13). The appropriation of the French language produced heteroglossia and hybridity in literature. Lionnet's concept of *métissage* in the work of multilingual writers, 'the layerings or stratifications of diverse language systems' (1989: 21), focuses on multiplicity, or the interweaving of languages, and cultural hybridity. Francophone autobiography played a central role in the representation of the subjectivity of the colonised, such as Assia Djebar's *L'Amour, la fantasia (Fantasia: An Algerian Cavalcade*, 1985) and *Nulle part dans la maison de mon père* (*Nowhere in My Father's House*, 2007); Abdelkebir Khatibi's *La Mémoire tatouée: autobiographie d'un décolonisé* (*Tattooed Memory: Autobiography of a Decolonized Man*, 1971) and *Amour bilingue* (*Love in Two Languages*, 1983); and the Morrocon writer Mohamed Choukri's *For Bread Alone* (1973) (*Le Pain nu*, 1980; *al-Khubz al-Ḥāfi*, 1982). Critics have noted that African and Caribbean Francophone autobiography poses the problem of writing for a local audience or the French literary market with the latter offering a much broader readership (Sankara 2011: 7).

By comparison, the case of Anglophone autobiography in the Arab world is limited but has witnessed a steady rise, especially in memoirs in the twenty-first century. Anglophone Arab memoirs include Edward Said's *Out of Place* (1999b); two volumes by Jean Said Makdisi, *Beirut Fragments: A War Memoir* (1990) and *Teta, Mother, and Me: An Arab Woman's Memoir* (2005);

Dreams of Trespass: Tales of a Harem Girlhood (1995) by the Moroccan Fatima Mernissi; and, more recently, a collection of Anglophone Palestinian memoirs that has grown out of the occupation of Palestine by writers such as Palestinian lawyer Raja Shehadeh.[23]

Contemporary Arab autobiography, drawing on a rich heritage, local forms, and European autobiography, reworked the conventions of autobiography in a plethora of forms – autobiographical novel, memoir, journals, and epic. Mohamed Makhzangi (Muḥammad Makhzanjī) revised conventional autobiographical forms in *Laḥaẓāt Gharaq Jazīrat al-Ḥūt* (*Memories of a Meltdown: An Egyptian Between Moscow and Chernobyl*), his 1997 memoir, or what he calls 'anti-memoir'.[24] Makhzangi relates the aftermath of the nuclear explosion of the Chernobyl plant in the Ukraine in 1986 through the realism of reportage interwoven with fiction. He traces the dissolution of his dreams of Moscow while studying medicine in Kiev, his grief distilled in moments in the irradiated city. Twenty-first century memoirs offer new forms and explore the role of autobiographical production in revolutionary movements: Mona Prince's *Ismī Thawra* (*Revolution Is My Name: An Egyptian Woman's Diary from Eighteen Days in Tahrir*, 2012); Radwa Ashour's *Athqal min Radwā: Maqāṭi' min Sīra Dhātiyya* (*Heavier Than Radwa: Fragments of an Autobiography*, 2013); and a new generation of Arab-American memoirs such as Najla Said's *Looking for Palestine* (2013).

Chapter 1, 'From Solitude to Stealth', examines the foundational three-volume autobiography in Arabic literature by Egyptian reformer Taha Hussein and an autobiographical novel by Egyptian writer Sonallah Ibrahim. The two works rework the form through important historical, cultural, and literary junctures. This chapter explores the ways in which Hussein's *The Days* and Ibrahim's *Stealth* blur the conventional borders between fiction and autobiography. One lays down the conventions of the autobiography of childhood and the other dramatically revises the genre. By focusing on a canonical autobiography and a seemingly conventional autobiographical novel, the chapter reads the reworking of the form from the twentieth to the twenty-first centuries in parallel with national developments and through the cultural status of the writers.

Chapter 2, 'Revolutionary Memoirs', focuses on the autobiographical novels and memoirs of two important twentieth-century Arab women writers who provide models for the adaptation of the genre in colonial and postcolonial cultures: *Fantasia: An Algerian Cavalcade* and *Nowhere in My Father's House*, two Francophone autobiographical novels by Algerian writer Assia Djebar, and *The Search: Personal Papers*, a memoir in Arabic by Egyptian writer Latifa al-Zayyat. By framing autobiographical production in anticolonial national movements, Djebar and al-Zayyat rework the genre to comment on postcolonial cultures. Both writers contest colonial formations and offer revolutionary representations of solitude in the postcolonial nation: the Francophone Algerian writer's challenge to the French archive of the Algerian War of Independence and the Egyptian writer's reexamination of national culture and the history of the 1940s student movement. In the chapter, solitude is read as an emancipatory opportunity when the writers rethink the language of the new nation through autobiography.

Examining the two writers' autobiography against two landmark 1960s novels, the chapter shows the effects of national movements on Djebar and al-Zayyat's literary production in colonial and postcolonial Algeria and Egypt. While Djebar focuses on colonialism and her vexed relationship with the French language, al-Zayyat frames self-liberation within the broader national struggle. Both writers appropriate and remake the genre through the solitude of the writer and her representation of national history.

Chapter 3, 'Palestine Song', explores a new form of poetic autobiography by Palestinian poets Mahmoud Darwish and Mourid Barghouti. The chapter explores the relationship of the poets to Palestine and its effects on autobiographical form in Darwish's *Memory for Forgetfulness*, his 1986 memoir of the Israeli siege of Beirut, and *Mural*, his 1999 autobiographical epic focusing on mortality and Palestine. Barghouti's memoirs *I Saw Ramallah* and *I Was Born There, I Was Born Here* explore the 'solitude of exile' (Said 2000d: 181), in the words of Edward Said, and the return of the poet to Palestine. Darwish and Barghouti rework the genre to explore the life of the poet in relation to Palestine and the tension between the poet's solitude and his public role.

Chapter 4, 'Revolutionary Solitude', examines Arab Anglophone memoirs by focusing on Edward Said's *Out of Place: A Memoir* (1999b) and Najla Said's *Looking for Palestine: Growing Up Confused in an Arab-American Family* (2013). *Out of Place* traces Edward Said's cultural and literary journey from Palestine, Lebanon, and Egypt to his education in the US, framing the story of his life in a form of 'revolutionary solitude' represented by the public intellectual. Edward Said's self-representation rests on the dichotomy of his solitude during his formation within a history of dispossession and his career. Rather than the Arab-American public intellectual, the memoir focuses on Said's youth, chronicling his history in counterpoint to the cultural icon. The chapter rethinks *Out of Place* through the burgeoning of the Palestinian national movement and Said's lifework. In the chapter, I compare Edward Said's youth in the Arab world and Najla Said's Arab-American background, Said's journey to the US and his daughter's return to her roots, to arrive at a rethinking of the genre that migrates across languages and cultures.

Chapter 5, 'Dreaming of Solitude', concentrates on new areas of exploration of testimony and memory in unconventional forms such as the prison diary by focusing on the narration of torture in *Fī Arwiqat al-Dhākirah* (*Dreaming of Baghdad*, 1990) by Iraqi writer Haifa Zangana and the prevalence of fear in *Al-Ajnabīyah* (*The Foreigner*, 2013) by Iraqi novelist Alia Mamdouh. *Dreaming of Baghdad*, written in London during the 1980s, revisits Zangana's experience of imprisonment in 1970s Iraq in complex ways. While *Dreaming of Baghdad* offers new forms for the exploration of the subjectivity of Iraqi revolutionary women by exploring the precariousness of memory and challenging taboos on testimony, *The Foreigner* subjects the subjectivity and trajectory of Iraqis in the diaspora to scrutiny, focusing on the effects of violence and the infringement of taboos.

Chapter 6, 'Tahrir Memoirs', examines new Arab memoirs and the effects of the Arab revolutions in the twenty-first century on the genre. The genre of the Tahrir memoir, a form that focuses on subjectivity in the broader movement rather than solitude, reworks Arab memoirs in the twenty-first century. Radwa Ashour (1946–2014) and Mona Prince (Muna Brins) (b. 1970) wrote new memoirs that chronicle the writers' involvement in Egypt's 2011 revolution. The chapter focuses on Ashour's *Athqal min Radwā: Maqāṭiʿ min Sīra Dhātiyya* (*Heavier than Radwa: Fragments of an Autobiography*, 2013) and the posthumously published *al-Ṣarkhah* (*The Scream*, 2014), including *al-Riḥlah* (*The Journey*, 1983) and *Aṭyāf* (*Specters*, 1999), with Mona Prince's *Ismī Thawra* (*Revolution Is My Name*, 2012). Both Ashour and Prince offer a new form in which writing, activism, the university campus, and Tahrir Square

are deeply intertwined, with parts that focus on the writers' medical or professional crises within Egypt's revolution.

The final chapter looks at the effects of autobiographical production in other languages and translation on the globality of national literatures and world literary study. It examines current theorisations of world literature and considers Arab autobiography within new literary systems and comparative literary studies.

1

From Solitude to Stealth: Taha Hussein and Sonallah Ibrahim

In 1926, during the controversy provoked by the publication of *On Pre-Islamic Poetry*, and ensuing developments, Taha Hussein retired to France where he dictated part I of his famous three-volume autobiography *The Days* over nine days (Hafez 2002: 10–11). Part I seems to be written in self-defence, helping him to re-evaluate the present by revisiting his boyhood.[1] Hussein, from his solitude in a village in the Haute-Savoie, traced his journey from an Upper Egyptian village to the city (and, subsequently over his trilogy, his rise to the pinnacle of Arab culture). France is emblematic of his East–West trajectory in his education, thought, and literature: he had travelled on a scholarship to France, and he would formulate an important framework by which Egypt formed part of the West and not the East in *Mustaqbal al-Thaqāfah fī Miṣr* (*The Future of Culture in Egypt*, 1938). In part I of his autobiography, the story of his youth and his embattled public life intersected. The autobiography responded to the crisis with an exemplar of a cultural Arab hero whose growth to prominence in national culture and cultural exchange can be traced to his revolt against the traditionalism of his education. Similarly, Hussein wrote part II, *The Stream of Days: A Student at the Azhar*, after another crisis occasioned his dismissal from Cairo University.[2]

The stature of Taha Hussein and his adaptation of the genre of autobiography to chronicle his passage from the village *kuttāb* to a secular education have earned *The Days* the status of a masterwork in modern Arabic literature. The autobiography frames two important encounters that appear in other Arab autobiographical production in subtle ways: the encounter with the West (such as his predecessors' the pre-eminent Egyptian intellectual, educator, and translator Rifā'a Rāfi' al-Ṭahṭāwī and Lebanese writer Ahmad Faris al-Shidyaq), and his encounters with the state or the establishment. Hussein epitomised revolution in his thought and his career is marked by a series of crises.[3] Not only does *The Days* chronicle his migration from the village to the Azhar to France, but also the movement from tradition to an Arab literary modernity influenced by secularism and the synthesis of an Arab heritage and European culture.

The cultural-historical background of *The Days* helps contextualise the three volumes: part I (*An Egyptian Childhood*) was serialised in *al-Hilāl* in 1926–7 and published in 1929 (Cachia 1997: 6) during the crisis in which he was embroiled; part II (*The Stream of Days)* appeared in 1939 in colonial Egypt; and part III (serialised in *Akhir Sā'a* in 1955, printed as *Mudhakkirāt Taha Hussein* in 1967, and later added to *The Days* (*A Passage to France* in English)) appeared in postindependence Egypt. *A Passage to France*, a chronicle of his education in France and his career at the Egyptian University upon his return to Egypt, is grounded in his career-long struggle for cultural and educational reform.

The Days offers a model inspired by the synthesis of an Arab heritage and Western education, scholarly freedom, and revolutionary thought.[4] Critics have described *The Days* as 'one of the foundations of modern Arabic literature' (Malti-Douglas 1988: 11), 'an important example of Third World autobiography' (13–14), and 'the first great classic of modern Arabic prose literature' (Allen 1982: 566). The relationship between East and West frames and informs the foundational autobiography in Arabic letters. Fedwa Malti-Douglas observes: '*Al-Ayyām* is an important example of Third World autobiography. Not only does it articulate a vision of East and West but, more importantly, it shows the East as it comes into a special contact with the West' (1988: 13). Taha Hussein's autobiography synthesises Egyptian and European cultures within a movement of Arab literary revival and revolutionary rethinking of Arabic letters.

The autobiography provides the most famous Arab model emulated in subsequent autobiographical production. It offers a model where fiction is not antithetical to autobiography, but a feature of the form (Eakin 1985: 7). Nor is it concerned with self-creation or the fictionalisation of autobiography. Rather, it lays the foundation for a form, drawn from a rich Arabic literary tradition that inspired its reworking over the past half-century. This chapter brings a contemporary autobiographical novel into conversation with a famous autobiography: *Stealth*, a 2007 novel by Egyptian writer Sonallah Ibrahim (b. 1937), reenvisions *An Egyptian Childhood*. Like Hussein's *An Egyptian Childhood*, *Stealth* focuses on the misadventures of a young boy and the ways he comes to understand his world in colonial Egypt. In contrast to *An Egyptian Childhood*, which details the youth's conquest of his blindness, important scenes focus on the young narrator's stealth, spying, or sight. While Hussein adapted a new literary form, Ibrahim infuses a modern genre with renewed narrative modes to revisit his youth and expose the parallels between a historical moment in which he grew up and a present one with which he unequivocally contends.

The Fiction of Autobiography

Fiction and autobiography intersect in ways that have provoked much critical attention: the relation of autobiographical form to subjectivity (Eakin 1985: 34); the role of creation and invention in autobiography;[5] and the forms of autobiographical fiction and fictional autobiography in modern Arabic literature.[6] The conventional borders between fiction and autobiography are tantalisingly blurred when autobiography employs the forms and conventions of the novel (295). John Paul Eakin argues that the autobiographical self is necessarily fictive and notes the interplay between the process of self-discovery and the art of self-invention (55). Novelists produce autobiography by re-ordering and framing experience within the form of a novel. To shape autobiographical material, they may adhere to the conventions of the novel. Memory plays an important role in the production of autobiography: the complexity, lapses, and imprecisions of memory influence the recovery and interpretation of experiences and events.

The autobiographical pact (*le pacte autobiographique*) is central to the reception of an autobiography. Philippe Lejeune distinguishes between autobiography and fiction by identifying an autobiographical pact, the conventional agreement between the author of autobiography, who offers his statement of intention, and the reader. The autobiographical pact confirms the identity between the author, the narrator, and the character (Lejeune 1982: 193). As Lejeune notes, the autobiographical pact appears in the title, the dedication, the preface, the author's note, or in interviews. Lejeune's definition of autobiography depends on a set of conditions: form, the life story, the identity between the author (whose name designates a real person) and the narrator, and retrospective narration (1989: 193). Occasionally, writers blur the borders between literary genres and contravene the convention of the autobiographical pact, when no such agreement, commentary, or paratexts (interview, title, preface, or testimony) frame the autobiography. Another form they rework is the novel of education and formation (*Erziehungsroman* or *Bildungsroman*) – examined by Bakhtin – in which a writer narrates the formative years of the protagonist (1986: 19). These writers review and rethink their youth from the vantage point of a mature narrator (or writer) who reports the adventures of a youthful character.

The relationship between *Bildungsroman* and autobiography is central to autobiographical novels that centre on the education and youth of the writers. Moretti's examination of the *Bildungsroman* 'between two epochs' may be adopted to illuminate Hussein's autobiography and Ibrahim's autobiographical novel. For Moretti, the rise of the *Bildungsroman* has to do with youth and modernity (2000: 5). *The Days* employs the conventions of the classical *Bildungsroman*, or what Moretti notes as the synthesis of *Entwicklungsroman*, or 'novel of 'development'', and *Erziehungsroman*, or 'novel of "education" . . . observed from the standpoint of an educator' (16–17), through the balance between vocation and education. The synthesis of the development of personality and the process of education is prevalent in *The Days* in the protagonist's learning in the *kuttāb* of an Upper Egyptian village, his journey to the Azhar, and passage to France. Moretti notes that the classical *Bildungsroman* traces the rise of the modern young hero and social change through 'the fiction of youth' (230). Although the classical *Bildungsroman* evokes the 'tension between the individual and his world' (23), it also traces the fulfilment of the young hero's aspirations. *The Days* traces the birth of the modern autobiographical hero during cultural and political change in turn-of-the-century Egypt.

The form of 'autofiction' offers further insight into Hussein's novelised autobiography and Ibrahim's autobiographical novel. Coined in 1977 by Serge Doubrovsky, 'autofiction' evokes both autobiography and fiction, a form of the autobiographical novel, although critical debates have distinguished between autofiction, on the one hand, and autobiography, the novel, and the autobiographical novel, on the other (Bacar 2014: 178, 183).[7]

Autofiction is neither autobiography nor novel (163). Like the autobiographical novel, it is a hybrid literary form that blurs the borders between fiction and autobiography. Unlike other forms, autofiction is autobiography where the name of the narrator is different from the author (188); it offers a double pact – autobiographical and fictional; and displays autobiography and novel on the cover (407) through such subtitles as 'sīra ruwā'iyya' (literally, novelised autobiography). It is a form that mingles autobiography and the modes of fiction to create works that contract to be both autobiographical and fictional.

Taha Hussein and Sonallah Ibrahim rework the autobiographical and fictional in an autobiography that employs the mode of fiction and an autobiographical novel, respectively. While Hussein employs third-person narration and distance from the protagonist, and other autobiographical features underline the genre of *The Days*, Ibrahim reworks autobiography into his novel. Hussein draws on the *Erziehungsroman* (novel of education) in an autobiography that closely follows his growth into an educator and reformer and traces the fulfilment of his aspirations. Ibrahim evokes his youth through his protagonist's intimately recounted boyhood in his autobiographical novel. Whereas Hussein set the foundations of the genre in modern Arabic literature through its productive relationship to fiction, Ibrahim would go on to produce a seemingly conventional novel whose literary history and role within his oeuvre betokens a complex autobiographical corpus.

The Autobiography of Youth

Hussein, a revolutionary thinker in modern Arab culture, was involved in the cultural movement of the Nahda or Arab literary renaissance. He earned a traditional Azharite and European education, adopted Western ideals, and famously declared a shared heritage for Europeans and Egyptians in the form of a Mediterranean culture in *The Future of Culture in Egypt* by which he resituated Egypt in the West, not the East.[8] One of the most important *Nahda* thinkers, Hussein founded the genre of autobiography in modern Arabic literature at the confluence of important cultural-historical forces in the Arab world: part I appeared when Egypt was colonised by Britain and European culture dominated the Arab world.[9] Hussein reworked a form with precedents in an Arab autobiographical tradition.[10] His history informs his adaptation of the genre: his migration from the village to Cairo, his criticism of the conservatism of the Azhar, his education in France, and his conception of Egypt within a cultural framework shared with the cultures of the Mediterranean. Although part I returns to the nineteenth century during the British colonisation of Egypt (1882–1952), it does not directly engage with colonialism. Rather, it delineates the forces of tradition and ignorance that profoundly changed the life of the young boy who was blinded from the age of two by the treatment of a local barber. From 1932 to 1952, plagued by party politics and dismissed from the university by the government in 1932 (he would return to the post of Dean of the Faculty of Arts in 1936), Hussein obliquely directed his criticism of the government in his literary production (Cachia 1956: 65–6).

The conventions of the *Bildungsroman* pervade the story of his boyhood and youth in an Upper Egyptian village and his formation at the Azhar. *An Egyptian Childhood* focuses on the solitude of a young blind village boy at the turn of the twentieth century. In volume I, Hussein narrates his formation in the Upper Egyptian village of Izbit al-Kīlū near the town of Maghāgha in poverty (Cachia 1997: 3), framing the story of his youth in the backwardness of the village. In one of the most widely quoted scenes in modern Arabic literature, a mature narrator, distant, detached, and ironic, commences the story with his evocation of a young boy who 'cannot remember' the day, but recalls a spot by the fence where he would contemplate and enjoy the recitations of a poet. The fence is symbolic of the boundary between his house in the village and the world, which he would cross with his journey to the Azhar.

In *An Egyptian Childhood*, the young boy is deeply aware of his blindness and his sense of isolation in an Upper Egyptian village and, in *The Stream of Days*, he suffers solitude in the dormitory at the Azhar seminary.[11] Early in *An Egyptian Childhood*, blindness is conjured in his sense of the soft light, the sensation of a cool breeze, the hushed movements in his surroundings, and the euphonious song of a poet; when his mother pours a liquid in his 'poor weak eyes'; and when his father entrusts him with prayers because he is a young boy and blind and thus favoured 'in the sight of God': 'How could God be pleased to turn a deaf ear to a blind lad' (*A1*, 102; *EC*, 62). The English translation offers the play on the words 'deaf' and 'blind' while the Arabic only alludes to the blind boy: '*sabiyyan makfufan*'. He learns of his infirmity when he hears his siblings describe sights of which he had no knowledge: 'Then he knew that they saw what he did not see' (*A1*, 18; *EC*, 16). The youth apprehends his world in *The Days* through auditory experience. While he feels the play of light and the outlines of the fence, he would strain his ears in his surroundings. *An Egyptian Childhood* abounds with recitation and the imagination: the Qur'an he recites; poetry to which he listens in the *kuttāb*; folktales; Sufi rituals in which he partakes; the sound and movement of his dying sister (for whom no one summons a doctor) as well as his mother's bereavement; and the sound of his elder brother's sickness – his groans, and silence when he is afflicted with cholera, while the young protagonist, isolated, 'silent', and 'downcast' rests in a corner of the room; and the preacher's sermons at the Azhar.

Hussein offers no conventional autobiographical pact that may identify the narrator by the author's name in volume I.[12] The narrator goes on to challenge the conception of his story as an 'example' or 'model' of the 'noblest of men' (and children) to be emulated (*A1*, 145; *EC*, 84). Rather, by the volume's end, the narrator offers a model of a fate he has laboured to spare his daughter. Malti-Douglas draws attention to a doubling and distancing produced by third-person narration (1988: 100). As Lejeune notes, autobiography 'in the third person' draws attention to an indirect character or a 'figurative narrator' (1989: 35), an observation that pertains to *The Days*. While autobiography is 'autodiegetic', the third person creates a 'distancing' to 'express an articulation (a tension) between identity and difference' (36). Lejeune notes that the alternations 'in which contemporary autobiographers indulge are the timid echo of the investigations of modern novelists into narrative voice and focalization' (37). In this sense, Hussein's alternation between the third person and autodiegetic narration or the split of the narrator 'produces an effect of unvoicing and of stepping back (an effect whose functions can be very diverse: protection, self-irony, solemnity)' (39). The enunciation 'splits' or 'distances', producing an effect by which autobiography is read 'from the perspective of the convention that it violates' (42). In the case of *The Days*, to use Lejeune's reasoning, the title and history of the autobiography impose an autobiographical interpretation. The alternation between the first and third person, although often unobtrusive, may be seen to create the effect of distance, repudiation, or modesty.

By *An Egyptian Childhood*'s end, the narrator notes to his daughter: 'He [her father, the youth] was conspicuous for all this [his poverty], but nevertheless pleasing to the eye when its gaze fell on him, notwithstanding his ragged state and sightless eyes' (*EC*, 86). The Arabic clearly imparts the pronounced appearance of his poverty: '*taqtaḥimahu al-'ayn iqtiḥaman*' (*A1*, 148) is rendered into 'Indeed he was conspicuous' (*EC*, 85), thereby removing the connotation of the eye's aversion to his dirty cloak, an allusion to the 'eye' that recurs three times in the same passage. Here '*taqtaḥimahu al-'ayn wa lakinaha tabtasim lahu*' (*A1*, 149) is rendered thus: 'He was conspicuous but pleasing to the eye' (*EC*, 86). The emphasis on 'the eye', a prominent allusion in the chapter, is part of the evocation of sight and sightlessness. The conflation of narrator and protagonist in this passage gestures to his present state: how he passed from poverty to prominence and what he provoked in the way of 'envy, hatred and malice' and earned by way of 'approval, respect and encouragement' (*EC*, 87). In this passage, the narrator imparts to his daughter his identity with the young boy as well as his blindness and his poverty and offers the insight of the mature narrator.

In *The Stream of Days*, the narrator's father sends him to study in the Azhar seminary in his brother's charge. The second volume details the young boy's education, solitary life in Cairo, and frustration with the conservatism of the Azhar. Pierre Cachia notes his experience of 'solitude' in his early months at the Azhar (1956: 47), a state furthered by his criticism of the Azhar's traditionalism.

The second volume, penned in Vic-sur-Cère during July and August 1939, opens with the imagination frequently evoked in volume I: 'It was more by imagination than by sense that he distinguished the three phases of his day' (*SD*, 105) – his room; the journey between his lodging and the Azhar; and the courtyard of the Azhar. On his way from the Azhar to his lodging, he has to pass through a narrow passage-way, assailed by odours and attentive to sounds, feel his way forward and then turn up a staircase.

In his room in Cairo, he would fall to an 'intolerable solitude' (*SD*, 131); when his cousin comes up to the Azhar to keep him company, his 'solitude' (*'uzla*) (*A2*, 109; *SD*, 178) ends, so much so that he sometimes longs for it, and he returns to his solitude at the Azhar and in the tenement when his cousin matriculates at Dār al-'Ulūm and feels 'condemned once more to the stony solitude which long before in the first months of his life as a student had caused him so much suffering' (*A2*, 180; *SD*, 230).

The Stream of Days traces the young Azharite's revolt against the Azhar. The author frames the chronicle of his education at the Azhar within the old and the new. *The Stream of Days* ends with his break with the Azhar; while he was enrolled at the Azhar, he began to frequent the Egyptian University and thus came to lead a 'double life' between 'the old world of the Azhar' and 'the new world of the University' (*A2*, 183; *SD*, 232), a doubleness that would characterise his oscillation between the old and the new, the conservatism of the Azhar and the secularism and humanism of the modern university.

The final volume, *Memoirs* (1967), republished six months before his death in October 1973 (Cragg 1997: 241) as part of the trilogy, enshrines his formation and education within the birth of the modern university, the pursuit of academic freedom, and the Egyptian–European encounter. The final volume chronicles his passage to France on a scholarship for doctoral study at the Sorbonne. Before France, in 1908 he enrolled at the newly established Egyptian University, where he was introduced to Western culture. On his return from France, he would be appointed a professor of ancient history at Cairo University, where his legendary lectures and subsequently his revolutionary thought would court controversy.

In France, he encounters a new education and languages (French and Latin) that differ from his learning of the Qur'an at the village *kuttāb* and his education at the Azhar. A reader, metonymically described as 'the sweet voice' (*A3*, 87; *PF*, 330), the woman who was eyes to him, later his fiancée and wife, reads to him. When he is encouraged to learn writing for the blind, he finds it difficult and uncongenial because he was accustomed to acquiring knowledge through his ears and reasons that it was more suitable to learn through his hearing. Throughout his education, he is unaware of others' signs; he notes that people are 'those whose voices he heard, and some of whose movements he felt, but he did not see them or know what lay behind these voices he heard and movements he felt' (*A3*, 114).

Politics creeps into volume III when he lampoons the sheikhs for their conservatism, servility to the Khedive, and co-operation with the British. This is the only volume in which he slips in a barb at British colonial rule. With the end of World War I comes 'the news that Egypt was seeking independence from the victorious occupying power' (*A3*, 137; *PF*, 378). Taha Hussein and Egyptian students abroad are full of aspirations and dreams of revolution: 'Our friend was given to solitude and rarely mingled with his fellow Egyptian students. Now he began to meet with them frequently and to engage with them in conversations about the revolution and revolutionaries' (*A3*, 137–8).[13] The events inspire him to complete his doctoral study to return to Egypt: 'Who knows? He might be able to play some part insofar as he is able to' (*A3*, 138). On his return, he notes his national aspirations and the revolution that rose in Egypt in 1919: 'It was little wonder that our friend returned to his country, believing in the revolution that had risen in it, and believing, too, that a large measure of the burdens of this revolution would fall upon the educated and the intellectuals of the country . . . they were able to lead the people forward' (*A3*, 158). A national struggle and controversy bring the volume to a close: in the wake of the 1922 Declaration, which granted Egypt nominal independence, he is keen to fan the flames of revolution because of his conviction that this would grow into a full-fledged independence from the British, and he would go on to advocate a democratic constitution that would make him fall out of favour with the Palace. Caught between the supporters of Sa'd Zaghlūl and the Palace, he notes: 'Thus our friend was up to his ears in politics' (*A3*, 163). Thereafter he would go on to reap the fruits of his entry into national politics.

The foundational Arab autobiography chronicles the rise to prominence from poverty, tradition, and blindness. *The Days* adheres to three important landmarks in Taha Hussein's trajectory: his education in the village, his departure to the Azhar, and his encounter with the West. His revolutionary thought and reform of education, language, and culture underwrite the solitude prevalent in his autobiography, but not in his public involvement as reformer, educator, and intellectual.

Solitude and Stealth

The status and experiences of Taha Hussein and Sonallah Ibrahim are markedly different: they have made different contributions to Arab literary and political culture; Hussein, a reformer and educator, holds a revered status in the highest levels of Egyptian culture while Ibrahim has long held a special role characterised by his independence on the Egyptian cultural scene, and both writers produced autobiographical examinations of rural and urban boyhoods, respectively. Nonetheless, a comparison between *The Days* and *Stealth* reveals some important similarities between the two writers: they struggled for independence from institutions and the state, adopted positions that were at odds with the establishment, and went through major political and cultural crises. They were deeply marked by contact and exchange with Europe: Hussein by his contact with French culture and Ibrahim by his cultural exchange in East Germany and the Soviet Union, including his reading of American, Latin American, and Russian literature in prison. Hussein worked to reform education and culture in Egypt; Ibrahim revitalised Arabic literature with innovative modern novels. Moreover, Hussein reoriented culture towards a literary modernity and Ibrahim produced a modern literary corpus. *The Days* offers the model of an original autobiography, whose protagonist is blind and solitary, and Ibrahim appropriates that model by focusing on a young narrator whose spying and stealth are diametrically opposed to his literary antecedent.

Ibrahim rose to prominence on the Egyptian literary scene with the publication of *That Smell* (*Tilka al-Rā'iḥa*), his 1966 semi-autobiographical novella. Ibrahim was a revolutionary, who served most of a seven-year sentence for his activity in the Communist Party in 1959 and was released in an amnesty granted in 1964.[14] Although Ibrahim is an emblem of the independent, solitary, and ascetic writer, he has been deeply committed to national and anti-imperialist movements. Richard Jacquemond notes that he 'has always been at the limit of what can be tolerated by the various censorship authorities', represents the ideal of 'fusing purity with commitment', and enjoys pre-eminence within 'the consecrated avant-garde' (2008: 258–9).

In *That Smell*, the narrator, like his author, a prisoner just released from prison, has to transact new relationships to the city. He circles around the city on the tram and returns to his flat at dusk to report to a policeman and sign his notebook. Little happens in *That Smell*: his failure to write, the curfew, impotence, and defeats punctuate the novel. The reception of *That Smell* was incendiary largely because it explicitly presented sexuality but most likely because it plumbed the depths of a general state of stagnation. Hoda Elsadda reads *That Smell* as the novel that 'inaugurates the character of the ineffectual, impotent male' and the modern 'defeated antihero' who has lost his revolutionary fervour and national dreams (2012: 124, 138) and Paul Starkey reads the narrator as a model for an 'anti-hero' who recurs in most of Ibrahim's novels (2016: 41).[15]

In the late 1960s, Ibrahim performed a revolution of literary style in *That Smell*: a statement signed by his friends Kamāl al-Qilish, Ra'ūf Mos'ad, and Abdel Ḥakīm Qāsim (his co-prisoners in al-Wāḥāt prison) declared the novel an expression of 'the experience of a generation' in the introduction:

> A generation born in the shadow of monarchy and feudalism, that went out marching to demand the fall of the King and the British, and that embraced the July Revolution with words and deeds. A generation that has witnessed the collapse of monarchy and capitalism and the construction of socialism – all this in a few short years. A rich and profound experience, full of contradictions and crises, a growing sense of self and knowledge of self. All this requires serious, courageous expression to articulate these experiences creatively and innovatively. (*TR*, 18; *TS*, 73)[16]

The 1986 introduction to the complete edition of *That Smell* proclaims his nationalism and his doubts about the production of a novel that is critical of the nation in the context of anti-imperialist movements: 'The Arab nation, with Egypt in the vanguard, was indeed in a dogfight with American imperialism and its Zionist stepdaughter, not to mention Arab conservatives. So it was natural for me to wonder whether I wasn't harming the country by publishing my work under such conditions' (*TR*, 19; *TS*, 74). Samia Mehrez, in her examination of the history of the production of *That Smell* and Ibrahim's introduction, notes his guilt towards the regime 'whose struggle and sacrifice he had respected' (1994: 122) by publishing a novel that was critical during the rise of Arab nationalism and the challenge to imperialism and Zionism (122–3).[17] The introduction proclaims: 'Rebellion was the spirit of the age, after all', inspiring the explosion of 'conventional forms' (*TR*, 13; *TS*, 69).[18] Youssef Idris called *That Smell* a revolution (*thawra*) 'of an artist against himself' (1986: 29). The publication of *That Smell* established Ibrahim's status as a revolutionary and an iconoclast known for his independence from the Egyptian literary establishment.

That Smell contains asides on the narrator's work on a novel whose description closely resembles *Stealth*. Although *Stealth* appeared much later, the novel can be read as a preliminary to *That Smell* and *Notes from Prison* (*Yawmiyyāt al-Wāḥāt*) (literally, Notes from the Oases Prison), a memoir based on Ibrahim's prison experience (1959–64). After the narrator wanders around Cairo on the tram, visits relatives and his co-prisoner's wife, returns to his apartment to report to a policeman, and attempts to write, he resumes another novel he had commenced in prison, which continues to exert an influence on him. As the introduction comments on the writing of *That Smell*:

> When I wrote *That Smell*, I had just gotten out of prison and was under house arrest, which required me to be at home from dusk to dawn. I spent the rest of the day getting to know the world I'd been away from for more than five years. As soon as I was back in my room, I rushed to record, in quick sketches, all those events and sights that had made an impression on me, that seemed to me completely out of the ordinary. Then I would put the diaries aside and get back to the novel I'd begun in prison, a novel of childhood. (*TR*, 12–13; *TS*, 68)

Stealth, a novel he wrote secretly in prison and shaped amid interruptions by the policeman's visits and his failure to write under house arrest, rests within *That Smell*. Although *That Smell* abounds in interruptions and non-action – the policeman's visits, reveries, smoking – it is suggested that the narrator has resumed a novel of childhood.

In his 1986 introduction, Ibrahim admits that he had begun to leaf through the drafts of a 'still unfinished novel of childhood' in the room he rented after his release from prison, 'asking myself what the point was of writing something that didn't engage the struggle against imperialism, the effort to build socialism' and the problems of 'terror, torture, prison, death' (*TR*, 15; *TS*, 70). Ibrahim's admissions express the unease with the genre of autobiography in the Arab world because the focus on subjectivity appears to preclude commitment to public roles and national movements. By contrast, politics pervades the novella: the police officer, the train bearing troops from Yemen, the surveillance of the narrator, and the arrest of the narrator on his release from prison all contribute to the politically charged atmosphere.

Notes from Prison (henceforth *Notes*), his 2004 memoir, recounts the story of the years he spent in prison through a diary (1962–4).[19] Ibrahim wrote his memoirs in prison and transferred his secret notebooks to cigarette paper and had them transported out of prison in November 1963. *Notes* is a series of journal entries written in his last two years in al-Wāḥāt prison camp in the Western Desert (1962–4). Part prison notebook and part creative work, the memoir includes notes on the formation of the writer, observations, excerpts from books, historical commentary, and reflections on Soviet, American, and Latin American literature.[20] Ibrahim's prison notebooks, in which he adopts Hemingway's objective reportorial style discovered in prison, anticipate his signature style employed in his autobiographical novel.

Stealth can be read as the novel of childhood to which Ibrahim alludes as the novel he began in prison. It tells the story of a young boy and his elderly father, Khalil Bey, a retired army officer, who live on his meagre pension in middle-class poverty. The young narrator explores his world by spying and eavesdropping on other characters (maids, tenants, neighbours, sister, brother-in-law, parents) but is often unaware of the implications of conversations, scenes, and memories. Like *That Smell*, he goes on a series of visits with his father throughout the novel to relatives, the coffeehouse, and the grocer and stays in the flat. Mostly the knowledge he accumulates eludes him: the history of his father's marriage to his mother, a younger woman whom he loved; his mother's psychological breakdown; and his father's need for female companionship.

Stealth plots a parallel between the early twenty-first century in which the novel appeared and mid-twentieth-century Egypt in which it is set (Ibrahim 2011b). Ibrahim returns to *Stealth* to resume the novel of childhood he began in prison and under house arrest. His challenges to colonialism and the state appear in two important historical moments that he reads in counterpoint: 1940s Egypt characterised by discontent with the monarchy, defeat in the Palestine War in 1948, and the decline of the middle class, on the one hand, and corruption and disenfranchisement in the early twenty-first century, on the other.[21] *Stealth* narrates the boyhood of the writer, offering the story underlying *Notes* and *That Smell*.

At the moment that Ibrahim completed his autobiographical novel, he had been involved in a recent crisis on the Egyptian literary scene that preserved his independence from state cultural institutions.[22] The literary and cultural landscape in which Ibrahim wrote *Stealth* is telling. On 22 October

2003, Ibrahim was awarded the Arab Novel Award by the Egyptian Higher Council for Culture at the Second Cairo Conference on the Arab Novel whose panel of judges honoured his ideals: asceticism, independence, ethics, and national commitment.[23] In a climactic speech, Ibrahim declined the state prize and excoriated the Mubarak regime.[24] The appearance of *Stealth* can be read in the context in which he declined the award – the story of his boyhood against his public confirmation of his freedom and independence from the state. Importantly, Ibrahim's subsequent works confirm a commitment to autobiographical literature: *Amrikanli*, a 2003 novel inspired by his visiting professorship at the University of California, Berkeley;[25] his 2004 memoir *Notes from Prison*; and the 2007 *Stealth*. *Notes* and *Stealth* fall into the genre of memoir and autobiography and, in a sense, represent an autobiographical project that is coterminous with his public encounters with state cultural formations. *Stealth* followed *Notes*, unconventionally revisiting his boyhood in a context in which Ibrahim declined a prestigious state prize, thereby confirming his autonomy and his stature on the Arab literary scene.

Ibrahim extends and rethinks the autobiographical tradition formed by Taha Hussein's autobiography in modern Arabic literature. Ibrahim maintains that *Stealth* is not an autobiography, but fiction inspired by memory (Ibrahim 2013b). Nonetheless, there is evidence that *Stealth* is autobiographical: *That Smell*, *Notes from Prison*, and *Stealth* contain references to his mother and a novel of childhood. Ibrahim does not adhere to Lejeune's autobiographical pact and the character is unnamed in *Stealth*. Nor are there authorial interventions or an introduction framing *Stealth* as autobiography. Nonetheless, the Arabic edition (and the first edition of the English translation) features on its cover a family photograph of a young boy and a suited father. In *Stealth*, the young boy looks at a postcard-sized photograph in his father's room:

> The other picture has my father sitting wearing a fez and a tie. Between his knees a small child wearing a two-piece shorts suit is standing. Its first piece starts at the neck, and its second goes all the way down to the knees. The picture is in black and white, except for the child's clothes. The suit is a blue-green color with two yellow stripes around the wrists and around the

> waist. On the back there's my name and father's name too. The handwriting is my mother's. (*T*, 77; *Sb*, 52)[26]

Other autobiographical allusions appear in paratexts: interviews, novels, and memoirs.[27] His statements about *Stealth*, therefore, both confirm and unsettle its autobiographical status.

Although Ibrahim breaks with the conventions of autobiography in *That Smell*, *Stealth* appears to be comparatively conventional. It departs from the iconoclasm of *Dhāt* (*Zaat*), his 1992 postmodern novel of the 1970s culture of post-Open-Door (*infitāḥ*) consumerism. The writer challenges himself by departing from the postmodern style characteristic of his other novels and reworking the conventions of autobiography with the unconventional autobiographical representation of stealth and sparse language, a rupture with rhetorical prose that departs from the lyrical style characteristic of the high-brow Arabic prose of Taha Hussein.

Ibrahim's quotation of a phrase by Hemingway, underlined in his prison diary in his notes on Hemingway's *The Green Hills of Africa*, helps to frame his autobiographical novel *Stealth*. The Arabic translation of the English 'But you ought to always write it to try to get it stated' reads: '*Uktub, uthbit ma tarāhu wa-ma tasma'uhu*' ('Write, set down what you see and hear') (*YW*, 95; *NP*, 90).[28] In *Stealth*, Ibrahim literally adheres to Hemingway's dictum and sets down what the narrator sees and hears. The reader reads the implications of what the narrator sees and hears in the world of the novel. The young narrator's observations and experiences offer deep insights into his relationship to his father and the absence of his mother. The young narrator understands his world through what he sees and hears in a novel whose title in Arabic, *al-talaṣṣuṣ*, means 'spying' or 'eavesdropping'. The word 'stealth' in the English translation denotes 'secrecy', 'furtiveness', and 'voyeurism', but also connotes furtive actions by the state in an evocation of the surveillance prevalent in *That Smell*.[29]

In contrast to *An Egyptian Childhood*, where the character remembers the play of light on the fence in front of his house in the village and contemplates the day, *Stealth* commences with the narrator walking with his father in an alley (*ḥāra*) at dusk. Unlike *That Smell*, where the narrator walks out of prison and has nowhere to go upon his release, the young narrator in *Stealth* holds his father's hand as they pass through the alley of a working-class district to which they have just moved, pass the café, the grocer's, the butcher's shop, and the shoe shiner, and head by tram to Midan al-Sayyeda where his father sells his pocketwatch. *Stealth* begins: 'My father stops for a second at the door to the house before we step into the alley' (*T*, 7; *Sb*, 7).[30] The young narrator evokes his father of whom the narrator-prisoner dreams, walking and embracing him, seeming 'strong' and 'solid', and complaining about last year's troubles in *Notes from Prison (YW*, 114; *NP*, 94). The young narrator evokes the squalor of the family's room, the challenges his father faces to live on a modest pension, and the memory of his mother in *Stealth*.

The city seethes on the eve of King Farouk's birthday and the founding of Israel in 1948. The narrator reports conversations that reflect the disaffection in Egypt where a wave of strikes and protests has spread under the monarchy and British colonial rule. Such conversations between his father and his circle in the coffeehouse highlight rising national tensions in 1948 that would parallel the regional catastrophe experienced with the loss of Palestine. Khalil Bey, asked if he would like to contribute a piastre with the rest of the group to buy the daily newspaper *al-Ahrām* for a month, observes: 'anyway, today's news is the same as yesterday's' (*T*, 52; *Sb*, 36). The response of the young lawyer Refaat Effendi in sheikh Abdel 'Alim's shop, where a picture of the King hangs on the wall, captures the political landscape of the narrator's boyhood:

> You can say that again. Look at the story today about the Yemeni Jews and how the English are smuggling them into Palestine. Ever since the partition, ships keep coming and going, gathering them up from near and far.
>
> Then he lowers his voice and adds that the university students tore up the king's picture and made fun of his fooling around. (*T*, 52; *Sb*, 36)

In this context, people no longer trust political parties or leaders. Characters, in this passage and others, survey the political mood: opposition to the king and assassinations by the Muslim Brothers; Egypt's involvement in the Palestine War; the siege of Faluja; the defeat of the Egyptian army; the Deir Yassin massacre in Palestine (*Sb*, 76; *T*, 110); and the Muslim Brothers' bombing of the Benzion and Gattegno department stores in Egypt. Evoking the national unrest upon the army's defeat in the Palestine War, the neighbourhood sheikh Abdel 'Alim proclaims: 'The streets are full of protests and people chanting: "Where's our food, clothes, and basic things, thou most womanizing of all kings?"' (*T*, 156; *Sb*, 108). Moreover, the young narrator takes part in a strike with students chanting 'Long live Egypt, Free and Independent!' and calling for further armed opposition to Zionism and for the withdrawal of the British from Egypt (*T*, 245; *Sb*, 169).

Unlike the third-person narrator of *The Days*, the first-person narration of the young unnamed narrator, whose understanding of his world is limited to eavesdropping and 'spying', offers an intimate portrayal of events and experiences. But Ibrahim's narrator is also the septuagenarian narrator who revisits his boyhood and offers deeper insight into the implications of the words and scenes that the young narrator accumulates as well as the parallels between two eras. In this sense, another mature narrator intimates the father's economic decline after his retirement and his desires after his young wife's psychological breakdown. Like *The Days*, a mature narrator looks back on the misadventures of his younger self, yet Hussein's third-person narration distances the writer and the narrator from the autobiographical youth, while Ibrahim's mature narrator intrudes upon his younger self.

In contrast to *An Egyptian Childhood*, Ibrahim reworks the trope of sight or stealth to lay bare the development of the narrator. Stealth or spying on others evokes the political landscape where men converse in hushed tones in cafés and represents the young narrator's ignorance of his mother's breakdown, his father's desires, and other characters' relationships. In a telling scene, Khalil Bey purchases a pair of old glasses for his son and the purchase is symbolic of the young narrator's observations and examinations of his world, but the amelioration of his sight does little to amplify his insights into relationships. Hereafter, the narrator notes his father's movements, ailments, and conversations. Although he observes actions, overhears conversations, and discovers desires, he is unable to piece together the details. Yet the mature narrator offers intimate knowledge to the reader, and, in a sense, intrudes upon the world of the young narrator. In *Stealth*, a mature narrator dominates the narration, producing the effect on genre that Lejeune describes: 'To reconstruct the spoken word of the child, and eventually delegate the function of narration to him, we must abandon the code of autobiographic verisimilitude (of the "natural") and enter the space of fiction' (1989: 53). This is the space of fiction that accounts for the split between a youthful narrator and a mature narrator who writes of events in retrospect and with full knowledge of the implications of the young narrator's experiences. Although the young narrator absorbs observations and confessions, the adults are unaware of his thoughts and interpretations, too.[31] The actions of the young narrator recur throughout the novel and serve to redirect attention to his sight: he steals looks through cracks in doors; sneaks out of rooms; peeks into rooms; peers through keyholes; and pricks up his ears to overhear conversations. He steals glances at Um Nazira the maid from a crack in the door and follows her around the house in scenes that evoke his relationship to his father and the family's social class. He recalls memories of stealing into and out of his parents' bedroom before his mother's departure. Other furtive actions express the young narrator's ignorance of the relationships and comportment of the characters at the same time that the reader is privy to them: he leaves doors open; peers into drawers; peeks through the keyhole of his sister's guest room; listens to his father's conversations; pauses in front of the door of the constable's room and puts his ears to the keyhole; looks at the neighbours' windows; and overhears conversations about his mother. The reader learns through the conversations the narrator overhears that his father has married another woman (the narrator discovers the marriage when his father brings his wife home) and that his mother has been admitted to a psychiatric hospital. But spying is not limited to the narrator: his father instructs him to spy on the new maid and the neighbours; his half-sister plies him with questions about their father; and the constable's mistress sends him to spy on others. These intrusions replicate the writer's intrusion on the young narrator and, in a sense, the reader's voyeurism. In a sense, *Stealth* is an analogue to *That Smell*, where the prisoner is taken into custody upon his release because he has no address, feels that he is being followed on his walk in Bab al-Hadid, his old neighbourhood, and is routinely interrupted in his room by the policeman after his curfew, but instead the narrator in *Stealth* is the interloper.

In spite of the narrator's solitude or because of it, he discovers complexities and contradictions that the reader can read with an eye and an ear to the writer-narrator's insights. Conversations, confessions, and observations intimate some knowledge of which the narrator is unaware, and the story is formed between the words he overhears and the scenes he observes, so that events rest in ambiguity and overtones. The absence of the narrator's mother is immediately apparent and a powerful memory in *Stealth*. The young narrator has memories of his mother bathing him and scalding him with hot water that has not been mixed with cold water in a pitcher and remembers his distraught mother on a visit to the zoological gardens, which all point to his mother's psychological state. Nonetheless, he is unable to account for her absence even by eavesdropping on his father but he is aware that adults refrain from speaking about her in his presence. He recalls a memory of sitting on his mother's lap and his mother pushing him away from her and remembers his mother in a large hall before a judge: '*Mother notices me. I can't tell if she knows me or not. She suddenly talks to me in a very normal voice, like we've never even been separated: "How are you?"*' (*T*, 176–7; Sb, 57–8; italics in translation and bold in original). He remembers visiting his mother at the hospital, his father clutching a bag of apples: '*An open hall with many beds. Mother is lying on one. She smiles quietly. My father holds the bag of apples out to her. She takes one of them . . . She feels my face with her fingers. She asks me about school but doesn't seem to care*' (*T*, 204; *Sb*, 299–300; italics in translation and bold in original). The narrator's memories are interspersed with events and appear in situations whose import he does not appear to have fully grasped.

In *That Smell*, the narrator visits the old house where the family used to live and to which there are allusions in *Stealth*: 'I decided to go look for that old house. Maybe my mother was still there' (*TR*, 89; *TS*, 59). He approaches the house from Faggala Street, 'just as my father and I used to do' (*TR*, 89; *TS*, 59), recalling the route they used to travel:

> *We would go by tram, taking it from the Midan just before it turned into Zaher Street. I loved that peaceful street ... We would get off at Faggala and my father would take me with his right hand as we crossed the street. We set off down an alley bordered by a high white wall . . . Then the street ended and the house appeared. My father sat on the bawwab's bench while I went up the long staircase, passing by the doors with their smells of cooking oil. Afterward, my father and I left along the same alley, walking next to the white wall.* (*TS*, 59–60; italics in translation)

That Smell ends with a scene in which the narrator asks his grandmother, 'When exactly did my mother die?' (*TR*, 96; *TS*, 62). He learns that a week before his visit his mother read the newspapers and carried on with her life and then fell sick and stopped eating whereupon he suddenly remembers his curfew and walks out to the metro station. The narrator's discovery of his mother's death, just a week before he pays a visit to the old house, and the reportorial narration of his actions call attention to the complexity of the representation of the traumatic effect of his mother's breakdown and death. These allusions offer further insight into the representation of the absence of the mother through the limitations of the young narrator's point of view in *Stealth*.

The young narrator's memory and stealth illuminate an event embedded in his experience of his mother's state. In a scene that echoes Hussein's narration of the illness and death of his sister in infancy, we learn of the death of the young narrator's sister also in infancy (*T*, 103; *Sb*, 72) when Khalil Bey notes that the death was traumatic for Rowhaya (his wife and the narrator's mother) and the young boy overhears the conversation. He overhears his father recount his memory of meeting his mother and the story of his love: 'I listened like I was under a magic spell' (*T*, 113; *Sb*, 78). In *An Egyptian Childhood*, the narrator recounts the death of the youth's sister in which he embeds the story of his blindness and foregrounds tradition and backwardness. In his description, the narrator dwells on the state of the infant: she is 'languid' and 'out of sorts' (*A1*, 120; EC, 71), but no one pays any attention to her because mothers in villages, the narrator notes, attend to chores and rely on the knowledge of other village women. But in the midst of the story of the death of the young protagonist's sister, the narrator embeds the story of his blindness: 'In this way our lad lost his eyesight. Ophthalmia attacked him, but he was neglected for some days. Then the barber was called in, and he treated him in a way that resulted in the loss of his sight' (*A1*, 120; *EC*, 71). In *Stealth*, the story of the death of the narrator's sister is embedded in his memory of his mother's state. The reader discovers the story of which the narrator does not have full knowledge and whose memory has not offered him insight: his father's marriage to a younger wife and her psychological breakdown following her daughter's death in infancy. *Stealth* recounts traumatic events and intimate details by way of the interplay between the young narrator's spying and the writer-narrator's insight.

Stealth adopts the features of the *Bildungsroman* to conjure a new hero whose narrative is not only symbolic of modernity (like Hussein's autobiography) but rests between epochs in which the autobiographical novel is set and written. Hussein chronicles the young boy's intellectual energy in the cultural and political landscape of turn-of-the-century Egypt. His revolutionary legacy and synthesis of a rich Arabic heritage and Western culture illuminate his novel of youth. Both novels feature a *Bildungsroman* hero: the young protagonist, narrated by the erudite narrator in *The Days*, and the young boy-narrator in *Stealth* grow up in rural and middle-class poverty and are caught between two epochs in turn-of-the-century and mid-century Egypt respectively. While the narrator offers insight into the young protagonist's misadventures in *The Days*, the young narrator takes in his world with an eye and an ear to glaring contradictions and absences in *Stealth*.

The two writers share a revolutionary sensibility: they represent a reformer and an iconoclast. Nowhere does Ibrahim offer an explicit autobiographical pact and *Stealth* purports to be a novel or *Bildungsroman*. While *The Days* chronicles the movement from tradition to an Arab literary modernity, *Stealth* invokes parallel national moments: 1948 and twenty-first century Egypt. Whereas Hussein narrates the story of the young blind hero whose journey ends with his rise to a revered cultural status, Ibrahim tells the prehistory of the modern revolutionary iconoclast featured in his other autobiographical writings. In many ways, Ibrahim reworks the autobiography of boyhood and recasts the focus of *The Days* through situations that call attention to the trope of stealth and the young narrator's lack of insight into his experiences.[32] While Hussein focuses on a trajectory from tradition and superstition to a synthesis of heritage and modernity inspired by European models, Ibrahim offers a history of anticolonial movements that underwrote his formation in mid-century Egypt and inspired his revolutionary activity and literary production in the twentieth and twenty-first centuries. Ibrahim, the innovator and the iconoclast, reworks a classic Arabic autobiography into the autobiographical novel in which a youthful narrator apprehends his radically changing world.

2

Revolutionary Memoirs: Assia Djebar and Latifa al-Zayyat

> [N]othing is familiar to her . . . not the palpitation of the new world to which she's going to belong, finally delivered from herself, from the tangles of her youth, from the plains of her solitude . . . while from here on in it's actually a question of her being born – of a true awakening.
>
> Assia Djebar, *Children of the New World*

In the 1960s, Algerian Francophone novelist Assia Djebar (1936–2015) and Egyptian writer Latifa al-Zayyat (1923–96) produced landmark national novels. *Les Enfants du nouveau monde* (*Children of the New World*), Djebar's 1961 novel of the Algerian Revolution (1954–62), appeared one year before Algeria's independence. *Al-Bāb al-Maftūḥ* (*The Open Door*), al-Zayyat's 1960 novel, which chronicles the Egyptian national movement in the 1950s at a moment of revolutionary fervour in 1960, is an analogue of *Children of the New World. Children of the New World* ends with Lila, the French-educated Algerian woman, sent to school by her father, who has not belonged to the Algerian revolution but has now been drawn to the movement, in a cell, soon to be interrogated and tortured to confess the Algerian guerilla network in Cherchell. Likewise, *The Open Door* ends with Layla, whose coming-of age parallels the national movement, en route to Port Said to join the popular resistance to the 1956 Tripartite Aggression. In the postindependence period, Djebar and al-Zayyat went on to produce autobiographical novels and memoirs, respectively, that focused on the subjectivity of the writer and offered an examination of national movements and postcolonial futures in Algeria and Egypt.

In the last half-century, Arab women have produced memoirs centred on the role of women in national movements. The memoir of the first Egyptian feminist Huda Shaarawi (Hudā Sha'rāwī) (1879–1947), *Mudhakirrātī* (*My Memoirs*), dictated in Arabic in the 1940s and posthumously published (and translated as *Harem Years: The Memoirs of an Egyptian Feminist*) (1986), chronicle her life from the world of the harem to the 1919 revolution.[1] *Harem Years* tells Shaarawi's story from a life of seclusion in the harem to her participation in the 1919 revolution and public unveiling in 1923.[2] The final years in her memoirs (1919–24) document the involvement of men and women in the national movement and her organisation of demonstrations in Cairo during the 1919 revolution to protest against the exile of the Wafd popular leader Sa'd Zaghlūl by the British. In 1919, the memoir tells us, Sharaawi leads nearly 300 Egyptian women of all classes in a march against the British occupation in Egypt in a scene in which veiled women, who had sewn crescents and crosses on green cloth to proclaim the solidarity of Muslims and Christians, march amid British troops through the quarters of Cairo.[3] *Harem Years* provides a foundation for the relation between feminism and nationalism in Arab women's memoirs by underlining Sharaawi's feminism through her involvement in the 1919 revolution.

The woman's movement played an important role in independence struggles in the Arab world in the twentieth century. The life and writing of al-Zayyat are framed within the politics of women's liberation in Third World national movements (Elsadda 2012: 98, 100). Indeed, Frantz Fanon maintains the centrality of women to anticolonial nationalism in *A Dying Colonialism*, an essay on Algerian women's involvement in the Algerian revolution.[4] Nonetheless, some postcolonial women writers prioritised the national movement over feminism (Ashcroft et al. 1989: 101–2). In fact, al-Zayyat privileged her national commitment over women's rights during her involvement in the 1940s student movement. While her involvement in the anticolonial movement redefined women's conventional social roles, she declared that nationalism and feminism are part of the same national struggle and asserted her belonging to a popular revolutionary movement that focuses on the collective rather than the individual and the subjective (al-Zayyat 1994b: 247).

Memoirs produced during anticolonial movements represent women's liberation within the broader national movement. These memoirs focus on the tension between solitude and nationalism, remaking the genre in contexts in which anticolonial nationalism is a powerful force. They reexamine colonial history by focusing on subjectivity and solitude, particularly in postcolonial moments. By exploring self-formation at important historical moments during involvement in national movements, Arab women writers focus on subjectivity and envision national history. Arab women's autobiography produced in colonial and postcolonial cultures inscribes women's life history within the national movement. In Algeria and Egypt, novel forms of autobiography intersected with national history in subtle ways: they focused on the modern revolutionary woman and the newly independent nation-state.[5] By chronicling the emancipation and agency of women within the national movement, they appeared to focus on self-formation within the anticolonial struggle.

This chapter offers a comparative reading of Djebar's 1985 Francophone autobiographical novel *L'Amour, la fantasia* (*Fantasia: An Algerian Cavalcade*) and 2007 autobiographical novel *Nulle part dans la maison de mon père* (*Nowhere in My Father's House*) and al-Zayyat's *Ḥamlat Taftīsh: Awrāq Shakhṣiyyah* (*The Search: Personal Papers*), her 1992 prison memoir in Arabic.[6] These autobiographical novels and memoirs offer reworkings of the genre within revolutionary national movements in the Arab world. While Djebar's *Fantasia: An Algerian Cavalcade* (henceforth *Fantasia*) blurs the borders of genre as she reworks autobiographical strands with the history of the French colonisation of Algeria in 1830 and the Algerian War of Independence (1954–62), *Nowhere in My Father's House* (henceforth *Nowhere*) focuses explicitly on her life. Al-Zayyat's *The Search* revisits her role in the 1940s student movement and her experience of prison in 1981. These reworkings highlight the influence of national movements on the growth of the genre and rework the form not only to envision the modern woman vis-à-vis the new nation, but also to compose the life history of the postcolonial subject. Whereas Djebar focuses on colonialism and the hybrid postcolonial subject, al-Zayyat explores the solitude of the writer who is characterised by nationalism and isolation in the postindependence period.

Autobiography, Archives, and Algerian Fantasia

The trajectory of Djebar is a story of a woman's liberation through her French education and literary production: she was admitted to the École Normale

Supérieure in France and would go on to be elected to the Académie française in 2005.[7] Her Francophone novels transgressed Algerian patriarchal culture and made a contribution to Francophone literature that brought Algerian writing into mainstream French cultural production. Djebar's autobiographical writing is framed in a long tradition of North African Francophone literature in general[8] and autobiography in particular, such as the Moroccan writers Abdelkebir Khatibi's *Tattooed Memory* and *Love in Two Languages*, Tahar Ben Jelloun's *Harrouda* (1973), and Mohamed Choukri's *For Bread Alone*.

In her early novel, *Children of the New World*, Djebar ushered in a new Algeria that would go on to gain independence in 1962. Set in the Algerian city of Blida, the novel focuses on Lila, a young Algerian philosophy student educated in French schools, a fictional antecedent of the narrator-historian in *Fantasia* (who closely resembles Djebar) and whose formation corresponds to the stages of development of the colonised intellectual in Fanon's *The Wretched of the Earth* (1963: 158–9). Lila, whose husband Ali has left to join the National Liberation Front (FLN) revolutionaries in the mountains, is uninvolved in the Algerian revolution when the novel opens and has assimilated the coloniser's culture. Subsequently, she is not integrated in the town's revolutionary network, feels isolated from her compatriots, and languishes in solitude. She remembers that her father rescues her from the fate of her cloistered kinswomen by insisting that she be educated and liberated. By the novel's end, she is arrested and shares the schoolteacher Salima's cell in a French jail, contemplates her commitment to the struggle, and by then has entered the revolution.

After a ten-year self-imposed literary silence (1969–79) attributed to 'political disenchantment' and the awareness of censorship in Algeria (Zimra 2005: 225), Djebar resumed her writing in French in 1980 and, in 1985, published her partly autobiographical novel, *L'Amour, la fantasia*.[9] The autobiographical novel, a revision of the history of the French conquest of Algeria in 1830 and the Algerian Revolution through the examination of French colonial archives and an inscription of Algerian women's testimonies, not only challenges French colonialism and Algerian patriarchy, but also provides a model of autobiography that recasts national history and postcolonial subjectivity.

For Djebar, autobiographical production in patriarchal Maghrebian culture and the colonial French language is fraught with taboos. In traditional Arab Islamic culture, taboos are imposed on women's self-expression. Born Fatma-Zohra Imalhayène, Djebar adopted a pen name and wrote autobiographical novels in French, a language with which she sought to elude the patriarchal strictures of Arab culture.[10] A pen name contravenes Lejeune's autobiographical pact (Moore-Gilbert 2009: 101). Moreover, the form of *Fantasia* is a pastiche or what Djebar calls an autobiography (1999: 107) and a 'preparation for an autobiography' (Mortimer 1988: 203). Djebar remakes the form by reworking indigenous sources and mixing genres such as history and ethnography in her autobiographical novel. As Moore-Gilbert reads her allusions to two early North African autobiographers: 'Her citations of the North African autobiographers St. Augustine and Ibn Khaldoun suggest that she also attaches herself to what she regards – in an implicit complication of the assumptions of Gusdorf and Pascal – as a long non-western tradition of self-representation' (2009: 95). By alluding to the *Confessions* of Saint Augustine of Hippo (354–430), born in North Africa, in Latin and the Tunisian sociologist Ibn Khaldun's *An Account of Ibn Khaldun*, written in Arabic, Djebar clearly invokes a literary genealogy and appropriates the form. Amid taboos on women's autobiography in Arab culture, autobiography can be read as an unveiling or denuding of subjectivity. Mildred Mortimer reads Djebar's practice of 'collective autobiography' as a way to elude patriarchal taboos (1997: 103).

By rewriting the history of the French colonial domination of Algeria and anticolonial nationalism from 1830 to 1962, Djebar frames her autobiography within national history. *Fantasia*, interweaving fiction, autobiography, and history, embeds her story in the narrator's re-examination of Algerian national and colonial history. As Mortimer notes: 'The writer contextualizes her own life story – presented as autobiographical fragments woven throughout the text – within this historical framework' (2013: 115). Part 1 of *Fantasia* integrates French memoirs, letters, and journals on the 1830 French conquest of Algeria while part 2 embeds the testimony of Algerian women on the War of Independence within the autobiographical novel. By examining obscure and forgotten French letters, memoirs, journals, and travelogues, and transcribing Algerian women's testimony, Djebar writes her life story within a revised national history. Not only does the narrator write her subjectivity within colonial history, but also through her translation of, and commentary on, French archival material and Algerian women's oral history.

The much-cited scene with which *Fantasia* opens evokes the complexity and ambivalence of Djebar's Francophone literature. In the very first scene of *Fantasia*, a little Arab girl walks with her father, a schoolteacher in the French colonial system, on her way to the French school, and her father's choice of a French education liberates her from the fate of cloistered Algerian women and opens a door to writing in the French colonial language. The scene that follows the narrator's allusion to writing autobiography in French returns her to the history of the arrival of the French in Algeria on 13 June 1830: 'But this stripping naked (*la mise à nu*), when expressed in the language of the former conqueror (who for more than a century could lay his hands on everything save women's bodies), this stripping naked takes us back oddly enough to the plundering (*la mise à sac*) of the preceding century' (*AF*, 182; *F*, 157). In this way, she pairs the language of the nineteenth-century conquest with that of the young girl who learns French (Zimra 1992: 184). Shaden Tageldin reads the pairing of the language of colonialism and patriarchy: French, a 'language of love, enters Algeria as a language of colonial brutality' and 'so too does French enter Djebar's life – through the contradictory actions of her father – as both the sign of love and that of its prohibition' (Tageldin 2009: 474). The violence of the conquest, where the invaders are 'lovers', underwrites the narrator's vexed relation to the language she has chosen for her self-expression or 'denuding'.

Critics have paused at the gendered ways in which Djebar describes the French conquest of Algeria.[11] Djebar examines nationhood and subjectivity through the representation of the colonisation of Algeria. The representation of the conquest evokes the trope of casting Algeria as woman in Fanon's 1959 essay 'Algeria Unveiled' in *A Dying Colonialism*. Fanon compares the colonial conquest of Algeria to unveiling (Faulkner 1996: 847; Woodhull 1993: 20).[12] This metaphor appears in the description of the conquest that follows the scene of a young Arab girl on her way to school with her father: 'la Ville Imprenable se dévoile' (*AF*, 18) [the Impregnable City sheds her veil] (*F*, 6). The scene represents the arrival of the French conquerors as a sexual conquest, 'an obscene copulation' (*copulation obscène*) (*AF*, 33; *F*, 19), and the invaders (*envahisseurs*) as lovers (*amants*) (*AF*, 20; *F*, 8). Further, Djebar cites from the letters of captains who speak of Algeria (*une Algérie-femme*) as a woman who cannot be tamed (*AF*, 73; *F*, 57).

For an Algerian writer, writing Francophone autobiography is fraught with tension and ambivalence. Djebar, who was educated in French schools in Algeria and France, retained the Amazigh language of her ancestors, adopted the French language, and abandoned Arabic, the language of a patriarchal culture and a national language imposed on ethnic groups in Algeria. French offers the narrator liberation from seclusion; she is exempted from wearing a veil because 'she reads' – or 'she studies' in Maghrebi Arabic. In the Postface to *Femmes d'Alger dans leur appartement* (*Women of Algiers in their Apartment*), 'Regard interdit, son coupé' (Forbidden Gaze, Severed Sound), Djebar conjures the seclusion and 'solitude' of the Algerian women's harem (1992b: 136) in contrast to her liberation through her education in the French system. Thus French, the language of the former conqueror and coloniser, is '*langue du père*' (paternal language) because her schoolteacher father sends her to the French school. French confers on her the anonymity and freedom to write autobiography in Arab-Islamic culture, allowing her 'unveiling' or 'denuding' in a language other than patriarchal Arabic (*AF*, 182; *F*, 157).[13] Nonetheless, French is a colonial and patriarchal language; the narrator's complex relationship with the French language is not only the product of the marginalisation of the North African Francophone writer, charged with complicity and betrayal,[14] in Algeria (and that of Francophone Maghrebian writers in France) but also the legacy of a brutal colonial history. This ambivalent relationship is further problematised by her liberation through the language of the coloniser and her subversion of French colonial archives by transcribing and translating Algerian women's oral history. Djebar writes for a French and Francophone audience, not because of 'the lack of an African reading culture', as Sankara suggests with regard to African Francophone autobiography, but rather because this is the language of her education and creativity. French is her 'stepmother tongue' (*langue marâtre*) (*AF*, 298) and her paternal language because of her father's encouragement. Djebar's appropriation and Arabisation of French highlight the challenge to colonialism and cultural domination inherent in her Francophone novels.[15]

For Djebar, the Arabic language is the language of patriarchal Arab-

Islamic culture that has imposed a fate of cloistering on her Algerian compatriots. She enacted a break with a language in a context of enforced Arabisation that followed independence and afterwards, as Tageldin notes, in a period characterised by Islamist attacks on Algerian Francophone writers in the early 1990s (Tageldin 2009: 468). Besides classical Arabic, there are multiple languages for Algerian writers: French, Amazigh, and Algerian Arabic. In *Ces voix qui m'assiègent*, Djebar elaborates on Francophone literature, the colonial gaze, and women's writing. The voices that 'assail' her – Arabic, Amazigh, and French – are those of women who challenge the prohibitions of patriarchy and the effects of colonialism. Djebar refashions French to rewrite colonial history through appropriation and polyphony. Her dialogic rewriting of Algerian history resists the monolingualism imposed by Algeria's 'enforced arabization' after independence (ibid.).

Fantasia has been variously read as a 'collective autobiography',[16] autobiographical novel, and novel. Djebar describes *Fantasia* thus: 'With *L'Amour*, I wanted to reintegrate my own autobiography' (Zimra 1992: 184). Djebar embeds the story of her education and her relationship to the French language in her reexamination of archival French sources in part 1 and her voice dominates the Algerian women's testimonies that she transcribes and translates in part 2. National history helps elude patriarchal prohibitions on women's self-expression and censorship in Arab culture.[17] While Djebar's autobiographical novel produces a communal story, her authorial interventions offer her account of Algeria's history. By transcribing and translating her exchanges with Arab and Amazigh Muslim women – Lla Zohra and Cherifa – she mediates between colonial history and oral culture.[18] By interrogating French colonial sources and re-integrating women's stories into the historical archives, she exhumes forgotten Algerian sources and rewrites national history through polyphony and translation. Her autobiographical project problematises colonial Orientalist representations of Algerian women and challenges Algerian patriarchal culture. Furthermore, her transcription and translation of Algerian women's oral history from Amazigh and Arabic into French helps to preserve and circulate the agency of women combatants in the Algerian War of Independence in her Francophone autobiographical novel.

Djebar problematises colonial, Orientalist representations of Algerian women, not only by superimposing the narrator-historian's commentary on French colonial archives, but also by examining the subjectivity of the Francophone writer in her novel. When the narrator cites the observations of the chronicler Bosquet, for example, she subjects his notes to the authority of her autobiography. Djebar rewrites the French disembarkment at Staouéli and fumigation of Algerian tribes in the Gorges de Dahra. She juxtaposes Baron Barchou's account of the battle of Staouéli on 19 June 1830 with her descriptions of the mutilation of women. Similarly, the narrator reconstructs the forgotten history of the fumigation of an Algerian tribe at Mount Nacmaria from the reports of French officers: she takes the report from Pélissier and reworks the history of her ancestors into her novel. The narrator-historian superimposes the history of her ancestors on to French reports in a palimpsest: 'Pélissier, speaking on behalf of fifteen hundred corpses buried beneath El-Kantara . . . hands me his report and I accept this palimpsest on which I now inscribe the charred passion of my ancestors' (*AF*, 97; *F*, 79). In spite of the superimposition of her commentary on to the reports, traces of them are still visible. The narrator directs and controls these exchanges, allowing Bosquet or Saint-Arnaud to write to each other, through her mediation, in a sort of 'cross-breeding' (*bâtardise*; *métissage*) (Lionnet 1998: 327). Further, the narrator appends to Lla Zohra's testimony the story of the murder of two *naylettes*, Fatma and Meriem, recounted by a French officer and reported by the French artist and writer Eugène Fromentin. By translating Lla Zohra's history in her French novel, she exhumes and circulates her story.

In the end, the narrator tells us that on a visit to Laghouat in the Sahel, after the siege of Algiers in 1853, Fromentin found the severed hand of an anonymous Algerian woman. The author intervenes to give the anonymous hand her '*qalam*' [pen] (*AF*, 259; *F*, 226) to write the woman into Algerian national history. The representation of Algerian women's history, she seems to suggest, is possible by taking the *qalam* from the Algerian patriarch and the French coloniser, the authors of Algerian national history. By exhuming the dismembered Algerian woman, the narrator appropriates the *qalam* to write a history of mutilation.

Djebar reworks the autobiographical form, palimpsestically writing Algerian colonial history. She interweaves memoirs, travelogues, archives, chronicles, diaries, journals, letters, testimonies, reports, correspondence, and epigraphs, reading them, hybridising them, and creating a palimpsest. The epigraphs enfold *Fantasia* in multiple literary traditions – Arab, Amazigh, Muslim, and French.

Djebar's autobiography is far from conventional; she brings together colonial history and autobiographical commentary in literary *métissage*. Structuring part 3 of the novel on Beethoven's sonatas 1 and 2 Quasi una fantasia in five movements produces a synthesis of polyphony.[19] The word 'fantasia' appears in Fromentin's *Une Année dans le Sahel* (1858) as an evocation of a cavalcade. Fantasia, therefore, alludes to a Western musical form that permits improvisation and indigenous communal forms.[20] The cultural forms fused in the fantasia are European and indigenous (Amazigh and Algerian). Djebar's use of the fantasy sonata, a musical composition featuring improvisation, underlines the orality and speech of her interlocutors. The production of sound is the opposite of the former aphasia or silence of Algerian women. Sound, speech, and testimony transgress patriarchal laws prescribing seclusion (*AF*, 232; *F*, 203). As Moore-Gilbert notes, the women she interviews offer a 'communal commentary' on 'contemporary Algeria' (2009: 96). Part 3 includes 'five movements' featuring autobiography, the testimony of women, and the author's interventions whereby Djebar exhumes her ancestors and restores the history of Algerian women's involvement in the War of Independence, writing her story through her ancestral history.

Nowhere in My Father's House, another autobiographical novel, is steeped in the tragic history of Islamist violence against Algerian Francophone writers in the 1990s. Extending her autobiographical project into the twenty-first century, Djebar redirects her attention from Algerian women's oral history to her youth. Mildred Mortimer has argued that the autobiographical novel represents a movement from 'a collective project' to 'a singular voice' (2013: 113). *Nowhere in My Father's House* narrates Djebar's adolescence within Algeria's colonial history, revisiting some of the writer's history in *Fantasia* such as her father's encouragement of her French education from her youth to the eve of the Algerian War of Independence, and, in a sense, circling back to *Children of the New World* but in the aftermath of the struggle between Islamic fundamentalism and the postcolonial government.

In her more recent autobiographical novel, Djebar returns to some of the material of *Fantasia* with more intimacy and directness. While *Fantasia* opens with a young Arab girl on her way to a French school with her father, *Nowhere* opens with the image of a young girl on her way to the public bath (*hammām*) with her mother.[21] The narrator's mother, young and veiled, needs her two-and-a-half year-old daughter to guide her across her hometown Cherchell (to which she alludes by its Roman name, Césarée) to protect her from the gaze of men. The narrator looks back to interpret her mother's dependence on her younger self:

> At present, I, her little daughter, hold her hand in the corridor of the ground floor, at her mother Mamane's. Young, wrapped up in a white satin veil from head to toe, needing a child to pay an afternoon visit in the little city. In the entrance, her mother covers herself slowly in the immaculate silk and wool-fringed *haïk*. I can still hear the rustle of fabric, enfolding her hips and motherly shoulders, while we paused in the penumbra, in front of the heavy door. (*NP*, 13–14)[22]

Rather than the father who escorts his daughter to the French school in *Fantasia*, the young girl holds her mother's hand to cross the town in *Nowhere*, and instead of the future of the modern woman that her father promotes and bequeaths to his daughter in *Fantasia*, her mother is enfolded in her traditional Algerian role.

> She whom I escort wears on her nose a triangle of organza exposing her eyes – this is the privilege of women of this port populated three centuries ago by Andalusian refugees. On the street, the white woman will walk, her gaze fixed to the ground, her eyelashes batting with the effort: me, I do not only feel I am her follower, but her companion who watches over her steps.
>
> My mother, Moorish bourgeois crossing the ancient capital, the woman not more than twenty years old, needs my hand. I, at perhaps three, then four, five, knew that once outside my role was to guide her before the masculine gazes. We follow several streets, first behind the church, then walk along the Roman amphitheatre: we go on in front of the column of ancient houses – each with a wooden door painted in green, blue and displaying a heavy hand-shaped bronze knocker. (*NP*, 14)

The young, veiled mother crosses the town, assisted by her daughter.[23] The crossing of the narrator and her mother evokes a scene in *Children of the New*

World, where the young woman Cherifa must cross the town to warn her husband, Youssef, an Algerian rebel of his imminent arrest by the French. She passes from the old Arab quarter to the centre of the city through rows of café-goers. Djebar writes, 'Middle-class women actually never frequent the streets in the center of town. When a woman must go out – only to go to the baths or for special ceremonies, parties, or days of mourning – the escorting spouse walks in front of her and guides her by a roundabout route to the appointed place' (*C*, 85–6). Cherifa attracts the gaze of the loiterers on the terraces and her veil offers no protection. In *Nowhere*, the little girl stands in for the husband, the woman's customary guide, and provides protection for her mother in the town where a woman's movement, like Djebar's writing in French, is comparable to public unveiling. In *Ces voix qui m' assiègent*, Djebar notes: '*J'ai utilizé jusque-là la langue française comme voile. Voile sur ma personne individuelle, voile sur mon corps de femme; je pourrais presque dire voile sur ma propre voix*' (Thus far, I have used the French language as a veil. A veil over my self, a veil over my woman's body; I can almost say, a veil over my own voice) (1999: 43; emphasis in original). She evokes the memory (and scene from *Nowhere*) of crossing the city with her mother, covered in her white veil, aware of the gaze of the men, on the weekly ritual visits to the public bath.

Nowhere focuses on the narrator's growth and formation in colonial Algeria. The narrator confesses autobiographical details: the death of a younger brother in infancy; the solitude of women; her education in a French colonial school in Blida; her father's modernity and adherence to Arab-Islamic tradition; and her romance in Algiers.

By *Nowhere*'s end, Djebar gestures to a postcolonial future that has implications for the narrator whose 'disinheritance' contrasts with the nation's independence. In the end, Djebar writes: 'I no longer have "my father's house." I have no place there, not only because my father died, weakened, in a country they say was liberated where girls are disinherited with impunity by their fathers' sons' (*NP*, 427).[24] Disinheritance reinforces the status of women in the postindependence nation and, in an autobiographical novel of youth on the eve of independence, written in postindependence Algeria, presages further struggle for enfranchisement and empowerment that recalls the Algerian revolutionary woman evoked by Fanon.

The Solitude of the Search

Al-Zayyat's 1992 prison memoir *The Search: Personal Papers* was a radical departure from *The Open Door*, her 1960s novel produced in the 1950s national landscape of independence and revolutionary fervour following the 1952 Revolution, the British evacuation, the nationalisation of the Suez Canal, and the popular resistance to the 1956 Anglo-French-Israeli attack.[25] While *The Open Door* chronicles the nationalist movement and women's liberation, *The Search: Personal Papers* traces a different historical moment in the 1970s and 1980s when al-Zayyat was concerned with the hardships endured by the individual and the fragmentation of the national project.[26]

The status of al-Zayyat in Arab culture is intimately intertwined with her role in the movements of anticolonial nationalism and women's rights. The twin forces of nationalism and feminism are central to al-Zayyat's oeuvre. Nonetheless, al-Zayyat has focused on the dominance of the nationalist movement in her writings, especially in moments of anticolonial and anti-imperialist struggle. Hoda Elsadda describes women's liberation, long thought to be the outcome of independence, as a 'political taboo' that did not allow criticism of gender inequality during national movements (2012: 116).

In *The Open Door*, spanning the period from 1946 to 1956, al-Zayyat addresses women's involvement in the nationalist movement throughout the 1950s. The reception of the novel in 1960 reveals its status as a work of women's liberation (Booth 2000: x). The novel tells the story of Layla Suleiman, a young girl from a middle-class Cairene family during an important decade of Egyptian history (1946–56) from anti-British demonstrations in 1946 to the resistance movement against the 1956 Tripartite Aggression in Port Said. The key moments of Layla's life develop in parallel to national events: a movement of popular opposition to the monarchy and British colonial rule; the 1952 Revolution; the nationalisation of the Suez Canal; and the 1956 Israeli-British-French attack.[27]

The Open Door opens with a conversation among a group of people from different social and educational cross-sections of Egyptian society about an anti-British demonstration in Ismailiyya Square. On 21 February 1946, men comment fervently on the street on the battle of 1946, a new stage in the national struggle, and one interlocutor notes: 'even the women came out of their houses. There were women all over the place in Bab al-Sha'riya' (*BM*, 1; *OD*, 4). Layla joins a procession of students from Khedive Ismail School in which they exchange slogans. In the procession, where the boys clear the way for the girls to take the lead, Layla feels that she belongs to a crowd of thousands in the march: 'Everything around her was propelling her forward, everything, everyone, surrounding her, embracing her, protecting her' (*BM*, 45; *OD*, 51). She feels she belongs to the crowd of thousands who shout slogans: 'No more imperialism!' Layla's struggle for freedom from her father's authority and bourgeois conventions – she is censured by her father for her role in anti-British national demonstrations – parallels the nation's struggle for independence (Elsadda 2012: 102). The novel parallels Layla's development with the nation, tracing the trajectory of Layla the young middle-class girl to the new Egyptian woman.

In the end, the novel completes Layla's liberation in parallel with the nationalist movement. Layla joins the popular resistance against the Israeli, French, and British attack following the nationalisation of the Suez Canal in 1956 in Port Said with a fellow activist. Layla's liberation from the social conventions of her bourgeois family is made possible through her emancipation and national independence. The novel chronicles Layla's formation into an independent woman during the nationalist movement, showing the relation between women's liberation and national independence.[28] In this way, the novel promotes a reading of the modern Egyptian woman in parallel with the change in women's status with the right to vote in 1956 and the 'Charter for National Action' (*al-Mīthāq al-Waṭanī*) in 1962 (Bier 2011: 24–5), which confirmed that women's liberation was indeed an extension of national independence.

Like Djebar, al-Zayyat wrote her memoir after a silence – a thirty-year silence – from the publication of her novel of anticolonial nationalism.[29] Al-Zayyat's silence is examined in a memoir focusing on self-reflection and the search for unity and community. *The Search* narrates the experiences of *The Open Door* differently: the memoir is centred on the narrator's anticolonial nationalism in 1940s Egypt, during which she was imprisoned, and her 1981 prison experience. Part 1 of the memoir revisits the narrator's involvement in the 1940s student movement at Fuad I University (now Cairo University) in 1942, where she develops through her political commitment, and part 2 focuses on a prison ward search of the women's wing in al-Qanatir prison in 1981. *The Search*, covering the 1940s and 1980s, plots al-Zayyat's story from 1940s colonial Egypt to her 1981 postcolonial prison experience, focusing on her political activism and national commitment rather than women's rights. Like *The Open Door*, *The Search* portrays the centrality of the broader national struggle, not only for the new Egyptian woman for whom involvement in the nationalist movement is a path toward women's liberation, but also for the postcolonial writer whose complex process of critical self-examination was seen to be part of the contemplation of the postindependence period.

Part 1 of *The Search*, in which al-Zayyat narrates her formative years in Egypt under the monarchy and British colonial rule, focuses on her Alexandria City prison experience. In 1949, she was arrested with her husband, a leftist revolutionary and university colleague who shared her national aspirations, for alleged membership in a communist organisation and accused of conspiring against the state. Like Djebar, who was on the run with her new husband from the French police and sought refuge in Tunisia in 1958 (Zimra 2005: 204) – during which she wrote *Children of the New World* – al-Zayyat and her husband were wanted by the police in 1948. Upon her arrest, al-Zayyat spent six months in solitary confinement in the Alexandria City Prison (her husband would be sentenced to seven years). This part of her memoir, centred on the significance of 1973 in her life and national history, interweaves personal and national events: the death of her brother and the 1973 War and her arrest with her husband and the 1948 Palestine War. Upon her release from prison in 1949, she undergoes what she describes as a change from a revolutionary to a woman who has withdrawn from the struggle during her second marriage (1952–65), a union that was radically different from her political partnership with her fellow activist in the 1940s student movement.[30] Like *The Open Door*, al-Zayyat creates a national framework for *The Search*, her memoir inspired by the 1973 October War and dedicated to her brother.

Part 2 of the memoir recounts the story of al-Zayyat's sentence in al-Qanatir Women's Prison in November 1981. In September 1981, al-Zayyat, then chair of the Committee for the Defense of National Culture, a group of writers whose members publicly opposed the peace treaty with Israel in 1979, was arrested, along with more than 1,500 prominent writers. The search conducted by the prison administration of al-Zayyat's ward is central to the memoir. In al-Qanatir women's prison, a group of political prisoners from both right and left share her prison cell – prominent professors and writers Amina Rachid, Awatef Abdel Rahman, and Nawal El-Saadawi among them. *The Search* juxtaposes her two prison experiences from colonial and postcolonial Egypt, focusing on the differences between them within anticolonial and anti-Zionist movements at different moments in the nation's history.

The Search opens with a revised autobiographical pact, confirming the identity between the author, the narrator, and the protagonist, while undoing its conventions. Al-Zayyat opens her memoir with an allusion to her dying brother Abdel Fattah in March 1973. From March to May 1973 (before the October War), with the death of her brother, she writes about her self-formation and imprisonment, ironically writing about life under the peril of death (Ghazoul 1994: 37). Moreover, she draws up the terms of her autobiographical contract by contracting to write her story (and all that entails of truth) and confessing that she has concealed from her brother the nature of his illness. The prologue–pact establishes the relation between memoir and mortality and prefaces an extended elegy for her brother and compatriots in the Mansura and Abbas Bridge massacres and the defeat of 1967. Elsewhere in the memoir, she mourns the reformer Taha Hussein, the father of modern Arab secularism.

The memoir is comprised of two parts framed by two important dates in the life of the writer: 1973, the year of her brother's death, and the Arab–Israeli War; and 1981, the year of her imprisonment. Part I recounts her youth from 1950 to 1973 and part II contains notes from al-Qanatir prison in 1981. Literary fragments, excerpts from unpublished novels from 1949 to 1981, appear in the memoir and furnish different autobiographical forms: part of her memoir written in 1973; a plan for a novel dated 1963; portions of an unpublished manuscript *In the Women's Prison* (based on her experience in the Alexandria City Prison) completed in 1950; fragments from an unfinished novel *The Journey* in 1962 (published as *The Owner of the House* in 1994); and writings from al-Qanatir prison. Her writings represent stages of her life and consequently integrate her literary history into her memoir (al-Zayyat 1997a: 12).[31]

The Search explores al-Zayyat's political formation (*tarbiyah siyāsiyyah*) in the 1930s and 1940s. The narrator's father opposed and discouraged her involvement in the nationalist movement because political commitment was seen to challenge women's conventional social and cultural roles. In 1934, the narrator observes the police open fire on twenty-four demonstrators in the procession of the leader of the Wafd Party Mustafa El-Nahhas, whom Prime Minister Ismail Pasha Sidki had refused permission to tour the provinces, from the balcony of her house in Mansura. She observes the repression of the struggle by the 'treachery' and inhumanity of the state. The event evokes a political coming-of-age in which the narrator discovers state oppression. When students of Fuad I University march on Abbas Bridge against the monarchy in 1946, the bridge is drawn up during the protest and the students are shot. The massacre furthers her political commitment as a student involved in the 1940s nationalist movement.

Writing her memoir in prison revisits the writer's self-examination by exploring the tension between isolation, solitude, and withdrawal from public life, on the one hand, and political action that has long dominated her life and career, on the other, or what Edward Said has described as 'loneliness and alignment' (1994: 22). The struggle between detachment, isolation, and exclusion, on the one hand, and the continual relation with others, 'a strong longing for communication with others' (al-Zayyat 1994b: 247–8) and unity, on the other, pervades the memoir. *The Search* draws a contrast between the revolutionary in colonial Egypt and the solitary postcolonial writer. The narrator notes that her sense of 'alienation' increases in November 1977, 'after Sadat's visit to Israel' (*HT*, 128; *S*, 92). In contrast, she describes the young witness of the Abbas Bridge massacre as 'powerful' and belonging to the nation. She explains her 'alienation' (*ghurba*) through the radical transformation of the Middle East with the founding of Israel. Her involvement in the national effort after the Abbas Bridge massacre, the 1940s student movement, and her work for the Committee for the Defense of National Culture underline her political action. Rather than represent isolation and solitude, prison inspires her introspection and renewal. The relation of subjectivity to political agency frames her prison memoir. Indeed, she writes the story of her life partly through national history in an evocation of Layla in *The Open Door*, but intimately examines her marriage and search for emancipation.

In this broader context, the narrator refocuses on the story of her marriage, tracing the strands of her private life and political activism. After her second marriage, she resumes her political work and refocuses on the broader national struggle. Her novel *The Owner of the House*, cited in *The Search*, tells the story of Samia and her revolutionary husband Mohamed who has sought refuge in a house from the political police and with whom she is reunited by his comrade Rafik. However, throughout the novel, Samia feels excluded and isolated from the circle of Mohamed and Rafik. The novel explores the isolation of the individual who is unable to change her world through political action. *The Search* traces the contours of the story by describing her marriage to a young Marxist revolutionary who was sentenced to seven years in prison in 1949 and the trajectory of the writer from isolation to self-possession.

Throughout *The Search*, first- and third-person narration creates a split, unstable subjectivity. Allusions to 'the child', 'the girl', and 'the young woman at university' offer insight into the narrator's youth and maturity by way of a distance from which she surveys all stages of her youth and growth. Al-Zayyat offers the mature writer's perspective of the young revolutionary: she evokes the young woman on the run with her husband between Cairo and Alexandria where they are arrested and describes the arrest in the third person, followed by the first person. The change in point of view lays emphasis on her isolation on the day of her arrest after the Palestine War. She also employs third-person narration to describe her experience in the prison cell and interrogation at the Alexandria City Prison. Revisiting her 1949 imprisonment in the postindependence nation, the narrator distances herself and comments on the youthful revolutionary.

Parts 1 and 2 of *The Search* are evocative of the landscape in which her novel and memoir were read. While *The Open Door* evokes the anticolonial nationalism of the 1950s, *The Search* can be read in a context in which the nationalism and Third World leftist politics of the 1950s and 1960s were marginalised in 1970s Egypt. Although *The Open Door* traces the relation between national independence and women's liberation, *The Search* focuses on self-examination. En route to al-Qanatir prison, the narrator notes her 'dreams of revolution . . . side by side with the President's holiday home from which the order for my arrest, and thousands of others, came' (*HT*, 115; *SP*, 84).

While prison memoirs are centered on communal life, al-Zayyat's memoir calls attention to her solitude more than her political activism in

1970s Egypt. Caren Kaplan argues that women's prison memoirs turn the focus from the individual to the group. [32] Although al-Zayyat's experiences of prison are framed in the national struggle – anticolonial nationalism in the 1940s and anti-Zionist activism in the late 1970s – the memoir focuses on the solitude of the search. The ward search inspires the self-examination of the writer in a prison memoir and her search for the self in her relations with others. Al-Zayyat's metaphorical search commences with the writing of a diary and ends with the completion of a memoir.

The prison memoir explores the struggles of the individual within the national struggle. The community in prison is symbolic of the broader struggle against the state (Harlow 1987: 129). Relations between the prisoners are central to that struggle and, because of al-Zayyat's charges, anti-imperialist movements. Though the prisoners occupy separate prison cells, they discover unity and belonging. As Harlow observes in her reading of African prison memoirs, solitary confinement is enforced to destroy relations between co-prisoners (Harlow 1987: 151). However, the two groups of prisoners, Marxists and Islamists, on whose ideological divisions the prison administration depends, form alliances by signing petitions and organising strikes. Collectively, the prisoners develop ways to survive and resist the administration. In this case, they are involved in a strike to prevent Amina Rachid from being subjected to disciplinary action for attempting to smuggle letters out of prison. Marxists and Islamists sign the petition. On 13 November 1981, a prison source alerts the prisoners to the ward search and the preparations of the prisoners show the measures that they take to thwart the wardens and the Commissioner.

The power of writing and reading appears in the prison's prohibitions on the prisoners and the preparations for the ward search. [33] Writing in prison evokes the experience of Sonallah Ibrahim who writes a novel on cigarette paper that he smuggles out of prison and for whom prison offers a school and library from which he reads and that the prison wardens periodically supply with books. Ibrahim and his co-prisoners take turns to borrow a copy of each of the books the wardens procure and set up plays in prison. Like Ibrahim in *Notes*, al-Zayyat conceals her diary before the arrival of the authorities to inspect the ward. She and her co-prisoners are able to devise ways to prepare for the routine prison inspection. To prepare for the ward search on 13

November 1981, the narrator conceals other forbidden material – Amina Rachid's diary, pens, books, and a newspaper. During the search, the narrator collects the headscarves of the Islamists who have sought refuge in the lavatory upon the arrival of the Commissioner. As she collects the clothing of the Islamists, she remembers the scenes she had observed from the balcony in Mansura and the corpses she had wrapped in the green Egyptian flag after the Abbas Bridge massacre. She recounts the prison search in the first person rather than the third person employed throughout the memoir. The memoir ends with her contemplation of the ward search in al-Qanatir prison; she is now able to re-read and re-write her Alexandria City Prison diary and rework her scattered papers into a manuscript. As al-Zayyat notes, upon her release from prison, 'I felt the need to discover how to use the material of these memoirs for literary narratives rather than publish it as it was' (al-Zayyat 1994b: 260). Inspired to revise her diary, she ruminates on her subjectivity, insisting on the continuity of her political commitment.

Al-Zayyat's memoir focuses on the legacy of a popular revolutionary movement and a postcolonial landscape where women (and men) began to experience isolation and defeat rather than belonging and agency. While *The Open Door* focuses on anticolonial nationalism and nation building in 1950s Egypt, *The Search* concentrates on isolation and loss in the 1970s and 1980s.[34] By focusing on solitude, al-Zayyat examines the ways she sought to belong to national movements and retains her self-liberation through national belonging and commitment. In *The Search*, she employs fragmentation to show the struggle for balance, synthesis, and unity and reworks her scattered papers into a memoir where the subjective and the national coalesce.

Solitary Song

In *Fantasia*, Djebar assembles a rich archive of Algerian national history that revises French historiographical practice and reenvisions a European autobiographical tradition by exhuming indigenous sources – North African autobiographical writing, mutilated corpses, oral culture, and the writer-historian's commentary. Her autobiography shows through a palimpsest of sources and a polyphony of multiple voices staged around colonial history: the writer-historian's appropriation of French archives, her autobiographical voice, and the hybridisation of Algerian oral culture with archival colonial history. The narrator's story and the relationship of French, Arabic, and Amazigh invoke a history and language dominated by colonial violence, but Djebar lends her own voice (Algerian Arabic and Amazigh transposed into French) to women from her ancestral tribe, allowing them to speak through her in a threnody of voices. In these polyphonic sequences, she includes her 'solitary song', writing of her ancestors: 'They summon me, encouraging my faltering steps, so that at the given signal my solitary song takes off' (*F*, 217). Djebar frames her subjectivity within her revisionary historiographical reconstruction of the 1830 French colonial conquest of Algeria and writes her ancestry through the anonymous women and communal memory of the Algerian War of Independence.

While Djebar ushered in a 'new world' in her early novel, al-Zayyat envisioned the modern woman in her postindependence novel, *The Open Door*. Both writers offer autobiographical forms drawn from a common 'Third World' revolutionary history, and Djebar, in particular, draws on an indigenous heritage in the form of North African autobiography and testimony. In this particular genre of autobiography, the writers rework inherited forms: Djebar reframes autobiographical history through *métissage*; al-Zayyat contravenes the conventions of autobiography by employing unconventional forms such as fragmentation that departs from the evocation of the national project in *The Open Door*. While Djebar subverts the colonial gaze by turning her gaze inward and produces autobiography through adaptation, appropriation, intertextuality, and interpretation, al-Zayyat offers a condensation of experience through revolutionary ideals and national culture. Both writers rework a postcolonial subjectivity embedded in national history: Djebar problematises postcolonial women's subjectivity and Orientalist representations by reworking her autobiography into her revision of colonial history; al-Zayyat examines her subjectivity within national history and the form of her autobiography mirrors the fragmentation of the postcolonial national project.

3

Palestine Song: Mahmoud Darwish and Mourid Barghouti

> 'Exile' carries with it, I think, a touch of solitude and spirituality.
>
> Edward Said, *Reflections on Exile and Other Essays*

> Solitude is good training for being self-reliant. He writes the phrase and looks at the ceiling. Then he adds: To be alone . . . to be able to be alone is an educational experience. Solitude is choosing a sort of pain, training to conjugate the verbs of the heart with the freedom of the self-sufficient . . . Solitude is a filter, not a mirror . . . Solitude is the choice of someone with an abundance of possibilities – the choice of the free.
>
> Mahmoud Darwish, *A River Dies of Thirst*

> Darwish . . . makes an explicit declaration . . . : 'Your cause and your life are one. And before all this – and beyond it – it is your identity.' This identification is part of the symbolist equation of himself and Palestine. It is as much a poetic identification as it is political; in other words, it is an equation of the poetic with the political.
>
> Ibrahim Muhawi, 'Foreword', *Journal of an Ordinary Grief*

In 1986, the pre-eminent Palestinian poet Mahmoud Darwish (1941–2008) secluded himself in his Paris apartment for three months to write *Dhākirah li-l Nisyān* (*Memory for Forgetfulness: August, Beirut, 1982*, 1986) (Muhawi 1995: ix–xiii). *Memory for Forgetfulness* (henceforth *Memory*) is a prose memoir centred on his experience of the Israeli invasion of Beirut in the summer of 1982. Ibrahim Muhawi notes that Darwish wrote his memoir under a three-month 'self-siege' in Paris to replicate the experience of isolation and siege (Muhawi 1995: xiv). More than ten years later, Darwish wrote his masterwork *Jidārīyya* (*Mural*, 1999), an autobiographical epic written after the poet's heart surgery in Paris. Similarly, Palestinian poet Mourid Barghouti (b. 1944) produced two memoirs between exiles: *Ra'aytu Rāmallah* (*I Saw Ramallah*, 1996) and *Wulidtu Hunāka, Wulidtu Hunā* (*I Was Born There, I Was Born Here*, 2009). These prose memoirs articulate the role of Palestine in the poets' poetic imagination and the solitude in which they produced poetry. Solitude is conceived as a state to which they have been compelled by exile or one to which they aspire as poets.

Darwish's memoirs ushered in a new form of Arab autobiography that opened up the genre to the historical, political, and cultural changes in the Arab world and global literary sources. The 1990s saw an explosion of Palestinian autobiographical writing in the aftermath of the 1982 Israeli invasion of Beirut and the signing of the 1993 Oslo agreements. Poets such as Darwish and Barghouti, whose fate was perennially shaped by dispossession and exile, adapted the genre. The writings they produced blurred the borders between poetry and autobiography.[1] At the same time, they reexamined the poet's relationship to politics. These memoirs rethought Palestinian literature with new literary, cultural, and political landscapes in the Arab world. Darwish explores memory under siege and mortality while Barghouti explores his return to Palestine and the migration of his poetry. Both poets created a new poetic autobiography characterised by generic innovations, the migration of the memoirs, and the synthesis of literary and cultural traditions – Arabic, classical, biblical, European, and Latin American.[2]

Poetry played an important role in the Palestinian national movement from the 1960s. These new memoirs extended the role of lyric poetry to prose memoirs devoted to particular historical moments in the life of the poet. Darwish and Barghouti transformed the genre by reworking the prose memoir, exploring the poet's memory in contemporary political junctures, and synthesising local and global literary sources. Although Darwish's *Memory* and *Mural* have been the subject of much critical attention, they have not been read together with Barghouti's two memoirs to examine the development of the genre in contemporary Palestinian autobiographical writing.[3] An examination of the poets' subjectivity and relationship to Palestine contributes to the study of the relationship of poetry and politics in Palestinian poetic memoirs and the rise of new autobiographical forms.

Poetic Autobiography

While the history and development of the genre of autobiography in the Arab world underscore a long-standing tradition that extends to premodern Arabic literature, it is important to address contemporary autobiography that has become central to important anticolonial movements in the twentieth and twenty-first centuries, especially in relation to Palestine.[4]

Poets such as Wordsworth, Goethe, and Yeats produced a form characterised as 'the autobiography of the poet'.[5] Memoirs by Darwish and Barghouti depart from the memoir or autobiography (*sīra*) because they do not offer a narrative of the external events through which the poets lived or a prose narrative focusing on the development of the poet's personality, but instead focus on particular monumental events experienced by the poets such as the siege of Beirut or the return to Ramallah and examine the private experience in poetic prose. In this sense, they represent a condensed experience rather than an extended narrative devoted to the totality of the poet's life and focus on introspection rather than the narration of events.

The memoirs are framed within global literary influences from Europe to Latin America. Darwish's influences span Arabic and global poetry from Badr Shākir al-Sayyāb, 'Abd al-Wahāb al-Bayātī, and Nizār Qabbānī to Pablo Neruda, and especially García Lorca, whom he read in Palestine, Derek Walcott, Seamus Heaney, Yannis Ritsos, and René Char (Darwish 2006: 106–7). In an interview, Darwish names some of the influences on his poetry: 'And in Latin American poetry my favorite poet is Pablo Neruda' (108).

The memoirs of Darwish and Barghouti are situated within a larger frame of modern Palestinian autobiography and autobiographical writing produced by poets such as Fadwa Tuqan and Jabra Ibrahim Jabra. They are representative of Palestinian autobiography in the sense that they revisit the experiences of the poet in Palestine in 1948 juxtaposed with the present of the poet, yet they are also marked by the evolution of poetic prose and, in this way, depart from the prose memoirs of Tuqan and Jabra. The memoirs of Darwish and Barghouti are broached through genre because they develop a form that evolves from the poetry they produced and belongs to a multiplicity of genres; they also metaphorically disrupt geographical borders.

Jacques Derrida's 'The Law of Genre' is important in the consideration of the forms of the memoirs. Derrida asserts that 'a text cannot belong to no genre, it cannot be without or less a genre. Every text participates in one or several genres, there is no genreless text; there is always a genre and genres, yet such participation never amounts to belonging' (1980: 65). The memoirs of Darwish and Barghouti do not adhere to 'the normative definition of the genre, to the law of genre' (67). Darwish's *Memory* is part memoir, journal, prose, poetry, history, and dream, crossing the borders between genres. Moreover, it introduces such concepts as memory, remembrance, and memoir, differentiating between them in the way the poet creates a dichotomy between memory and forgetfulness, remembers particular events and wishes to forget others, and brings together the experience of the siege, his encounters with poets, his memory of Palestine, and his ruminations on the Arab political landscape. Memory is an important concept that recurs in Darwish's corpus in relation to the rupture created by the 1967 War and refers to the memory that Arabs have, the remembrance of 'a homeland that was lost' (*JO*, 32). It further alludes to a 'struggle between two memories' (*JO*, 33) whereby memory is analogous to Palestine and 'a way of mobilizing nationalist sentiment' (*JO*, 33). Darwish notes: 'What is homeland? To hold on to your memory – that is homeland' (*JO*, 37). In this way, the occupation of homeland extends to an assault on memory. The term 'memoir' is never used to categorise *Memory*, but the poet recounts his experience of the siege and his statements confirm its production in response to the event.

Critics have examined the relationship between exile and nationalism, noting the centrality of the nation in exile. Benedict Anderson's reflections on 'long-distance nationalism' in *The Specters of Nationalism* examine the effects of migration, diaspora, and 'revolutions in communications' on nationalism, provocatively posing questions about the national affiliations of diaspora communities (1998: 26). Anderson alludes to a kind of haunting, *el demonio de las comparaciones* or the spectre of comparisons between local and global models of nationalism (2). For him, "nationality' arose from exile', from the situation in which one could no longer dream of dying where one was born (60). For Anderson, long-distance nationalism includes the contribution of the migrant to the movements in his country from the nation in which he resides. Said notes the development of nationalism as an extension of the condition of exile: 'All nationalisms in their early stages develop from a condition of estrangement' (2000d: 176). Poets 'are cut off from their roots, their land, their past' and, therefore, contemplate the fate of a people; however, Said further notes that while nationalism concerns groups, 'in a very acute sense exile is a solitude experienced outside the group' (177). This implies the dichotomy with which the poet continually engages: poetry and politics.[6]

The memoirs produced in exile rework the poet's memory of Palestine against the systematic erasure of the *Nakba*, fusing communal history and poetic memory. The form of contemporary Palestinian memoirs differs from other post-1948 prose marked by the rupture created by the loss of Palestine.[7] Poets such as Darwish and Barghouti grew up during the *Nakba* and revisited its effects as they responded to other historical ruptures such as the 1967 War and the 1982 Israeli invasion of Beirut.

Jean Franco asserts: 'It was poetry rather than the realist novel that narrated Latin America's fragmented history as an epic adventure with the poet, not the politician, as prophet' (2002: 4). Similarly, poetry played a central role in the struggle for Palestine and helped poets examine the experience of dispossession. Poets adapted autobiography to explore the relationship of poetry to politics and poet to Palestine.

Memory and Memoir

> I am besieged by land and air and sea and language.
>
> Mahmoud Darwish, *A River Dies of Thirst*

Darwish would go on to rework the genre in a sequence of autobiographical writings ranging from diaries, journals, and prose poems: *Yawmiyyāt al-Ḥuzn al-'Ādī* (*Journal of an Ordinary Grief*), his 1973 diary dedicated to Gaza and the victims of the *Nakba*;[8] *Memory for Forgetfulness: August, Beirut, 1982*; *Ḥālat Ḥiṣār* (*State of Siege*, 2002), a poetic diary written under the Israeli blockade on Gaza and reoccupation of the West Bank during the 2002 Second Intifada; *Fī Ḥadrat al-Ghiyāb* (*In the Presence of Absence*, 2006), a lyric prose meditation composed as self-elegy; and *Nahr Yamūt min al-'Aṭash* (*A River Dies of Thirst*, 2008), a journal of poems, fragments, musings, and entries written in Ramallah during the Israeli attack on Gaza and Lebanon in the summer of 2006.[9] *Memory* and *Mural*, each of which marks an important moment in the life of Darwish, stage the drama of poet and Palestine, so recurrent in his poetry, in different autobiographical forms: prose memoirs and epic poem.

Critics have noted the tension between the political and the poetic, the national and the individual, in the poetry of Darwish throughout his career (Bernard and Elmarsafy 2012: 1).[10] Edward Said writes, 'In Darwish, the personal and the public are always in an uneasy relationship' (1994: 12). Said's comments on the status of Darwish as the national poet of Palestine and his 'political independence' imply the relationship of the national poet to the solitary one. Palestinian cultural production is embedded in the experience of dispossession and exile; Salma Khadra Jayyusi notes that Palestinian poets explored the personal tragedy and national history (2008: viii). Although Darwish was committed to the struggle, he aspired to produce poetry exploring his humanity. Darwish explored the poet's burden in his poem 'Who Am I, Without Exile?' in which the poet focuses on the centrality of exile and the occupation to his identity and poetry (2007: 90, 91). He stages the combination of solitude and intensely communal life that would characterise his poetry throughout his career.

The poetry and prose memoirs of Darwish explore an elusive state to which the poet has been compelled or drawn, a state of solitude to which the poet alludes in his poetry and that he pursues in the poems of *The River Dies of Thirst*, a diary of prose entries and poem fragments. In diary entries recorded during the Israeli aggression in the summer of 2006, the poet addresses the victims in Gaza, the West Bank, and Lebanon, but the poet also goes on to search in his 'desk drawers' for the self. These fragments are an evocation of his journeys in writing and encounters (with Derek Walcott and García Lorca's granddaughter) where the poet muses on poetry and memory. Solitude is a state he contemplates and parses: in the fragment cited in the epigraph of the chapter, the solitary poet in a study records his observations that solitude is 'training' for self-reliance and 'the choice of the free'. More important, the poet's writing gestures to how solitude is an elusive state, frequently interrupted, and a choice to which he aspires. The word 'solitude' in Arabic has multiple equivalents: '*al-wiḥda*', '*al-ʿuzla*' (the word used by Darwish in *Memory*), '*al-waḥsha*', and '*al-ghurba*'. Darwish observes: 'Many people complain about solitude (*al-ʿuzla*). As for me, I have grown addicted to solitude, I have nurtured it and made an intimate friendship with it'

(2006: 133). To define solitude, he focuses on self-containment and equates the state to the self: 'Solitude is one of the greatest tests for one's ability for self-possession (*al-tamassuk*) . . . and I feel that if I lost solitude I lost myself. I am careful to remain in this solitude; and this does not mean being cut off from life, reality, and people' (ibid.). Interruptions of solitude are staged in his memoirs where the poet addresses his lover and other poets. In *Journal of an Ordinary Grief*, the poet evokes another state of solitude where he is forbidden a travel permit to visit his mother and father in his village on a feast day and where his day at the beach evokes not the freedom that he should feel but a sense of imprisonment: 'In solitude you lie on warm sand in the open air . . . All around you people speak a language you understand, but your sadness and your loneliness and your alienation intensify' (*JO*, 70). Elsewhere he describes exile as a form of solitude required for his writing: 'Therefore, when in crowds, you long for yourself and for the solitude to write' (*PA*, 109).[11]

The production of *Memory* constitutes a reenactment of the siege of Beirut.[12] Darwish recalled the siege in a three-month self-imposed solitude in Paris.[13] In 1973, Darwish moved to Beirut where he settled for ten years until the Israeli invasion during which he moved to Tunis and then to Paris where he settled for more than a decade until his return to Ramallah in 1996. The memoir is the work of the poet in his study and the memory of the poet in the apartment overlooking the sea during the bombardment of Beirut. *Memory* is also based on the memory of the poet of the siege and his boyhood. In *Memory*, the poet cites from his poems and his name appears when an interlocutor addresses him in what can be read as his 'signature' (Hallaq 1998: 199).

Memory for Forgetfulness appeared in Arabic as *The Time: Beirut/The Place: August*, a memoir focusing on the poet's experience of the Israeli siege of Beirut in August 1982 (Muhawi 1995).[14] Amal Amireh reads *Memory* as an evocation of the poet's experience and Palestinian exile (Amireh 1995: 859). The poet experiences the Israeli bombardment of Beirut in his apartment overlooking the sea. He lights a gas lamp and walks over to his study in his glass-façade apartment besieged by jets, navy, and artillery. The poet revisits the encounter with death under the siege with irony: he is amused at the thought of death at the age of forty and wants to make love on the balcony – before the jets, boats, artillery, and Ashrafiya – to defy death and 'the fear of war'.

Memory opens with the poet's recurrent dream: 'Out of one dream, another dream is born./*Are you well? I mean, are you alive?*' (*DN*, 7; *MF*, 3).[15] The opening suggests that the prose memoir has been recalled from sleep, dream, and wakefulness. In *Memory*, the poet focuses on the paradoxes of memory, dreams, and desire during the siege. The poet crosses the hallway of his apartment to prepare a cup of coffee during the bombardment. As he notes, 'The conclusion is, I'm alive; or, more accurately, I exist' (*ana ḥayy . . . ana mawjūd*) (*DN*, 10; *MF*, 5). The poet, on the eighth floor of a building overlooking the sea under siege, expresses a desire for coffee: he wants 'a five-minute truce for the sake of coffee' (*DN*, 11). For him, this represents the promise of peace and 'solitude' (*'uzla*) (*DN*, 11–12; *MF*, 7). The use of the pronoun 'I' in *Memory* differs from its use in *Journal of an Ordinary Grief*, for example, where the 'I' can refer to both the poet and Palestinians (Muhawi 2010: x). Ironically, on a day when the news announces the bombardment of Beirut without conveying the scope of the event, the poet also wants a newspaper. Looking for a paper rescues the poet from a 'solitary to a collective death' (*DN*, 28; *MF*, 24). The poet walks slowly in the street and feels as though he is walking in a funeral in the graveyard of Beirut. He takes shelter in a bombed building and notes that his office (he was the Director of the Research Center of the Palestine Liberation Organization (PLO) in Beirut) has been destroyed.[16] Invoking T. S. Eliot's 'April is the cruelest month', the poet notes: 'August is the cruelest month. August is the longest of months. And today is the cruelest day in August, and the longest' (*DN*, 119; *MF*, 118). It is a day in which the echoes of Shakespeare's Hamlet assume tragically collective proportions: 'To be, or not to be. To be, or to be. Not to be, or not to be' (*nakūn aw lā nakūn. Nakūn aw nakūn. Lā nakūn aw lā nakūn*) (*DN*, 120; *MF*, 118). The plural form of the Arabic '*nakūn aw lā nakūn*' (to be, or not to be) transposes Hamlet's question to the Arab nation (or Palestinians, especially Palestinians in Lebanon). It is not a question of death; rather, the poet fears non-being. He presages, on the anniversary of the Hiroshima bomb on 6 August 1982, during the bombardment of Beirut: 'Hiroshima is tomorrow' (*DN*, 88; *MF*, 85).

Language, poetry, and solitude are besieged in *Memory*. When an American journalist at the Hotel Commodore asks Darwish about writing poetry during the siege, he responds: 'I'm writing my silence' (*DN*, 65; *MF*,

61). Writers proclaim under the siege: 'If the poem is not born "now," then when will it be born? And if it's to be born later, what value has it "now"?' (*DN*, 66; *MF*, 63) This evokes his 'poetic' response to the Beirut siege in Paris (Rahman 2008: 322). Darwish remarks on the impossibility of poetry under siege: 'I have yet to write it [the story or the siege] or forget' (*DN*, 168; *MF*, 163). Replying to expectations that he produce poetry under siege, he observes: 'I would ask: Is poetry possible?' and 'the poet wants his solitude' (321–2). Language eludes the poet during the siege. In Paris, Darwish subjects his poetry to a state of siege to replicate the calamity (Muhawi 1995: xvi). It is implied that the poet can only recall language and produce poetry after the event.

For Darwish, memory is a mode of life. The memoir explores the memory of the arrests, imprisonment, harassment, and return to Palestine after 1948 against the forgetfulness of the siege. *Memory* contemplates the poet's mortality and future during the summer of 1982. As the title suggests, *Memory* explores paradoxes: memory and forgetfulness, presence and absence. Muhawi outlines the implications of the title: 'a use of memory *for the purpose of* forgetfulness, for purging the violent emotions attached to the events described. The poet wanted to forget' (Muhawi 1995: xix; emphasis in original). Yet *Memory* clearly reconstructs the poet's memory. It is implied that 'memory' alludes to Palestine and 'forgetfulness' alludes to the siege. Muhawi also suggests that 'memory is for forgetfulness – to be forgotten' (xxiv). *Memory* acquires the status of history for Palestinians, who are born in refugee camps without 'birth certificate or name registration' (*DN*, 18; *MF*, 14).

Revisiting one day of the siege, the poet notes the importance of memory for existence: 'No one wants to forget; more accurately no one wants to be forgotten' (*DN*, 19; *MF*, 15). In Beirut, where he endured a ten-year exile after he left Palestine in 1971, he retraces the path of the young boy he has forgotten. Darwish remembers his departure from his village al-Birweh in Galilee to Lebanon in his boyhood, a memory he explores at length in *Journal of an Ordinary Grief*. In 1948, he fled from his village with his mother to Lebanon and moved to the refugee camp in Damur, where the children 're-created the homeland'. They left him in al-Burj Square where he rode a streetcar. Darwish asserts the importance of his memory and experience: 'I'm searching for a boy here, not for a homeland' (*DN*, 92; *MF*, 89).[17] *Memory* recounts the story of his return, a year later, and discovery that the Israeli army had razed his village whereupon he returned to Galilee without a citizenship in the new state where returnees held the status of 'present-absentees' under the occupation (*J*, 14) and became itinerants and refugees (*PA*, 45). Remembering his exile, he resumes: 'Did I forget to return, or did I forget to remember?' (*DN*, 178–9; *MF*, 172). *Memory* encompasses the poet's history and communal memory.

In *Memory*, the language of the poet is under siege. In parts of *Memory*, prose breaks down into poetry and different forms of speech (monologue, dialogue, essays, and interviews) (Gonzales-Quijano 1998: 187). Form in *Memory* evokes the rupture marked by the invasion and the expulsion of the Palestinians from Beirut.[18] *Memory* does not adhere to conventional generic categories: it contains musings and fragments of essays on the discourse of pan-Arabism and Arab nations' silence. Darwish also alludes to important Arab poets: Palestinian poet Muʿin Bseiso (Muʿīn Bsīsū) whose fate haunts him; the Lebanese poet Khalīl Ḥāwī; and Palestinian writer ʿIzzeddīn al-Qalaq with whom he imagines a conversation (Reigeluth 2008: 316).

Love during the siege reinforces the poet's focus on existence and memory and also serves to respond to criticism of his love poetry. The poet returns to the Israeli lover of his early poetry, a lover with whom 'sharing a silence would be a solitude' (*DN*, 132; *MF*, 130).

In the end, the poet invokes his famous 1964 poem 'Identity Card' ('Biṭāqat hawīya'): 'Put this in your record: I'm Arab!' ('*Sajjil/Anā ʿArabī*') (*DN*, 180; *MF*, 174).[19] 'Identity Card', written in his early poetic career, grew out of his experience from 1961 to 1969 when he would regularly report to the police station in Haifa under the occupation. No poem explains the relationship of citizenship to existence more than 'Identity Card': without a citizenship or a certificate of existence, he must prove he exists (Muhawi 1995: xiii). In *Journal of an Ordinary Grief*, the young poet goes on to parse the paradox of identity and existence he discovers through the control of mobility under the occupation:

> You ask for a passport, but you discover you are not a citizen because your father or one of your relatives had fled with you during the Palestine War.

> You were a child, and you discover that any Arab who had left his country during that period and had stolen back in had lost his right to citizenship.
>
> You despair of the passport and ask for a laissez-passer. You find you are not a resident of Israel because you have no certificate of residence. You think this is a joke and rush to tell your lawyer friend: 'Here, I'm not a citizen, and I'm not a resident either. Then where and who am I?' You are surprised to find the law is on their side, and you must prove you exist. You ask the Ministry of the Interior, 'Am I here, or am I absent? Give me an expert in philosophy, so that I can prove to him I exist.' (*JO*, 66)

In *Journal of an Ordinary Grief*, this self-examination is part of a series of encounters that show the poet's quotidian problems with citizenship and recurs in a series of rhetorical questions framing encounters with the Israeli state, denials of travel permits, house arrests, interrogations, and detention: 'You want to travel to Jerusalem?' 'You want to travel to Greece?' 'You want to celebrate your birthday?' 'You want to rent an apartment?' 'You want to visit your mother on a feast day?' (*JO*, 64–70) In 'Identity Card', he declares to an Israeli officer: 'Put this in your record: I exist!' As Darwish explains, 'I said it in Hebrew to provoke him' (*DN*, 180; *MF*, 174). But when he reworked the words into a poem, he proclaimed his identity and existence across the Arab world. Edward Said noted the importance of the poem: 'If there is anything written by a Palestinian that can be called a national poem, it would have to be Mahmoud Darwish's short work *Bitaqit Hawia*' (1979: 155). Muhammad Siddiq reads the extraordinary encounter between the young poet and the Israeli official dramatised in the poem:

> The poem dramatizes an encounter between a Palestinian civilian and an Israeli official, perhaps in the office of the military governor, where, between 1948–1966, the Arab citizens of Israel had to go every so often to secure an official, written permit to travel from one village or town to another within Israel. The encounter often involved a spurious 'interrogation' of the Palestinian applicant, intended more to harass and humiliate than anything else. This is likely a setting as any for the dramatic action of the poem. In an astounding rhetorical feat the young poet – twenty-three at the time – turns tables on the interrogating officer and 'dictates' to him not only the term of the terms of the present 'exchange' between them but also that of all future

> relations between the two national entities metonymically represented by the two interlocutors. (Siddiq 2007: 494)

In Beirut, the poet is compelled to reiterate the command: 'Write this down!' It is a statement that he exists – not in the absence of papers – but under the siege by land, air, sea, and language.

Memory circles back to the topos of death with which it commences (and that the poet addresses in *Mural*). The poet asserts: 'And here, I didn't die. I haven't died here yet. Ten years I've lived here. I've never before lived in a place for ten years' (*DN*, 184; *MF*, 178). However, *Memory* anticipates his departure and the evacuation of Palestinian *fidayīn* from Lebanon. Darwish writes: 'we'll take our martyrs with us to sea' (*DN*, 155; *MF*, 151). It further anticipates changes in the poet's trajectory and poetry after Lebanon.[20] The memoir ends with a scene of love and allusions to the sea, recalling the poet's recurrent departures. The final scene contains an encounter and exchange between the poet and a fighter that questions the relation between private poetic language and the common language. The poetic speaker (named when his interlocutor addresses him as 'Brother Mahmoud' (*DN*, 185; *MF*, 179)) encounters a fighter from Haifa born in a refugee camp who asks him about the meaning of the 'sea', a word that in Arabic denotes both the sea and a meter of rhythmical poetry, to whom he responds: 'My sea is your *sea*, and your sea is my *sea*' (*Baḥrī huwa baḥruk, huwa baḥrī*) (*DN*, 186; *MF*, 180; emphasis in translation). The speaker asserts that his sea is the same sea his compatriots know, concluding on a note that he speaks a common language through his poetry.

Mural and Memoir

While *Memory* recounts a day in the life of the poet under the siege of Beirut, *Mural*, his autobiographical epic, focuses on his mortality. Solitude is a state under siege in *Memory* and on the threshold of death in *Mural*. Rather than the more communal elegy in *Memory, Mural* has been read as self-elegy, a memorialisation of the poet's own death.[21]

Darwish wrote *Mural* after undergoing heart surgery in Paris in August 1998. He began to write because he feared that he had forgotten language (Khoury 2009). *Mural* was written as a final work focusing on the mortality and humanity of the poet (Akash 2000: 46). The epic adapted a rich cultural inheritance represented by Arab-Islamic, biblical, Mesopotamian, and Western mythology and various poetic sources.[22] *Mural* can be read as his self-elegy, his poetic challenge to death, and a summation of his poetry, conceived through his synthesis of mythologies and cultures.

Mural is a late work exploring the dichotomy of the private and the public running through Darwish's poetry (Joudah 2009b). It offers an exploration of mortality by focusing on the poet's encounter with death. The poetic speaker addresses death, nurses, and doctors as his wardens, interrogators, and torturers in prison (ibid.). Describing his hallucinations in the hospital after his heart surgery in *In the Presence of Absence*, Darwish evokes a scene in which he addresses a prison guard, 'but nothing comes out', gestures that he wants a pen and paper, and writes 'I have lost my language' (*PA*, 102). He describes a visit by Elias Khoury ('the author of *Gate of the Sun*') at the hospital and his hallucination wherein he narrates the story of his torture and asks his visitors to help smuggle him out: 'Soon, when the guards are distracted, take me with you! Get me out of this prison!' (*PA*, 103). Embedded in the poet's relationship to Palestine, the poem focuses on his subjectivity and a synthesis of traditions that embody the broader history of his humanity.

The form of *Mural* is central to its role in the corpus and life of the poet. It is an extended poem in the form of an epic, but, to use the words of Derrida, it 'participates in several genres' such as the short poem (*qasīda*) and the epic (*malḥama*) (Ghazoul 2012: 39).[23] But this participation precludes a belonging to genre; in other words, the poem may take part in these genres 'without belonging' (Derrida 1980: 59; Ghazoul 2012: 41). Ferial Ghazoul notes that the genres of lyric and epic produce the 'topoi' of the poems where the lyric expresses the individual and the epic recounts the national (2012: 39). Darwish's poem belongs to the epic or the mural (Bernard and Elmarsafy 2012: 9), forms that imply a communal story. The classical epics such as *Gilgamesh*, Homer's *Iliad* and *Odyssey*, or Virgil's *Aeneid* focus on heroes whose exploits are related to the founding of a nation. The genre of epic is implied in the title of the poem because the word 'mural' evokes an extended collective narrative, but that of autobiography is implied in the subtitle containing the poet's name '*Jidārrīyat Maḥmūd Darwīsh*' (Mahmoud Darwish's Mural) (Ghazoul 2012: 39). In this sense, *Mural* synthesizes and extends forms: lyric and epic, poetry and autobiography. It furthers the interplay of the personal and the political, the autobiographical and the national. Murals preserve communal memory as they represent historical events in the fate of a community and they are often produced collectively as a public archive (41). As Ghazoul reads the rich cultural resonances of Darwish's adaptation of the form of the mural:

> Darwish uses the term 'al-nashid al-malhami' (the epical hymn) in his *Mural (M* 131–2/*J* 39) as if he is drawing attention to his own poem/epic. Darwish explained in his address why he chose the title: 'The mural is an artistic work, carved or painted and hung on a wall, in the belief that the work can be seen from far and can survive geographically and historically.' He went on to ask rhetorically if that indicated his obsession with immortality behind choosing a title equivalent to *al-mu'alaqa*, the poem selected to be hung on the kaaba in pre-Islamic Arabia for its excellence. He added: 'No, the obsession that took hold of me, namely, that I will not live to write another work. That is why I called it *Jidariyya* as it was meant to be my last collection that would condense my poetic experience, constituting a panegyric to life.' (Ghazoul 2012: 42)

In this passage, Darwish asserts that he was not concerned with immortality conferred by a poem of the stature of the Arabian odes (*mu'allaqāt*), but with his mortality, his final work, and the condensation of his poetry. *Mural* opens with a scene that recurs throughout the poem: the poetic speaker addressed by a nurse in a hospital room. The poem opens with the poet's name stated by the nurse in a scene evocative of a naming ceremony. The scene is telling because the poet's name opens an epic poem, infusing the national form with the autobiographical story.

> This is your name
> a woman said
> and disappeared in the spiraling corridor. (*J*, 9; *M*, 101)[24]

As the poetic speaker contemplates his state of delirium, evoking the 'nothingness' and 'whiteness' enshrouding him, he expresses his existence in a state between being and non-being: 'I was/and I wasn't' (*M*, 101) (*kuntu, wa lam/akun*) (*J*, 10). Echoing his statement in *Memory* in the plural '*nakūn aw lā nakūn*' (translated as 'to be or not to be'), the poetic speaker speaks in the first person, declaring that he was and he wasn't. The first person 'I' dominates the second stanza, where he rests in an 'eternal whiteness' (*J*, 10; *M*, 101). He repeats for emphasis on subjectivity and solitude: 'I was alone in whiteness,/alone' (*J*, 10; *M*, 101). With the exception of the nurse, his interlocutor, in the short opening stanza, there are no interlocutors to interrupt his solitude, no angel, none of the virtuous or sinners who populate Dante's *Divine Comedy*, in 'non-place, in non-time,/or in non-being' (*J*, 11; *M*, 102). Although the speaker observes 'It's as if I had died before now' and suspects 'I'm still alive in some place, where/I still know what I want' (*J* 11–12; *M*, 102), he declares: 'One day I will become what I want' (*J*, 12; *M*, 102). This declaration is repeated nine times in the following stanzas, once as 'One day I will become a poet' (J, 13; *M*, 103), followed by the use of the first-person plural: 'One day we will become what we want' (*J* 16; *M*, 104). Clearly, the use of the first-person plural invokes the future of Palestine. The poet in a state between life and death is 'the synecdoche for Palestine' (Ghazoul 2012, 39). While the verb used in these lines is 'to become' in Arabic, the line in which the speaker turns to the collective 'we' reverts to the verb 'to be' in Arabic. The English translation repeats the verb 'to become' for poetic repetition. However, the Arabic '*sanakūnu yawman mā nurīd*' ('One day we will be what we want') (*J*, 16) alludes to the preceding allusions to being and non-being, 'I was and I wasn't', and the plural of 'to be or not to be' that haunts the besieged narrator in *Memory*. Further, the stanza in which the poet declares 'One day I will become a poet' reworks the allusion 'to be or not to be' with its subversion; the poet writes: 'I am who I was and who I will be' (*M*, 103). Rather than the existential question posed by the narrator of *Memory*, the speaker expresses certainty in *Mural*: he is who he was and who he will be. The line in Arabic (*ana man kuntu aw sa'akūn*) (*J*, 14) plays upon the phrase 'to be or not to be' (*nakūn aw lā nakūn*) in *Memory* where the speaker addresses his poet-friends in the midst of the siege with echoes of the Hamletian 'to be or not to be' that take on a note of mourning: 'They have gone, the ones you love. Gone./You will either have to be/Or you will not be' (*fa' imma an takūn aw la takūn*) (*DN*, 62; *MF*, 59). The nurse interrupts his dream, hallucination, delirium, and solitude, instructing him to remember his name:

This is your name
a nurse said[25]
and disappeared in her corridor's whiteness:
This is your name, remember it well!
And don't disagree with it over a letter (*J*, 15; *M*, 104)

The nurse's imperatives – that he 'remember', not 'disagree with', write and pronounce his name – lay emphasis on the speaker. The speaker responds by invoking the communal through the first-person plural: 'One day *we* will be what *we* want' (emphasis added). Subsequently, he expresses his search for the self in others so that his dilemma is not 'to be or not to be' but to be himself or the multitude:

Whenever I searched for myself I found
the others. Whenever I searched for the others I found
only my stranger self in them,
so am I the one, the multitude? (*J*, 23; *M*, 107)

The poet dreams of a French doctor opening his 'cell', his father on his return from Hajj, René Char 'sitting with Heidegger' (*J*, 30; *M*, 111) and drinking wine; the Arab poet al-Ma'arri expelling critics from his poem; and his mother's loaf of bread. *Mural* abounds in allusions to the land and the nation: 'Green, my poem's land is green' and 'There is no nation smaller than its poem' (*J*, 33; *M*, 112). Recalling his land, the speaker invokes Narcissus, the mythical analogue of the poet contemplating himself in his poem: 'I have/the narcissus contemplating the water of its image' (*J*, 41; *M*, 115). The speaker addresses Death to express his concern about language and mortality, declaring: 'And I want to live, I want to live' (*J*, 55; *M*, 122). His concern with language dominates his dialogues and interior monologues: the poet who 'forgot speech' in his state is concerned with the language spoken in 'the eternal whiteness' and 'timelessness' and the return of his language: 'And what's the spoken language there:/colloquial for all, or classical Arabic?' (*J*, 51; *M*, 120) and 'bring life back to my language' (*J*, 66; *M*, 127). In *Mural*, the solitary poet, exhausted by politics, aspires to a return to language, not the land or the beloved (Wazen 2006: 54) in an echo of Darwish who notes: 'Go to the Arabic sentence, and you will find self and homeland' (*JO*, 138).[26] In *Memory*, the narrator is concerned with the fate of his corpse and wants 'a calm, orderly funeral' with 'wreaths of red and yellow roses' and no violets (*DN*, 29; *MF*, 25). In *Mural*, the speaker sets down his funeral wishes: 'Don't place violets on my grave: violets are/for the depressed, to remind the dead of love's/premature death. Place seven green ears/of wheat on the coffin instead, and some/anemones, if either can be found. Otherwise, leave the roses/of the church to the church and the weddings' (*J*, 50; *M*, 119). The speaker's interlocutor lays bare the anxieties of the poet and the conflation of Palestine with the poem:

> My nurse says: You used to hallucinate
> often and scream at me
> I don't want to return to anyone,
> I don't want to return to any country
> after this long absence . . .
> I want only to return
> to my language in the distances of the cooing
>
> My nurse says:
> You would hallucinate for a long while and ask me:
> Is death what you are doing to me now
> or is it the death of language? (*J*, 67; *M*, 127–8)

Darwish's allusions feature sources drawn from global mythology in an adaptation of classical epic into Arabic poetry and perform a synthesis of biblical, classical, and Arab-Islamic traditions that extend the national to the human and the universal. Darwish includes allusions to the Old Testament, Osiris, Imru' al-Qays, Anat, Gilgamesh, Enkidu, the Song of Songs, Majnun Layla, Homer, Penelope, Christ, and Adam. Each of these allusions has a relation to the predicament of the poet: the wandering Odysseus and Penelope; Imru' al-Qays, 'who was scattered between Caesar and rhyme' (*M*, 130), dramatises the dichotomy of politics and poetry;[27] Osiris and Christ are symbols of resurrection; Gilgamesh endures 'from one epoch to another' (*M*, 134) and the fate of Enkidu is death ('Enkidu slept but didn't wake' (*M*, 134)); and Majnun Layla at the ruins of the beloved's camp epitomises loss. In an interview, Darwish commented on the import of the content and form of *Mural*: 'In *Mural*, I wrote about a personal experience that was a way for me to go on to the question of death, from the oldest texts that concerned death, among them the epic of Gilgamesh which also concerned immortality and life' (2006b: 93–4). He further details the autobiographical shards of the epic, confirming its status:

> This experience was for me a narrative framework or what resembles autobiography (*al-sīra al-dhātiyya*). At the moment of death life passes before you in flashes. I lived this and saw it. All the visions I wrote about in the poem were real: al-Maʿarrī and the meeting of Heidegger and René Char . . . I saw a lot and did not write everything. But I noticed that the poem was drawn to the question of life more than the question of death. And in the end, the poem was a song for life. (Darwish 2006b: 94)

Jeffrey Sacks writes, 'The weariness of the poet entails a relation to the days of Imru' al-Qays and his language' (2015: 70). He reads the stanza where the poet is 'tired' of what his language 'says or doesn't say', where language is divided 'between Caesar and rhyme' (*M*, 130). The speaker invokes death, 'immortality' (*M*, 136), and 'eternity' (*M*, 137). *Mural* calls attention to the importance of local influences in Darwish's poetry: biblical and Qur'anic mythology and an Arab literary heritage such as Imru' al-Qays, Ṭarafa Ibn al-ʿabd, Abū al-ʿAla' al-Maʿarrī, and Ibn Ḥazm al-Andalusī's *Ṭawq al-Ḥamāmah* (*The Collar of the Dove*). Darwish reworks biblical language from Ecclesiastes in the poem (Wazen 2006). These allusions point to the incorporation of 'some classical forms into the new Arabic poetic sensibility' that predate colonialism (Aboul-Ela 2010: 745).

Beyond the biblical mythology rooted in the land, other inherited forms incorporated in *Mural* include the Sufi and the metaphysical. Darwish admits that he read Sufi literature such as Ibn ʿArabī: 'I do not look at Sufism intellectually or philosophically; I look at it poetically in terms of the adventure of going to the furthest ends and a different way of relating to the universe and an attempt to search for what is beyond that universe, nature, and existential questions. I am not concerned in the Sufi experience with its meaning as much as I am concerned with its attempt in language and knowledge to reach what other adventures do not reach' (2006b: 92).

Another interlocutor is a prison warden who tells the speaker that he is a prisoner. The poem closes with the pronunciation of the poetic speaker's name Maḥmūd, or 'writing of the poet's name' (Sacks 2015: 70). The stanza in which his name appears names the things that the speaker repossesses – the sea, the air, surat al-Rahman, the key (an important symbol for abandoned houses in Palestine) – and ends with his name: 'and my name,/even if I mispronounce it/with five horizontal letters, is mine' (*J*, 102; *M*, 144):

> *Meem*/the infatuated, the orphaned, the finale of what has passed.
> *Ḥā*/the garden and the beloved, two puzzles and two laments.
> *Meem*/the adventurer, the readied and ready for his death,
> the one promised exile, and desire's ill patient.
> *Wāw*/farewell, the middle rose, loyal to birth wherever possible,
> and the pledge of parents.
> *Dal*/the guide, the road, the tear of a meadow that has perished, and a house
> sparrow that spoils me and bleeds me. (*J*, 102–3; *M*, 144)

The speaker lays claim to his body ('absent or present'), 'two meters of earth', and his name; 'and my name,/even if I misspell it on the coffin,/is mine' (*J*, 104; *M*, 145).[28] Sacks reads the stanza in which Darwish spells his name and the closing lines ('I am not mine') through loss and return: 'Rather than a return to a place, the serene belonging of self or a language in place, Darwish's text scripts returns that come back under one name and then another'; 'If Darwish in a certain sense possessed his name . . ., this possession becomes a form of repetition and nonbelonging ("I am not mine/I am not mine/I am not mine")' (72). The speaker here also spells and writes what he possesses, or what belongs to him, in a clear movement from being and nonbeing ('to be or not to be') to belonging (in Arabic, 'ma kāna lī . . . wa mā sayakūnu lī' – 'what was mine . . . and what will be mine').

> But I,
> now that I have become filled
> with all the reasons of departure,
> I am not mine
> I am not mine
> I am not mine. (*J*, 104–5; *M*, 145)

The closing lines establish a contrast between his possession of self, language, or place and his nonbelonging. Concluding the play on being and belonging recurring throughout *Mural*, these lines represent an enigma that betokens departure and separation. Darwish explains that 'I am not mine' connotes exile (*ghurba*), and notes: 'Nothing remains of the poet but some of his poetry' (Darwish 2006b: 153) and 'In the end, he is ephemeral (*zā'il*) and language is eternal (*bāqiyah*).'[29] He further adds: '"I am not mine" on the personal level, but I might "be mine" (*akūnu lī*) on the poetic level, and if I have any value then it will not be my own (*lan takūnu lī*), but for language and others' (154). Like *Memory*, *Mural* closes with all the reasons for the speaker's departure, or disappearance in the spiral path of whiteness with which the poem opens.

Mural elaborates the concerns of *Memory for Forgetfulness* with being and belonging, offers another form that richly draws on global sources, and features clear autobiographical features such as Darwish's name. Like *Mural*, *In the Presence of Absence* focuses on death and self-elegy, and sheds light on allusions to solitude prevalent in Darwish's poetry.

Migrant Memoirs

In *Memory*, Darwish recounts one day of the siege in exile. In *I Saw Ramallah*, Barghouti revisits his twelve-day visit to his village of Deir Ghassaneh after a thirty-year exile. While *Memory* is set during the occupation of Beirut and the departure of Palestinians from Lebanon, *I Saw Ramallah* explores the poet's exile from Palestine after the 1967 War and his return to Ramallah in 1996. In this sense, Darwish's memoirs rehearse the departures of the poet whereas Barghouti offers narratives of return.

Barghouti re-animated Palestinian autobiographical writing and further developed prose memoirs. The forms he reworks in the memoirs are multifarious: memoir, poem fragments, anecdotes, and travelogue. The memoirs are situated between Egypt and Palestine: they evolve from the exile and return of the poet.[30] The poet also situates his memoirs in an Arab autobiographical tradition, invoking Fadwa Tuqan's *A Mountainous Journey: An Autobiography* and the arrest of Latifa al-Zayyat among 1,536 writers in September 1981 (narrated in *The Search: Personal Papers*). Moreover, *I Saw Ramallah* and *I Was Born There, I Was Born Here*, his 1996 and 2009 memoirs, represent a memoir of the poet on his return to Palestine and another of his son on his journey to Palestine; one tells the story of his separation from his family in Palestine and the other tells the story of his separation from his family in Egypt. The movement of poet and migration of memoir between Cairo and Ramallah challenge the regulation of movement in Palestine and Egypt epitomised in experiences of deportation, checkpoints, and curfews. Indeed, the memoirs metaphorically defy the firmly drawn borders imposed by Israel through migration between Egypt and Palestine. They underline the relation of the poet to Palestine even as he asserts his independence and autonomy.

Barghouti shared the 'solitude of exile' recurrently examined by Said and Darwish. Born in the Palestinian village of Deir Ghassaneh in 1944, Barghouti would move to Egypt in 1963 to attend Cairo University, later settling in Egypt after the 1967 War and Israeli occupation of the West Bank until 1977. That year, he was deported on the eve of Egyptian president Anwar Sadat's trip to Jerusalem, living in exile in Budapest and Beirut until he was allowed to return to Egypt in 1995, penning poetry and memoirs. *I Saw Ramallah* and *I Was Born There, I Was Born Here*, metaphorically and literally, revisit Palestine after decades of exile. Clearly, Barghouti's memoirs are embedded in a national movement; his story is shaped by the communal story from the loss of Palestine in 1948 to the return of the poet in 1996.

In 1995, after his return to Egypt, Barghouti wrote *I Saw Ramallah*, a memoir that narrates a visit to his village after an extended exile and underscores the centrality of his exile after the 1967 War and the Israeli occupation of the West Bank to his life and poetry. Edward Said describes the memoir as 'one of the finest existential accounts of Palestinian displacement that we now have' and 'an account of loss in the midst of return and reunion' (2000a: vii, x).

I Saw Ramallah opens with the poet's return to Palestine after thirty years: 'Here I am crossing the Jordan River' (*SR*, 1). The poet contemplates the Jericho Bridge (formerly Allenby Bridge), a checkpoint between Jordan and the West Bank on which exiles are interrogated and that he crossed from Ramallah to Amman on his way to Egypt in 1966. The narrator cites the names of the Bridge in colonial history and common language:

> Fayruz [the famous Lebanese singer] calls it the Bridge of Return. The Jordanians call it the King Hussein Bridge. The Palestinian Authority calls it al-Karama [Dignity] Crossing. The common people and the bus and taxi

> drivers call it the Allenby Bridge. My mother, and before her my grandmother and my father and my uncle's wife, Umm Talal, call it simply: the Bridge. (*RR*, 15; *SR*, 10)[31]

In 1996, the poet stands on the Jordanian bank on the lookout for the signal to cross the bridge and enter Palestine. This is a moment of return narrated through his perception of the bridge, which becomes 'a metaphor for endurance' (Bernard 2007: 666). The bridge recalls the memory of the poet's return to Cairo in 1966 and the event in 1967 that would commence his exile. He was about to graduate from Cairo University in 1967 but on the morning of 5 June 1967 he learns from Voice of the Arabs radio station that 'Ramallah is no longer mine and that I will not return to it. The city has fallen' (*RR*, 7; *SR*, 3).[32] Forbidden entry into Palestine, he discovers 'displacement' in the summer of 1967.[33] Thirty years later, the poet on the west bank of the Jordan River declares: 'This then is the "Occupied Territory"?' (*RR*, 10; *SR*, 6). Rather than his poetry, the poet comes into contact with the reality of Palestine upon his return: 'It is no longer "the beloved" in the poetry of resistance . . . it is not an argument or a metaphor' (*RR*, 11; *SR*, 6). This is an unknown beloved adored by generations created by the Occupation (*SR*, 62). The poet – 'I the individual, the stranger who leaned toward silence and solitude' (*SR*, 65) – returns from exile, where he perfected 'his solitude' (*BT*, 170), to Palestine.

I Saw Ramallah narrates a return and rediscovery of the geography of Palestine in parallel with a contemplation of the status of the poet through residence and repatriation. The poet was not allowed an identity card and is therefore not a citizen of the Occupied Territories; he is unable to enter Jerusalem; and the purpose of his return is to apply for a 'reunion' identity card to grant him the right to citizenship after thirty years and to obtain a visa for his Cairo-born son Tamim (the Palestinian-Egyptian poet Tamīm Barghūtī) to visit Palestine. The poet notes: 'I no longer know the geography of my own land' (*SR*, 10). When he returns to his ancestral village Deir Ghassaneh, he observes the Israeli settlements: 'The Settlements are the Palestinian Diaspora itself' (*SR*, 30). Throughout his visit, he notes the expropriation of land and water.[34] In a restrained elegy – one the narrator may affiliate with Neruda in *I Saw Ramallah*, where he remembers that 'in

Ghassan [Kanafani]'s world there was room for the poems of Neruda' (*RR*, 22; *SR*, 16) – he focuses on the elemental details of Palestinian life.[35]

I Saw Ramallah focuses on the fellowship with poets and writers in the world of Barghouti. The poet-narrator preserves an iconic image of the Palestinian writer Ghassan Kanafani (Ghassān Kanafānī) in his office in Beirut and the posters plastered on the walls of emblems of liberation movements in Asia, Africa, and Latin America invoked in the struggle for Palestine: 'The star on Guevara's beret'; Neruda, 'the words of Cabral . . . and the vision of Fanon' (*RR* 22; I 16). Further, he alludes to the Turkish poet Nazim Hikmet's poetry of exile (*RR*, 51, 41); *A Mountainous Journey: An Autobiography* by Fadwa Tuqan, who visited him in Amman (*RR*, 120, 99); and Latifa al-Zayyat who was imprisoned in September 1981 with 'Awatif 'Abd al-Rahman, Amina Rachid, Safinaz Qazim, Farida al-Naqqash, and Shahinda Maqlad (*RR*, 152, 128).

Another story of exile and return is narrated in parallel in *I Saw Ramallah*: his return to Cairo. In 1977, he was visited by six plainclothes policemen of the State Security Service on the morning of the feast and deported. In 1995, he was permitted to return to Egypt after a seventeen-year prohibition. In this sense, the poet is poised between 'the clarity of displacement' and 'the uncertainty of return' (*SR*, 73).

The death of his brother Munīf haunts his crossing of the bridge; the narrator remembers that his brother was turned away from the bridge twice, and concludes: 'Being forbidden to return killed him' (*RR*, 44; *SS*, 35). In Deir Ghassaneh, he visits the family house Dār Ra'd, where he begins his elegy for his brother Munīf, whom he wishes to restore to his village with his poetry. Between his deportation from Cairo in 1977 (when his son was five months old) and his return to Ramallah in 1996, he elegises the exile of displaced Palestinians refused by the capitals of the world. The memoir elegises three Palestinians: his brother Munīf al-Barghūthī who died a 'solitary, lonely, mysterious death in the Gare du Nord' (*RR*, 196; *SS*, 163); the Palestinian political cartoonist Nājī al-'Alī, shot on 22 July 1987 in London; and the Palestinian writer Ghassan Kanafani assassinated on 8 July 1972 in a car explosion in Beirut. Edward Said notes that the deaths 'haunt' the memoir and account for 'the grieving, sorrowful tone of the book, otherwise so exuberant and celebratory' (Said 2000a: x). In *The Work of Mourning*,

Jacques Derrida is concerned with 'what it means to reckon with death' as he mourns his friends and intellectuals (2003: 2). For Barghouti, *I Saw Ramallah* becomes a work that mourns his friends and compatriots. Significantly, the narrator refers to his brother's grave in Amman, Kanafani's office in Beirut, and Nājī al-'Alī's grave in England. The deaths that he mourns in the memoir further emblematise constellations of the poet's exile and poetry.

Barghouti's second memoir *I Was Born There, I Was Born Here* narrates the poet's second return to Ramallah to introduce his son Tamim to his family and village. Originally published in Arabic in 2009, and then in English translation in 2011, his memoir revisits his son's arrest in Egypt for participating in demonstrations in Tahrir Square in 2003 after the US invasion of Iraq, and his subsequent deportation from Egypt. The theme of exile is doubled in the memoir: before his deportation to Jordan, his son is held in the Cairo prison where he himself had been held before being deported to Iraq in 1977.

In *I Was Born There, I Was Born Here*, he and his son arrive in Jericho – the journey from Cairo to Amman and to the bridge, which he crosses after his original crossing in 1996, after thirty years of exile, a symbol of 'discrimination, distance, disunion' (*WH*, 49; *BT*, 33). He crosses the bridge with Tamim two years after applying for an entry permit for him: he returns 'Palestine to Tamim, and Tamim to Palestine' (*WH*, 63; *BT*, 44). The poet notes: 'Jerusalem has been a city since it was forbidden to us' (*WH*, 102; *BT*, 75). Tamim, who has encountered Jerusalem, through his father's reflections, now visits Jerusalem: 'Now it belongs to him' (*WH*, 104; *BT*, 77). The narrator writes that he was born 'there' (in Deir Ghassaneh) and upon arrival in his village, he will say, 'I was born here' (*WH*, 105; *BT*, 79).

When the poet learns to coexist with his forgetfulness, his existence is disrupted by the Egyptian State Security, who deports his son for participating in demonstrations against the invasion of Iraq in 2003. He is held in al-Khalifa Deportations, the prison where Barghouti had been held in 1977. *I Was Born There, I Was Born Here*, which begins with his second return to Ramallah with his son, and ends with his son's activism in Tahrir Square – a moment that is also Barghouti's own double experience of deportation and exile – reinforces this sense of commitment through poetry. Barghouti's memoirs migrate, insisting on a continuity of poetic dedication between Egypt and Palestine.

The memoirs of Darwish and Barghouti offer forms that are evocative of what Khaled Furani calls, citing Darwish, 'this dismembered land' (2012: 113) and explore the subjectivity and solitude of the poet through the work of remembering dispossession and displacement. The memoirs offer iterations of solitude and the relationship of the poet to Palestine. Both poets invoke the personal and the national, the poetic and the political, through the appropriation and reworking of the autobiographical literary form to restage the drama of loss and return. Darwish is the lover who forgets and the poet who remembers. Barghouti neatly divides his world into two: the 'here' where he was born and 'there' where he must live and be reborn. But the memoirs also suggest that these states cannot simply be partitioned into memory or forgetfulness, Palestine or Egypt, in part because these productive intertwinings animate the relationship of the poets to Palestine.

4

Revolutionary Solitude: Edward Said and Najla Said

Nationalisms are about groups, but in a very acute sense exile is a solitude experienced outside the group.

Edward Said, *Reflections on Exile*

In the preface to his monograph *Joseph Conrad and the Fiction of Autobiography* (1967), Edward Said (1935–2003) notes that he examined Conrad's letters 'because it seemed to me that if Conrad wrote of himself, of the problem of self-definition, with such sustained urgency, some of what he wrote must have had meaning for his fiction. In short, I found it difficult to believe that a man would be so uneconomical as to pour himself out in letter after letter and then not use and reformulate his insights and discoveries in his fiction' (2008: xix). He further notes his discovery of a public personality Conrad created to cover the anxieties and tensions in his fiction: 'I was able to discover, recorded in the letters, a curious phenomenon in Conrad's life. This was the creation of a public personality that was to camouflage his deeper and more problematic difficulties with himself and his work' (ibid.). Reading his early book as an antecedent of the interplay between his scholarship and *Out of Place: A Memoir* (1999b), this chapter argues that his lifelong contributions to literary criticism and his advocacy for Palestine may offer better insights into his memoir.

In *The Fiction of Autobiography,* Said reads Conrad's letters in an effort to illuminate the exclusions of his fiction. Said wrote a memoir devoted to his early years between Palestine, Egypt, and Lebanon before his career in the United States. His criticism illuminates the exclusions of his memoir and his public personality offers us deeper insights into his private life. In contrast to the exchange between Conrad's short fiction and his letters, Said's literary scholarship and political activism inform and illuminate his memoir, creating a fuller narrative of his life. In this regard, his lifework adds to his intimate memoir, his literary criticism and political engagement overlaying his 'pre-political life' (Said 2000d: 568). While Said reads Conrad's fiction through his correspondence, his memoir can be read through his public life. Like Gabriel García Márquez's long-awaited memoir, *Living to Tell the Tale* (2003), which concludes with a young Gabriel en route to Europe after he has dispatched a letter to his future wife Mercedes with a proposal and a request for a reply,[1] Said's memoir ends with the start of his career.

It is fitting that Said wrote his monograph on Joseph Conrad, his developing character, and the unresolved anxieties in his fiction, and later penned a memoir exploring the tensions related to nation and language in his life and work. Both writers experienced exile and estrangement in language and would arrive and settle in new worlds.[2] As Said notes, Conrad was a 'self-conscious foreigner writing of obscure experiences in an alien language' (2008: 4). Exploring his affinities with Conrad, he notes the centrality of exile and estrangement to his fiction: 'No one could represent the fate of lostness and disorientation better than he did' (2000d: 554).

This chapter examines the complexity of writing an Anglophone Arab memoir, which echoes Conrad's 'self-conflict' in language, and reads the effects of colonialism and dispossession on the recreation of Said's youth, Palestine in the autobiographical imagination, and the trajectory of his revolutionary solitude from youth to his public life in *Out of Place*. Drawing upon the conventions of European autobiography, Said narrates an unconventional Arab and Arab-American life and unobtrusively traces the growth of his activism. It is a memoir that grew out of his education in European and American institutions and traditions and his solitary understanding of Palestine. Reading his solitude as freedom and autonomy, the chapter argues that his memoir represents the dissonances and displacements that would become the dissent, freedom, and independence of the engaged or public intellectual, and that his memoir can be read through his advocacy for the rights of Palestinians, and his awareness of contrapuntal juxtapositions in language and culture. Focusing on another memoir, Najla Said's *Looking for Palestine: Growing Up Confused in an Arab-American Family* (2013), this chapter examines the other trajectory of his daughter's youth in the US and discovery of Palestine.

Out of Place recounts the story of Said's beginnings in Palestine, Egypt, and Lebanon and evokes his formation in an unstable historical and political landscape. The memoir covers his life from 1935 to 1962, offering a chronicle of his life in the Arab world of the 1940s and 1950s. Born in Jerusalem, he attended school in Palestine in 1947, lived in Cairo, and spent summers in the Lebanese resort town of Dhour el-Shweir from 1943 to 1969 and then left Egypt for the United States in 1951. *Out of Place* concludes before the onset of his career at Columbia University and his public life in 1962.

While Said enters a long tradition of Palestinian memoirs by Mahmoud Darwish and Mourid Barghouti (examined in Chapter 3), among others, his Anglophone memoir draws on canonical Western autobiography and holds the status of an important Anglophone Arab memoir produced by the most prominent Arab critic in the West.[3] It belongs to a genre of Palestinian memoirs whose concerns and commitments are intimately intertwined with a history of colonialism and dispossession.[4] Hossam Aboul-Ela reads *Out of Place* within a local context of the popularity of the confessional American memoir during the 1990s (2006: 24) and Waïl S. Hassan reads it as an example of immigrant or 'ethnic American autobiography' (2011: 120, 114).

Out of Place offers an example of the appropriation and 'displacement' of the form within transnational frameworks. Broadly, the memoir adheres to the European autobiographical tradition of James Joyce's *A Portrait of the Artist as a Young Man* (1991) whose final journey is a voluntary departure from family and nation.[5] In his criticism, Said demonstrates a familiarity with canonical Western autobiography (Moore-Gilbert 2009: 115): he affiliates himself with a European canon as he describes a 'Virgilian sadness' imbued with his contemplation of an existence that had passed and the memoir as a 'Proustian meditation' (Said 2000c: 420).[6] Moore-Gilbert reads *Out of Place* as 'a seemingly unexceptional, traditional, example of literary autobiography' influenced by his education and the conventions of the genre in the West (Moore-Gilbert 2009: 115), yet Said adopts the classical conventions of autobiography to narrate an unconventional life. *Out of Place* relates to the tradition of Jean Jacques Rousseau's *Confessions* and Joseph Conrad's autobiographical fiction. Moreover, for a writer whose public life largely dominated his work, Said turns to the beginnings of that life, which has important implications for understanding his status in the US and the Arab world. *Out of Place* appeared in English and therefore largely for a Western readership unfamiliar with the Arab world he conjures up and reads as a chronicle of an unconventional Arab, or Arab-American, life.

Said, in his reflections on the publication of his memoir, invokes an Arabic autobiographical tradition of al-Ghazali's *al-Munqidh min al-Ḍalāl* (*The Deliverer from Error*) – an exemplar of political, educational, or religious reserved autobiography concerned with the protection of the institutions of family and religion. His comparison of that tradition with the confessional memoirs of Rousseau and John Stuart Mill offers his memoir as a departure from the Arabic autobiographical canon for its treatment of family, 'sexuality', 'disgrace', moments of failure, and vulnerability, placing it squarely in a Western tradition (Said 1999a). Although readings of *Out of Place* have dwelled on its adoption of the conventions of a Western-style memoir (Moore-Gilbert 2009), his references to Arab antecedents challenge that reading. Said (1999a) notes the treatment of family in Taha Hussein's *al-Ayyām*, one of his 'favorite books', with 'reverence, if not piety'. Significantly, there are points of comparison between the story of Taha Hussein, the reformer who travels to the West and has a profound influence on Arabic letters, and Said's chronicle of intellectual growth and important contributions to Western culture. The similarities of their trajectories are more pronounced than would appear; they refashion the cultures of East and West in the genre of autobiography: a foundational Arabic autobiography and a new Anglophone memoir. Said, steeped in Western and Arab traditions, creates a new genealogy for his memoir drawn from his contrapuntal reading of two canons. The influences on his memoir include reading European literary antecedents, framing the memoir within a tradition of Arabic autobiography, and reading the memoir as Arab-American.

Critics have focused on *Out of Place* in a global frame, reading the memoir within the framework of Arab-American cultural production exploring the transnational status of writers who grew up in the Arab world and immigrated to the United States.[7] The question of language opens up the study of its readership. By writing a memoir in English, Said addresses a global public. The circulation of the Anglophone memoir in international networks and its global reception resituate *Out of Place* within transnational literature, a reading supported by Said's mobility and transcultural youth.

In this way, multilingualism and transnationalism inform the ways in which *Out of Place* addresses the global reader and accrues interpretations through contrapuntal reading between cultures and languages. Aboul-Ela reads *Out of Place* as an Arab-American memoir, while Fadda-Conrey reads it within the frame of a transnational understanding of US citizenship (2014: 125). Fadda-Conrey traces Said's belated acceptance of his 'inherited US citizenship' and self-invention to his relocation to the United States in her study of Arab-American literature within a transnational framework from the Arab world to the United States (127).[8] Nonetheless, *Out of Place* is a memoir that engages with the political and historical developments in the Arab world, the history of his family during the years 1947 and 1948, and the disappearance of the worlds in Palestine, pre-civil war Lebanon, and the 'colonial, monarchical Egypt' that he had known (Said 2000d: 568).

Out of Place offers the history of Edward Said's public personality. His status as a famous public intellectual is important to the reception of his memoir as a chronicle of his life between the Arab world and the West and as an important contribution to the Palestinian national movement. Importantly, *Out of Place* is his only memoir and attends to the concerns to which he devoted his career.[9] It animates a body of work that has typically been read through the biographical history of a Palestinian Arab educated in the West by illuminating the beginnings of his work.

The quandary posed by the private and the public is a state Said contemplates in his reflections on 'the hazards of publishing a memoir', or the unexpected publication of a memoir he completed at the moment he apprehended his mortality and therefore expected would appear posthumously (1999a). As Said notes, a memoir is not private since the moment it is published it enters a public world (1994). The voyeurism the memoir represents onto the early life of a celebrated public intellectual added to his misgivings about its publication. Though a prominent Palestinian American critic famous for his representation of the rights of Palestinians, he purports to trace his youth unpolitically in *Out of Place*. Said's intention to revisit his early life between pre-1948 Palestine, Egypt before the 1952 Revolution, and Lebanon before the Civil War (1975-1990) shows his overriding desire to provide a record of 'now lost or forgotten worlds' (Said 1999c). Although he had signed a contract for the memoir in 1989, the memoir appeared amidst personal and historical upheavals that undoubtedly coloured his 'intimate history': his cancer-stricken mother's death; his diagnosis with leukaemia and the onset of his chemotherapy treatment; the emergence of a new order with the Madrid Conference and the Gulf War; and the 1993 Oslo Accords. He began to work on *Out of Place* in May 1994 while he was recovering from chemotherapy treatment for leukaemia following his diagnosis in 1991, so his return to parts of his life, literally and metaphorically, is intimately intertwined with stages in the struggle for Palestine. The publication of *Out of Place* predated the invasion of Iraq and narrates his life from Jerusalem to the United States.

Of all the memoirs included here, *Out of Place* adheres most fully to the form of a memoir in which the focus is on events and worlds the author has known or experienced.[10] Unlike Darwish, who revisits the invasion through which he has lived, or Barghouti, who dwells on his return to Ramallah, by poetically re-ordering experiences and events, Said chronicles his formative years in a forgotten world. In his preface-pact, he concedes that it is 'a record of an essentially lost or forgotten world' (*OP*, xi) and notes that his life from 1935 to 1962 'had some validity as an unofficial personal record of those tumultuous years in the Middle East. I found myself telling the story of my life against the background of World War II, the loss of Palestine and the establishment of Israel, the end of the Egyptian monarchy, the Nasser years, the 1967 War, the emergence of the Palestinian movement, the Lebanese Civil War, and the Oslo peace process. These are in my memoir only allusively' (*OP*, xiii). Although Said would later maintain that he wrote a 'pre-political' memoir, he concedes the influence of the political landscape on *Out of Place*: 'Yet my political writings about the Palestinian situation, my studies of the relationship of politics and aesthetics, . . . must surely have fed into this memoir surreptitiously' (*OP*, xi). He observes that he has written a 'subjective chronicle' and his pact offers a disclaimer: 'I, and only I, am responsible for what I recall and see, not individuals in the past who could not have known what effect they might have on me' (*OP*, xv). While writing his memoir, he retained his interest in and commitment to public life.

While Said recalls a story embedded in the broader history of Palestinian dispossession and inherently the beginnings of his awareness of his roots after 1948, his self-discovery rests on solitude in Cairo and subsequently in the US. Although the memoir is a personal record, he embeds his chronicle in the history of Palestine, tracing his growing awareness and entry into public life. Said devotes most of his memoir to his early years in Jerusalem, Cairo, and Beirut and history pervades his account. He focuses on the solitude of the young Edward in his colonial community and his parents' circle in Cairo, his anxieties about his belonging as well as his intransigence, and his solitude in the United States. Solitude takes on a metaphorical character when he develops his revolutionary thought and advocates for Palestinian rights. The tension between his solitude and the commitment that distinguished his career commences in his youth.

The Languages of Solitude

While *Out of Place* traces the influence of European autobiography such as Rousseau's *Confessions*, the conventions of the European *Bildungsroman* are also clearly visible in the portrayal of the young Edward. This is the novel of formation and education or, in the words of Franco Moretti, the novel of youth. Clearly, Said further adopts the conventions of the *Künstlerroman*, the novel of formation of the young artist such as Joyce's *A Portrait of the Artist as a Young Man*. Anna Bernard notes the influence of the conventions of the classical and the postcolonial European *Bildungsroman* in Said's memoir (2013: 43). Moretti's rediscovery of the European novel of youth as the product of the decline of old worlds is important to his interpretation of European modernity. For Moretti, youth is symbolic of European modernity advanced through the synthesis of aspirations and disenchantment in the world. He interprets the *Bildungsroman* as the exemplar of nineteenth-century Europe and reads the collapse of the *Bildungsroman* in the years of World War I in advance of modernism. Moretti looks at the birth of a new hero, the young man of the modern world, in the European novel during the nineteenth century (2000: 3). 'Youth,' writes Moretti, 'or rather the European novel's numerous versions of youth, becomes for our modern culture the age which holds the "meaning of life"' (2000: 4). This modern hero is characterised by 'mobility' and 'interiority', or yearnings for exploration and restlessness, making him symbolic of modernity (4–5).

Moretti defines the *Bildungsroman*'s symbolic roles in the long nineteenth century: 'It had contained the unpredictability of social change, representing it through the fiction of youth: a turbulent segment of life, no doubt, but with a clear beginning, and an unmistakable end. At a micro-narrative level, furthermore, the structure of the novelistic episode had established the flexible, anti-tragic modality of modern experience. Finally, the novel's many-sided, unheroic hero had embodied a new kind of subjectivity: everyday, worldly, pliant – "normal"' (2000: 230). Yet *Out of Place* more fully corresponds to Moretti's notion of the late *Bildungsroman*, 'with its rootless heroes and inhospitable environments' (2000: 231). The late *Bildungsroman* is the novel of homelessness, loneliness, and isolation (ibid.). Banished by his father to Mount Hermon, a boarding school in the United States, young Edward's fate evokes Joyce's Stephen Dedalus's departure.

Said's *Out of Place* offers a model of a transnational *Bildungsroman* in its evocation of his youth in Egypt, Palestine, Lebanon, and the United States, chronicling his sense of failures and dislocations in advance of his pre-eminence. Bernard notes 'the contemporary association of the *Bildungsroman* as a genre with non-metropolitan and first-world minority struggles for enfranchisement' (2013: 53). Drawing upon the genre to revisit his youth in Palestine, Egypt, and Lebanon, *Out of Place* takes part in a process that advocates for the rights of Palestinians (ibid.). It is a *Bildungsroman* in which the political takes centre stage and therefore can be read as an extension of 'the Palestinian national novel' (61).

Drawing upon the *Bildungsroman* in a memoir that should bring his life to a close is no paradox. Memoir and mortality intersect in an echo of Darwish's *Mural.* Said spent five years of work on his manuscript during periods of illness or treatment in New York, Paris, and Cairo. He returned to Palestine in 1992 after a forty-five-year exile and visited Egypt in 1993 to collect material for a record of his youth. The motivation for his memoir was to chronicle his life in the Arab world and to 'defend himself' against the effects of his chemotherapy and 'debilitating sickness, treatment, and anxiety' (*OP*, xi).

The reception of *Out of Place* politicised the story of his youth. However, Said promulgated a 'pre-political' interpretation of his memoir, observing on occasion that his memoir would implicitly gesture at the political world he grew up in. Yet *Out of Place* returns to his roots in Palestine to revisit the country of which he had been dispossessed. He chronicles his family's mobility and exile after 1948: his education in Egypt; summers in Lebanon; and departure to the US. *Out of Place* appeared in 1999 against the backdrop of the Oslo agreements at a moment that marked the culmination of Said's long-drawn struggle for Palestine. It was emblematic of the fate of dispossession and was therefore read as part of his longstanding political activism.

Said describes exile as a debilitating solitude and a loneliness. In contrast to the expatriate or *émigré*, the exile is ennobled by 'a touch of solitude and spirituality' (2000d: 181). He writes of the solitude of estrangement in his community, language, and citizenship. Said's reflections on nationalism and the 'solitude and estrangement of exile' echo Anderson's reflections on long-distance nationalism. He juxtaposes nationalism and exile contrapuntally (Iskandar and Rustom 2010: 8). Said observes: 'Nationalism is an assertion of belonging in and to a place, a people, a heritage' (2000d: 176). In his reflections, he is concerned with ways to surmount the solitude of exile without submitting to nationalism. Solitude epitomises isolation and detachment, but it also evokes independence. In his memoir, he evokes the fate of the solitary writer, who is unaffiliated to institutions, and the isolated son.

Out of Place commences with his reflections on self-invention and intransigence, an echo of his monograph on Conrad: 'There was always something wrong with how I was invented and meant to fit in with the world of my parents and four sisters' (*OP*, 3). The invention of the young Edward underwrites his displacement and the sense of his interrupted selfhood: 'Being myself meant not only never being quite right, but also never feeling at ease, always expecting to be interrupted or corrected, to have my privacy invaded and my unsure person set upon' (*OP*, 19).

Said metonymically evokes his displacement by parsing his name:

> Thus it took me about fifty years to become accustomed to, or, more exactly, to feel less uncomfortable with, 'Edward,' a foolishly English name yoked forcibly to the unmistakably Arabic family name Said . . . For years, and depending on the exact circumstances, I would rush past 'Edward' and emphasize 'Said'; at other times I would do the reverse, or connect these two to each other so quickly that neither would be clear. The one thing I could not tolerate, but very often would have to endure, was the disbelieving, and hence undermining, reaction: Edward? Said? (*OP*, 3–4)

While the appearance of his name clearly adheres to the traditional autobiographical pact, infusing his memoir with his authority and contract, it also sets the scene for his history of displacement. His displacements in Cairo pervade his memoir: he is 'Palestinian-Arab-Christian-American' (*OP*, 268). Born in Jerusalem and educated in Cairo, where his father owned a private business, he inherited his father's US citizenship, without ever having been to the United States, and without an American name or appearance, he overturns expectations of community and citizenship: he is an Arab and an American citizen in British colonial schools in Jerusalem and Cairo; a Palestinian American in colonial Cairo; an Anglican Christian Arab among an Orthodox and Coptic Christian minority within a Muslim majority in Egypt; and an Arab-American educated in the United States; he spoke Egyptian Arabic in Palestine and Lebanon; and belonged to an affluent Palestinian family in Cairo after the dispossession in 1948. As he notes: 'I have retained this unsettled sense of many identities – mostly in conflict with each other – all of my life, together with an acute memory of the despairing feeling that I wish we could have been all-Arab, or all-European and American, or all-Orthodox Christian, or all-Muslim, or all-Egyptian, and so on' (*OP*, 5). Furthermore, he writes of his displacement and departures: his family's departure from Jerusalem prior to 1947; his departure for the United States in 1951 to attend Mount Hermon and later Princeton and then Harvard; and his final departure from Egypt in 1960 (he would return in 1977).

Said retains his dislocations in languages and cultures: he remarks on the 'overtones, the accents, the slippages, the sense of being in and out of language, being in and out of worlds, the skepticism, the radical uncertainty' (2000d: 421). An Anglophone memoir that chronicles youth in the Arab world in the 1940s would ordinarily evoke displacement in cultures and languages. Besides his name, with which *Out of Place* commences, he contemplates the unsettled problem of language: 'I have never known what language I spoke first, Arabic or English, or which one was really mine beyond any doubt. What I do know, however, is that the two have always been together in my life, one resonating in the other, sometimes ironically, sometimes nostalgically, most often each correcting, and commenting on, the other' (*OP*, 4). His description presents two languages jostling with each other in dialogue, conflict, and coexistence. They are concurrent, coexistent, and parallel to each other or, to use his term, contrapuntal. In writing of his formative years in English, he captures the languages or registers of his early years, each with its own particular set of experiences and contexts. The language of his formal education in Cairo is English and the Arabic spoken by his family is a Palestinian dialect. Importantly, Said's multilingualism precedes his exile because his father settles in Cairo well before the dispossession in 1948.

His awareness of his mediation between two languages rests on an early memory of 'the musical intimacy' of his mother's Arabic (*OP*, 4) and her inflection of his English name 'Edward', an echo of her Damascene (*Shāmī*) Arabic and English in Cairo. Arabic is his maternal language and permeates his memory of his exchanges with his mother: her endearments, intonations, and idiom. Yet English is a language that evokes a literary sensibility shared with his mother. When he and his mother read *Hamlet* together in Cairo, her voice would become 'exceptionally fluent' (*OP*, 52). Similarly, at a performance of *Antony and Cleopatra* in London in the early 1990s, echoing the 'Shakespeare readings' in Cairo (*OP*, 155), he feels they share 'the language and communion despite the disparity in our ages and the fact that we were nevertheless mother and son' (*OP*, 53). His mother is his interlocutor and his reflections on her words enact a return to his concern with discourse and language.[11] He continually translates between Arabic (his native language) and English (the language of his education and scholarship) in *Out of Place.*

Contrapuntally, Said offers the story of his youth in two cultures and two languages. Culture is used by Said 'to suggest an environment, process, and hegemony in which individuals (in their private circumstances) and their works are embedded' (2000d: 226–7). Two languages cross over in his contrapuntal reading of Arab and American cultures. The dialogue between languages, the continual translation, and the creation of new idioms animate his writing in English. He is aware of having to translate experience in a different language: the life he lived in Arabic and the split between Arabic, his native tongue, and English, the language of his formal education and future scholarship: 'and so trying to produce a narrative of one in the language of the other' (*OP*, xiii–xiv). He experiences displacements in languages and, moving from one language to another, longs for Arabic in the United States: 'There was always a feeling that what I missed with my contemporaries was other languages, Arabic mainly, in which I lived and thought and felt along with English' (*OP*, 233).

When a Lebanese friend introduces him to his classmates in Dhour el

Shweir, he senses that the jokes and anecdotes exchanged were 'in an Arabic dialect that was clearly their language, and just as clearly not mine' (*OP*, 176). Although he understands the language, he notes a separation and isolation because of his classmates' Lebanese accent and his Egyptian-inflected Palestinian dialect. The complexities of language in his youth are just as clearly informed by a colonial education as they are by his life between Arab capitals. Arabic is prohibited at his colonial English schools, so it becomes 'a criminalized discourse where we took refuge from the world of masters and complicit prefects and anglicized older boys' (*OP*, 184). Therefore, the use of Arabic becomes an insurrectionary gesture. Observing the languages that enfolded his existence in Cairo and would go on to attract him as he moved seamlessly between equivalents and analogues, he notes: 'The three languages became a pointedly sensitive issue for me at the age of about fourteen. Arabic was forbidden and "wog;" French was always "theirs," not mine; English was authorized, but unacceptable as the language of the hated British' (*OP*, 198). Arabic is the language of the natives, French is that of an elite, and English is a colonial language in the cultural landscape of 1940s Cairo. But in the present of his writing he interjects that 'only now' over sixty can he feel 'more comfortable' speaking or writing in those languages and can he overcome his 'alienation from Arabic caused by education and exile' (*OP*, 198).

Throughout his youth, Said writes, a young Edward created by his parents disrupts his sense of self: 'And thus I became "Edward," a creation of my parents whose daily travails a quite different but quite dormant inner self was able to observe, though most of the time was powerless to help' (*OP*, 19). The complexity of his subjectivity inheres in a split into an Edward and 'non-Edward self': 'the "Edward" whose making my family, teachers, and mentors contributed to' and 'my inner, far less compliant and private self, who could read, think, and even write independent of "Edward"' (*OP*, 165). His non-Edward self is Edward's other and different from the centred European self. The decentred subjectivity of young Edward evokes the dislocations and dissonances that Said would celebrate at the end of *Out of Place*.

Evoking youth, Said captures the failures and 'disgrace' of the young Edward in a context of the dying empire. *Out of Place* evokes the late *Bildungsroman*, with the lost illusions and defeated expectations of young Edward in the waning community to which he belongs in 1940s Cairo. The decline of his community's way of life is prevalent in his allusions to the fragility of the existence of the colonial elite after the burning of Cairo in early 1952. He dwells on what he describes as his failures and, frequently, his disgrace and the defeat of the ideal his parents envision. His father's aspirations dominate the early part of his life and, when the young Edward is expelled from Victoria College for his unruly behaviour, the dreams of youth have been exhausted, and he portrays his expulsion from Victoria College and departure to the United States as a culmination of his failure. His separation from family and nation is different from Stephen Dedalus's because it is involuntary. Another memoir exploring the anxieties of language and the failures of youth is J. M. Coetzee's *Boyhood*. Similarly, *Boyhood* adopts the conventions of the late *Bildungsroman* with the young John Coetzee's anxieties about language, heritage, and alignments in South Africa during the 1950s. The word 'disgrace', which Said writes is 'an English word that hovered around me from the time I was seven' (*OP*, 58), recurs in Coetzee's *Boyhood*.

Nonetheless, the failure of youth in the vanishing old order inaugurates his self-invention upon his relocation to the New World and concomitantly his self-discovery. The solitary young Edward at the Mount Hermon library develops his critical readings of literature. The trajectory of his formation and education, whereby he discovers his critical facility and subsequently his advocacy for Palestine, can be read as the inspiration for his lifelong activism and independent criticism.

Colonialism and Dispossession

Said's contrapuntal readings of canonical literature offer ways to read the colonial encounter with which he engages in the landscape of his youth between Palestine and Egypt. Reading his early years through the British mandate and Zionist colonialism in counterpoint to his burgeoning awareness of Palestine, and framing his story within the legacy of colonialism, the history of dispossession, and the growth of neo-imperialist interests in the Middle East, he offers an anticolonial reading of his youth. His early years can be read in relation to his scholarship on empire and exile. As he excavates and uncovers the facets of his existence in a context of colonialism and dispossession, his memoir may be read through the colonial encounter.

Although partly excluded by the author's preface framing the memoir, his self-examination and challenge to imperialism throughout his career extend his critical scholarship to his reading of his youth.

In his reading of his colonial education, through which he comes into contact with the remnants of colonialism and the changes that swept the empire during World War II and the loss of Palestine in 1948, his encounters replicate 'the colonial encounter' (*OP*, 44) and challenge colonialism. His behaviour at Victoria College symbolically challenges colonial authority and practices. In the present, he recalls his anxieties about his name and his desire for a stable, centred self. His family is Levantine ('Shawam') (195) or foreigners (*khawagāt* in the Egyptian colloquial dialect) in 1940s Cairo, a perception at which he chafes because of his sense of being an Arab. Although his family belongs to the expatriate community and thus holds the status of Europeans in Cairo, he is construed as Arab at his colonial schools. Similarly, Ahdaf Soueif notes that he is 'a Palestinian in the United States and an American in the Arab world' (2000: 95). Consequently, his family's situation, his father's citizenship, and his familial history create an unsettled self-perception. Moreover, he is both the Oriental and the colonised in spite of his American citizenship and colonial education. As he notes, 'the consciousness of being an Oriental goes back to my youth in colonial Palestine and Egypt' and the 'impulse' is 'nurtured' during a context of the end of the British occupation and the rise of Arab nationalism (Said 2000d: 200). One day on his way home from the Gezira Club, young Edward is 'accosted' by an Englishman who, unaware that he is a member, chides him for being at the club and orders him to 'get out', proclaiming: 'Arabs aren't allowed here, and you're an Arab!' (*OP*, 44). The Englishman's racialisation is for him a coup de grâce, an enforced epiphany at odds with his self-perception within the cosmopolitan Cairo community and a public discovery of his Arabness. Forced into a self-discovery, Said observes: 'If I hadn't thought of myself as an Arab before, I now directly grasped the significance of the designation as truly disabling' (*OP*, 44). Nonetheless, his adolescence abounds with instances of anti-authoritarianism and insurrection that overcome the discomfort with his name. His revolt against the colonial institutions sets him 'against a wounded colonial power' (*OP*, 184).

Out of Place offers an example of Palestinian literary self-representation that becomes central to the project of countering dispossession and displacement. Said notes the importance of Palestinian autobiographical production in *The Question of Palestine*: 'One of the features of a small non-European people is that it is not wealthy in documents, nor in histories, autobiographies, chronicles, and the like. This is true of the Palestinians, and it accounts for the lack of a major authoritative text on Palestinian history' (Said 1979: xxix). Implicit in his observation is the assertion that such memoirs and chronicles constitute a body of national literature that is central to the preservation of the history and existence of Palestine. In capturing the Jerusalem–Cairo–Beirut nexus of his youth, *Out of Place* traces the young Edward's formation and understanding of the dispossession that has uprooted and dispersed his family. Inasmuch as he examines the Cairo colonial community through contrapuntal reading, he traces his formative years through his political activism and the growth of his understanding of his Palestinian heritage in his memoir. When he visited Jerusalem in 1998, a network of towns and villages where his family had once lived – Jerusalem, Haifa, Tiberias, Nazareth, and Acre – was a series of Israeli locales and Palestinians had self-rule in parts of the West Bank and Gaza, but the Israeli army retained control (*OP*, xii). In 1992, he visited Palestine but could not enter the family-owned house where he was born in West Jerusalem and the house in Nazareth where his mother grew up after forty-five years since his family's departure in 1947. His visit to Palestine before the completion of *Out of Place* is not only an effort to contribute to the histories, memoirs, and chronicles that together preserve the history of Palestine, but also represents his reading into his early years the beginnings of his activism. This can be read as a literary investigation of Palestinian dispossession within the 'national-cultural community' of which he is dispossessed, one that he belatedly understands (Said 2000b: 226).

In *Out of Place*, Said offers a representation of Palestinian subjectivity against misreadings and misrepresentations of Palestine in Western culture in the vein of his study *Orientalism*. Moore-Gilbert notes that *Out of Place* 'plots his formation' in relation to 'collective national aspirations' (2009: 195). By chronicling young Edward's reading of Palestine, *Out of Place* traces the formation of the public intellectual whose work is characterised by deep commitment to Palestinian rights. More important, it offers a self-representation and an examination of Palestinian subjectivity whose importance is more pronounced in a context in which the rights of Palestinians have been repudiated; it is a response to 'injustice and oblivion' (Said 2000d: 566). Commenting on the material produced since the invasion of Beirut, Said notes that it is 'a small archive to be discussed in terms of absences and gaps – in terms either prenarrative or, in a sense, antinarrative' (Said 2000b: 256). Tracing the family's genealogy and his split geography between Palestine, Egypt, and Lebanon, he recreates his Palestinian selfhood. Moore-Gilbert reads the family portraits in Jerusalem included in *Out of Place* as documentary material that confers authority upon his narrative, establishing a relationship between memoir and history.[12] Iskandar and Rustom read the intersection between representation and 'empowerment' that can advocate for Palestine (2010: 12).

Although Said chronicles his life in Cairo and summers in Dhour el Shweir, Palestine is a forceful presence in his history and topography. His family house was in Talbiyah in West Jerusalem and, in 1947, Said attended St George's school in Talbiyah, where he observed the city's division into zones, and left in December before the dispossession. Said writes in Cairo that 'Palestine acquired a languid almost dreamlike aspect for me. There I did not feel as acutely the solitude I began to dread later' (*OP*, 21).

Paradoxically, the loss of Palestine is uneventful for the young Edward in Cairo and Said chronicles the *Nakba* (catastrophe) through the effects on his extended family. On his twelfth birthday in Jerusalem in 1947, the young Edward is unaware of 'our conflict with the Zionists and the British' but recalls that his cousins in Palestine bemoan the eve of the Balfour Declaration as 'the blackest day in our history' (*OP*, 107). Although the *Nakba* disrupts his family, he notes his parents' prohibition on the subject of Palestine. Said's retrospective commentary on the suppression of the subject of Palestine at a dramatic historical moment underscores the disjuncture between his Cairo milieu in 1948 and the American landscape in which he writes: 'It seems inexplicable to me now that having dominated our lives for generations, the problem of Palestine and its tragic loss, which affected virtually everyone we knew, deeply changing our world, should have been so relatively repressed, undiscussed, or even remarked on by my parents' (*OP*, 117). The disjuncture between his family's exile and enforced silence plays a central role in the formation of the adolescent whose experience of the split between his Arab allegiances and the international reception of the 1967 War has a profound effect on his development. He muses over his early distance from Palestine: 'The remoteness of the Palestine I grew up in, my family's silence over its role, and then its long disappearance from our lives, my mother's open discomfort with the subject and later aggressive dislike of both Palestine and politics, my lack of contact with Palestinians during the eleven years of my American education: all this allowed me to live my life at a great distance from the Palestine of remote memory, unresolved sorrow, and uncomprehending anger' (*OP*, 141). His aunt Nabiha's philanthropy in Cairo after the loss of Palestine introduces him to the desolation of dispossession, the disappearance of Palestine, and the rights of Palestinians through the fate of the refugees: 'the desolations of being without a country or a place to return to, of being unprotected by any national authority or institutions' (*OP*, 120). Although the subject of Palestine was taboo, the dominance of the problem of Palestine and the dispersion of Palestinians permeate his memory of his youth.

The burning of Cairo and the destruction of Cairo Standard Stationery Company owned by his father on Black Saturday in January 1952 while he was at Mount Hermon in the United States have a profound influence on the growth of his pan-Arab affiliations and his critical engagement. Said alludes to the same historical backdrop of *The Search*: the guerilla skirmishes in the Suez Canal Zone to which the British had withdrawn and the 26 January 1952 fire. He does not gesture obliquely at the backdrop of his memoir, but the upheavals are part and parcel of his self-development in the United States.

The memoir enshrines his formation after 1967 and his discovery of the status of the Arab-American literary scholar in the United States. In contrast to the effects of 1948 on young Edward, the Suez War of 1956 and the 1967 War he follows in the United States have profound implications for his lifelong involvement in the Palestinian national movement:

> 1967 brought more dislocations, whereas for me it seemed to embody the dislocation that subsumed all the other losses, the disappeared worlds of my youth and upbringing, the unpolitical years of my education, the assumption of disengaged teaching and scholarship at Columbia, and so on. I was no longer the same person after 1967: the shock of that war drove me back to where it had all started, the struggle over Palestine. I subsequently

> entered the newly transformed Middle Eastern landscape as a part of the Palestinian movement. (*OP*, 293)

He experiences the globality of the 1967 War at Columbia University in the summer of 1967 that would radically change his relationship to the Middle East (Said 2000c; Aboul-Ela 2006: 24).

Revolutionary Solitude

By 1967, Said would perform a self-reformulation or what Sabry Hafez reads as his 're-orientation' towards his Arab culture (2004: 76), so that his self-invention is also coterminous with his reassessment of his culture. Little is present in *Out of Place* of his experiences at Princeton and Harvard in the 1950s in comparison to his frequent returns to Cairo and Dhour el Shweir. The keynote of the conclusion of the memoir is his isolation from his own language and culture in the United States when he began his career at Columbia University in 1963 (Said 2000d: 560).

Representations of his youth in the memoir focus on a sense of solitude and displacement while anticipating the paradox of solitude and an intensely committed life that develops out of his exile and his reflections as he writes contrapuntally between 'my life today and my life then' (*OP*, xiv). He expresses his frequent experiences of 'enforced' or 'miserable solitude' in Dhour el Shweir or at school. Sent to the Mount Hermon boarding school in the United States in 1951, he felt a 'paralyzed solitude' (*OP*, 244). He does not attend to the priority of the national or tribal, no matter how 'solitary' that made him (*OP*, 280). For Said, solitude has a plethora of connotations: estrangement, exile, dislocation, dispossession, and separation, on the one hand, and commitment, independence, and autonomy, on the other. The dispossession gives him 'a discouraging sense of being solitary' (*OP*, 142). When he was 'most miserably solitary' (Said 2000d: 561), he writes, he held on to his distance in culture and language. Iskandar and Rustom comment on Said's 'considerable loneliness and solitude, a perpetual state of criticism that is interminably in exile' (2010: 9). Yet *Out of Place* captures the tension between commitment and autonomy by tracing his affiliation with Arab culture, critical engagement, and the 'independence' of the public intellectual (Said 2000d: 504).

In *Representations of the Intellectual*, Said addresses relations between the intellectual, institutions, and the state, one defined by his displacement and dissent. Said investigates the role of the intellectual 'to speak truth to power' and his relationships with institutions whose 'principal intellectual duty is the search for relative independence from such pressures' (1996: xvi). The subjectivity of the intellectual rests on dissent and opposition 'as exile and marginal, as amateur, and as the author of a language that tries to speak truth to power' (ibid.). The intellectual is involved in struggles on behalf of the underrepresented and the disenfranchised. He asserts: 'the challenge of intellectual life is to be found in dissent', which he describes as a 'lonely condition' (xvi, xviii).

Out of Place captures an Arab heritage and Said's commitment to Palestine in a form that can be read in relation to national struggles (Luca 2006: 125). Fadda-Conrey notes that the political upheavals in the Arab world delayed his acceptance of his inherited citizenship and his arrival in the US in 1951 provoked a process of self-invention and improvisation, one that is central to his development (2014: 127). Bayoumi and Rubin read his 'ambivalent relationship with two cultures often at odds with each other (American and Arab)' (2000: xiv). The memoir represents a reformulation of a Palestinian subjectivity that was central to his intellectual engagement.

Out of Place illuminates Said's commitment to the struggle for Palestine. At the same time, it fully attends to the story of his youth and simultaneously the freedom of exile. Said notes the 'anxiety and marginality of no "dwelling"' and the intellectual's solitude but also the rewards of exile that enable him to challenge the mainstream and co-optation (Said 2000b: 377). Exile affords him freedom, he notes:

> My search for freedom, for the self beneath or obscured by 'Edward', could only have begun because of that rupture, so I have come to think of it as fortunate, despite the loneliness and unhappiness I experienced for so long. Now it does not seem important or even desirable to be 'right' and in place (right at home, for instance). Better to wander out of place, not to own a house, and not ever to feel too much at home anywhere, especially in a city like New York, where I shall be until I die. (*OP*, 294)

Said juxtaposes the rupture and disruption with the states of rest and stability inherent in his mortality. In the end, he celebrates his displacement and freedom: 'I occasionally express myself as a cluster of flowing currents. I prefer this to the idea of a solid self, the identity to which so many attach so much significance . . . With so many dissonances in my life I have learned actually to prefer being not quite right and out of place' (*OP*, 295).

Said reworks cultural exchange and the form between his youth in the Arab world and the United States. Contrapuntally, *Out of Place* reads his youth and subjectivity, cultures and languages against and with one another, opening up the production of transnational Anglophone Arab memoirs in anti-imperialist movements and the formation of an Anglophone Arab autobiographical canon concerned with Palestine. Said reanimates Palestinian memoirs in English by looking at Palestine between the Arab world and the US to which he relocated in the mid-twentieth century and elaborating the form further in the struggle for Palestine at the turn of the twenty-first century.

Looking for Palestine

Another Anglophone memoir in a growing body of Arab-American memoirs is the newly published *Looking* for *Palestine: Growing Up Confused in an Arab-American Family* by American-born writer and actress Najla Said (b. 1974). Born to a prominent Palestinian father, Edward Said, and a Lebanese mother, Said grew up in 1980s New York at a moment of intense political instability in the Middle East and misrepresentation of the Arab–Israeli conflict in the West. Her memoir belongs to a literary corpus made up of the memoir of her celebrated father and a new twenty-first century generation of memoirs focusing on Arab-American and Arab subjectivity vis-à-vis Palestine. Adapted from her play *Palestine*, *Looking for Palestine* focuses on her confusion and self-conflict about her cultural background in 1980s and 1990s New York. Her confusion, an echo of Said's being out of place in Egypt and the US, reworks the trajectory of *Out of Place* through the examination of her Arab-American adolescence in New York, where her parents' identification with Palestine and Lebanon is at odds with the world of her youth, and her visits to Lebanon and Palestine through which she discovers her Arab roots.

In *Looking for Palestine*, Said works to reconcile her Arab-American girlhood with her parents' identification with Palestine and Lebanon in a process by which the young Najla has to continually take the measure of her subjectivity through her father's secular humanism and her parents' Arabness as well as rising anti-Arab sentiments and the Arab–Israeli conflict. A Christian Palestinian-Lebanese-American growing up in a Jewish neighborhood on the Upper West Side in the 1970s, she is aware of the complexities of her identity in ways that echo Edward Said's self-awareness of the differences between his family and the Cairene and colonial community of 1940s Cairo in *Out of Place*. The memoir opens with an unequivocal statement: 'I am a Palestinian-Lebanese-American Christian woman, but I grew up as a Jew in New York City. I began my life, however, as a WASP' (*LP*, 2). She goes on to chronicle her White Anglo-Saxon Protestant (WASP) girlhood, growing up with Jewish friends, and 'steeped in secular, humanist thought' (*LP*, 133). Throughout her youth, she learns the complexities of categorisations of culture and nationality and works through prevalent cultural stereotypes.

Set in Manhattan's Upper West Side, her home frequented by the Western world's prominent writers and figures of the Palestinian Resistance, and Chapin School (a private Upper East Side all-girls independent day school) on the Upper East Side of Manhattan, where she feels her otherness through her appearance, nationality, name, and the conflation of ethnicity with religion, or Arab with Muslim, *Looking for Palestine* focuses on her Arab-American background in the United States. She then parses the complex set of filiations in her youth – Arab and American – while being unaware of the political landscape of the Middle East prior to her visits to Palestine and Lebanon. In her youth, she enacts a separation from her Arab heritage and the representations that have characterised the Orientalism on which her father's oeuvre is founded. A baptised Episcopalian, she attended Chapin, where she grew up 'absorbed in the world of Jewish culture' (*LP*, 126). A Chapin schoolgirl, she has 'an instant awareness' of her 'differences' (*LP*, 2) and works to understand her world, culture, and family amid perceptions of Arabness as 'barbaric' and 'backward' (*LP*, 3). She notes that her awareness of her 'physical awkwardness' was at a moment of rising tensions and growing instability in the Middle East in the 1980s (*LP*, 82). On her return from Lebanon, in the summer of 1982, and her experience of the bombing of Beirut, she notes: 'I began to realize that even if I didn't entirely identify with Arabs as they were presented to me in America, I actually was one of them just as much as I was an American from New York' (*LP*, 99).

The scenes in which the young Najla recalls her father's explanations of the politics of representation made famous in his 1978 *Orientalism* in her youth evoke shared moments and, at the same time, underscore her confusion about her Arabness and his advocacy for Palestine in her world. The young Najla seems affected by her father's revolutionary critical practice insofar as she works to make sense of the reality of Palestinian and Lebanese affiliations in the New York of her youth. *Looking for Palestine* shows an Arab-American adolescent, confused about her father's identifications and uncertain of her Arabness, who rediscovers her roots. Although surrounded by Arabic and aware of her parents' identification with Arab culture, she is assailed by Orientalist images on TV. She writes, 'While my father was writing books about this very subject, I was looking at the images of Arabs on TV and in the movies and then looking back in the mirror, confounded' (*LP*, 63).

Said chronicles the family's return to Palestine upon her father's diagnosis with leukaemia and a visit to Gaza's Jabaliya refugee camp. An acceptance of her heritage follows her visit to Palestine. On her visit, she notes that the landscape is riddled with small Arab towns surrounded by settlements. She recounts her awkwardness and incongruity in Jerusalem and Gaza: 'The Arabs spoke to me in Hebrew, or Italian, or Spanish, but never in Arabic, and I smiled awkwardly, unsure of how to explain myself' (*LP*, 160). Nonetheless, she asserts the centrality of Palestine after her 1992 tour: 'Though I have never returned to Palestine, Palestine always returns to me' (*LP*, 250).

The 9/11 attacks on the World Trade Center and the ensuing American responses elicit a response that departs from her distance and separation from her Arab background in the 1980s. She recalls feeling the moment when people in the vicinity came to the 'collective, silent conclusion' that the perpetrators were Arabs and notes: '*that* was the moment my life changed forever' (*LP*, 214; emphasis in original). In post-9/11 America, she becomes an Arab-American, a term about which she expresses ambivalence: 'I don't feel entirely American, never have, but it's not because I don't want to or because I don't seem it – I do want to, I do seem it. I don't feel entirely Arab though either, for the same reasons. But I also certainly don't feel like any *combination* of the two' (*LP*, 217; emphasis in original). She joins a group of theatre artists of Arab descent to work on a documentary theatre project and her work with the group expresses her self-understanding in the aftermath of the 9/11 attacks: 'in America, there is no doubt that since 9/11, I am officially an Arab, bridging the gap between two worlds that don't understand each other' (*LP*, 251).

Tracing her subjectivity, she intimately revisits the final moments with her father.[13] It is also a moment that underscores the narrator's understanding of the politics her father espouses. Writing about her father's passing, she embraces his legacy of secular humanism and political activism.

Looking for Palestine contemplates the experience of growing up in an immigrant family in the US and the journey to the understanding of a new hyphenated Arab-American identity in a world that changes from rampant misrepresentations of Arabness during the Palestinian struggle and the Lebanese civil war (1975–90) to the post-9/11 climate of burgeoning anti-Arab sentiments. When she runs into a protest of young women wearing 'Free Palestine' T-shirts while walking up Broadway, she is beset by the intense feeling she experiences when the word 'Palestine' is spoken aloud and feels 'immensely grateful' that they are protesting for her and for Palestinians and wants to join them and 'be a revolutionary' (*LP*, 252). In a climactic moment, she notes her intense identification 'because I am this girl, this young woman . . . this . . . *me*, I am this *Palestinian*' (*LP*, 252; emphasis in original). Although she creates theatre as an Arab-American, the Upper West Side is her world. She asserts, 'None of it changes the fact that I started and finished school in America, that English is my first language, that I still live in New York' (*LP*, 253). By the end of the memoir, she has become Arab-American in concert with that particular post-9/11 historical moment and, although she has found solidarity with an Arab-American theatre group, she directs her creative energies to a solo show devoted to Palestine.

In the tradition of the *Bildungsroman*, Said chronicles her turbulent youth and a complex trajectory towards self-knowledge, embodying a new form of subjectivity in a world that has changed. In the post-9/11 world, second-generation Americans have increasingly found new ways to express a mixed cultural inheritance. For Said, her discovery is as much an acknowledgment of the hitherto-overlooked flows of Arab and American in her self-formation in the US as it is an understanding of Palestine.

5

Dreaming of Solitude: Haifa Zangana and Alia Mamdouh

> Prison is density. No one spends a night there without training his throat on what resembles singing, for that is the way one is allowed to tame solitude and preserve the dignity of pain . . . You sing, because the prison cell tempts you to speak of what you lack in perfect solitude to the world outside.
>
> Mahmoud Darwish, *In the Presence of Absence*

While the memory of colonial violence and national traumas has been the subject of a vast body of postcolonial and contemporary Arabic novels, the effects of torture and the challenge of taboos have offered new areas of exploration in the genre of memoir. In the twentieth and twenty-first centuries, the effects of communal trauma and prison have influenced autobiographical production, producing forms such as the prison diary, journals, notebooks, and testimony. In the twenty-first century, atrocity in Palestine and Iraq has produced a new wave of autobiographical production ranging from testimony, autobiographical novels, and memoirs. Although there has been a sustained effort to narrativise the recent history of violence in Iraq and Syria in contemporary Arabic novels, memoirs are comparatively scarce. These new autobiographical forms elaborate new languages and forms of narrativisation of atrocity. Two contemporary memoirs are *Fī Arwiqat al-Dhākirah* (*Dreaming of Baghdad*, serialised in the journal *Literary Exile* (*al-Ightirāb al-Adabī*) in London (1986–9) and published in 1995)[1] by Iraqi writer Haifa Zangana (b. 1950) [2] and *Al-Ajnabīyah* (*The Foreigner*, 2013) by Iraqi writer Alia Mamdouh (b. 1944). While the prevalence of violence has led to the rise of new literary forms in Iraq, Palestine, and Algeria, such memoirs can be seen as a continuity of a form that has flourished in Arabic literature, has been further influenced by contexts where violence has escalated, and has developed in response to dictatorships, war, and occupation.

Iraqi literature and culture have contested the US occupation and have elaborated novel forms to examine violence and atrocity in contemporary Iraq.[3] This chapter examines the ways in which *Dreaming of Baghdad* and *The Foreigner* offer new forms for the exploration of subjectivity and cultural memory by disrupting taboos on women's writing and self-representation. *Dreaming of Baghdad* explores the impossibility of narrating memory, torture, and prison. In *Cruel Modernity,* Jean Franco focuses on 'the incalculability of loss' (2013: 21) in the genres of testimony and memoir that narrate atrocity in the context of Latin America. *Dreaming of Baghdad,* I argue, not only disrupts taboos on the narration of prison and torture but also addresses broader anxieties over women's subjectivity, revolutionary action, and the future of Iraq. A reading of the memory of torture and the testimony of the writer focuses on the role of memoir in intervening in the discourse of human rights and minority rights in Iraq not only under the Saddam Hussein regime, but also in contexts ranging from the US occupation and the ensuing sectarian strife. Mamdouh's autobiography, *The Foreigner*, offers a continuity and extension of Zangana's memoir that focuses on the evocation of fear and terror in the diaspora. Focusing on postcolonial Iraqi memoirs, this chapter explores new forms and the remaking of the genre to narrate the effects of atrocity.

Zangana has noted that Iraqi writers who have not left Iraq have limited options: 'to write what the authorities approved of, to stop writing altogether, or to adopt an allegorical style'.[4] Both Zangana and Mamdouh, who write and publish in the diaspora, have produced postcolonial autobiographical works that are concerned with emancipation, the preservation of memory, history, and national dreams, and the obliteration of taboos in Arab literary autobiography.

Literary Testimony

In her study of the practices of cruelty in Latin America in the twentieth century and the relationship between literature, culture, and human rights in *Cruel Modernity*, Franco explores how Latin American modernity has been founded on practices of cruelty – kidnapping, torture, mutilation, dismemberment, disappearance, and murder. As she argues, 'Cruelty, a word that suggests a deliberate intention to hurt and damage another, is not only practiced by governments, including democracies, that employ torture and atrocity for many different reasons – from the extraction of information, to the suppression of dissident and ethnically different groups' (Franco 2013: 2). Franco, writing on the phenomenon of violence and the cruelty of modernity, notes: 'Neither cruelty nor the exploitation of cruelty is new, but the lifting of the taboo, the acceptance and justification of cruelty and the rationale for cruel acts, have become a feature of modernity' (ibid.). Drawing on testimony and forms of art, Franco examines the effects of cruelty and its institutionalisation of 'extreme masculinity' expressed in violence visited upon women. Her examination of testimonial archives explores the nature of cultural memory and the 'long-lasting memory traces' left by cruelty (9). Reading Arab memoirs through Franco's study helps us to examine how memoirs represent the atrocity and violations perpetrated by regimes and the ways in which they blur the line between self-representation and testimony. *Cruel Modernity* can be used to read the role of Arab writers in the subversion of a culture of state-sponsored violence in the postcolonial world. This can work to lay bare the ways in which Arab women's memoirs lift taboos on the representation of subjectivity, torture, and the effects of repression.

Autobiography can highlight the violence exercised by the state against dissidents and embody attempts to work through trauma. Gillian Whitlock notes the politics of the production and reception of Middle Eastern autobiography and argues that autobiographical works enable writers to foreground the nature of 'ethical justice'. At the same time, the consumption of autobiography in the West can enforce particular interests and promote misconceptions about the Middle East. Whitlock notes: 'Autobiography circulates as a "Soft weapon." It can personalize and humanize categories of people whose experiences are frequently unseen and unheard. To attend to a nauseated body at risk in Baghdad, or to hear a militant feminist body beneath a burka, to attach a face and recognize a refugee is to make powerful interventions in debates about social justice, sovereignty, and human rights. Life narrative can do these things. It is a "soft" weapon because it is easily co-opted into propaganda' (2007: 3). In the process, Whitlock examines the importance of autobiography in local culture and the different political purposes it can serve through its reception and consumption by a Western audience.

Self-representation and the evocation of trauma are central to memoirs centred on violence. Leigh Gilmore turns her attention to the relationship between trauma and self-representation, focusing on the limits of autobiography – the border between fiction and autobiography; autobiography and history; 'autobiography and legal testimony' (2001: 14). Gilmore notes the demands of autobiography that may limit self-representation 'through its almost legalistic definition of truth telling, its anxiety about invention, and its preference for the literal and verifiable, even in the presence of some ambivalence about those criteria' (3). In other words, self-representation and the narration of trauma are entangled with law as a 'metaphor' for 'veracity' (7), which explains some writers' tendency to depart from conventional autobiographical forms to elude the complexity and elusiveness of memory. Other obstacles to the representation of trauma include 'disruptions in memory', or a memory 'that expresses itself in flashbacks and fragments' (26, 29) and the recurrence of dreams.

Gilmore notes two obstacles to the representation of trauma: 'the subject of trauma refers to both a person struggling to make sense of an overwhelming experience in a particular context and the unspeakability of trauma itself, the resistance to representation' (46). Importantly, she argues that trauma demands 'alternative forms' of autobiography (143) because of the ethical questions inherent in the representation of trauma and poses important questions about how the marginalised can represent trauma, how the experience eludes language, and the ways in which writers eschew conventional autobiography to broaden the limits of the form.

In the words of Franco, 'testimony and memoir are the genres in which stories of atrocity are usually narrated' (2013: 195). The relationship between memoir and testimony inheres in the exploration of memory and the attempt to represent events that have been elided or occluded from the public record. Whitlock distinguishes between memoir and testimony: 'The memoir is traditionally the prerogative of the literate elite; alternatively, the testimony is the means by which the disempowered experience enters the record' (2007: 132). The distinction between memory and testimony is particularly relevant to marginalised groups – women and ethnic minorities – whose autobiographical production chronicles experience that offers testimony of practices of repression and extermination.

Baghdad Dreams

> If you dream, it's because memory remembers what you have forgotten of the obscure.
>
> Mahmoud Darwish, *In the Presence of Absence*

While other Arab writers have explored the experience of prison, Zangana's *Dreaming of Baghdad* offers an unprecedented attempt to examine the effects of violence on the survivor through confession and moments of silence. Torture and revolutionary anticolonial struggle are the subject of the famous 1966 film, *The Battle of Algiers*, directed by Gillo Pontecorvo. Set in the 1950s, the film offers an unprecedented cinematic representation of the torture of Algerian FLN members in French jails during the Algerian War of Independence. Torture has been amply documented by Ibrahim, Djebar, al-Zayyat, and Darwish, all of whom recount torture through the fate of characters or narrators of autobiography. Sonallah Ibrahim slips a brief mention of torture in prison in the pseudo-autobiographical novella *That Smell* and dwells on its effects in *Notes from Prison*. Djebar narrates atrocity in *Fantasia* by unearthing archives that offer testimony to the dismembered corpses and mutilated bodies in a history of colonial violence: the French conquest of 1830, the massacre of the Ben Menacer tribe, and the fumigation of the Ouled Riah tribe in 1845. In *Children of the New World*, women and men in the Algerian town of Blida are imprisoned and tortured in French jails in 1956. In *The Search*, al-Zayyat hears the screams of the tortured in solitary confinement in 1949 Egypt. In *Journal of an Ordinary Grief*, Darwish plumbs his experience of house arrest, interrogations, and prison. The poet describes mock courtrooms, military tribunals, house arrest, detention periods, and daily appointments at the police station where he has to prove he exists. In *The Presence of Absence*, Darwish reports the torture and massacre of Palestinians by the Israeli army in the Sabra and Shatila refugee camps on 16–18 September 1982 in a public spectacle: 'Killers had carried out the operation, but numerous torture squads were probably the ones who split skulls, slashed thighs, cut off arms, hands and fingers, and dragged the dying and disabled by ropes, men and women who were still alive' (2011: 77).[5] These works have documented torture in the prison camp, the solitary cell, interrogation rooms, caves, and refugee camps.

Haifa Zangana, an Iraqi writer, Kurdish revolutionary, former political prisoner, and survivor of torture under the Baath regime in 1971 for her activity in the Communist Party, left Iraq upon her release from prison, moved to Syria and Lebanon where she worked for the PLO, and settled in London in 1976. After the US invasion of Iraq in 2003, she joined the anti-war movement and wrote nonfiction works about the US occupation.[6] She has published two works inspired by her imprisonment, torture, and exile, *Dreaming of Baghdad* and *Nisā' 'alā Safar* (*Women on a Journey: Between Baghdad and London*, 2000), a novel about Iraqi refugees in London following the 1991 Gulf War. Her subsequent publications show her activism and concern with the unknown history of women's rights in Iraq and torture: *City of Widows: An Iraqi Woman's Account of War and Resistance* (2009), a history of women in Iraq from the early twentieth century through the US occupation, and *The Torturer in the Mirror* (2010, with Ramsey Clark and Thomas Ehrich Reifer), an essay collection about the inhumanity of torture. Recently, Zangana expressed her longing for fiction: 'I miss the freedom of solitude and dream . . . Fiction gives you the power to create a world that does not deny you access to the past . . . It feels like the Iraq that I miss' (2012). In this interview, Zangana invokes lines by Pablo Neruda from 'Explico Algunas Cosas' ('I Explain a Few Things'), a poem written about the Spanish Civil War, included in his poetry volume *Tercera residencia* (*Third Residence*) (1934–45), to explain the impossibility of fiction during the occupation, the imagery of violence obscuring poetry:

> You will ask: why doesn't his poetry
> speak to us of dreams, of leaves
> of the great volcanoes of his native land?
>
> Come and see the blood in the streets.
> come and see
> the blood in the streets,
> come and see the blood
> in the streets![7]

In May 2015, Zangana spent a month in Palestine where she ran workshops in cultural journalism and creative writing for former women prisoners in Israeli prisons.[8] As these publications and activities show, Zangana has long held a deep interest in the little-known history of violence and Arab women's revolutionary activity during war and occupation.

Zangana wrote *Dreaming of Baghdad* from 1986 to 1989 in London where she followed developments in the Iran–Iraq war and where she subsequently resided during the 2003 US invasion. *Dreaming of Baghdad* is an important contribution to Iraqi prison literature for the challenges the representation of prison and torture poses to the limits of the genre, its unprecedented exploration of prison and the survival of torture, and its rare insight into the long-drawn struggle for democracy, human rights, and sovereignty in postcolonial Iraq. The narrator-writer narrates her memory, dreams, and nostalgia for Baghdad. Further, *Dreaming of Baghdad* turns attention to the development of the genre to adapt to the ethical demands of the representation of torture in memoirs. It offers a sustained effort to examine minority rights, human rights, and women's rights through an examination of Zangana's experiences of prison and torture. *Dreaming of Baghdad* dwells on the violence and violations perpetrated by the state, recalled in another context – that of the Iran–Iraq war – and published in English once in 1991 and again in 2009, and therefore embedded in the practices of a postcolonial dictatorship and the US occupation. It examines the effects on the survivor's subjectivity in both contexts. Although set in Iraq in the early 1970s, with the publication of the English translation in 2009, the notorious prison of Abu Ghraib, in which Zangana was held, invokes the recent atrocity of the US invasion. By lending form to her memory, Zangana contributes to prison literature and addresses the fate of Kurdish nationalism, ethnicity, and ideology in postcolonial Iraq.

Zangana was imprisoned when she was a student at the University of Baghdad for distributing leaflets for the Communist party and attending political meetings in its headquarters. *Dreaming of Baghdad* follows the narrator from Qasr al-Nihaya, the detention centre for political prisoners, a palace ironically converted into a prison, to Abu Ghraib, the notorious general prison, to al-Za'afaraniya, a prison for prostitutes. Focusing on the young Iraqi revolutionary, the memoir details the experience of the Left and the struggle against the regime in Iraq, tracing the dissolution of the Communist Party, whose members were detained or who sought refuge in the Kurdish mountains (Ibrahim 2007). *Dreaming of Baghdad* explores the tragic fate of a group of members of the Communist Party whose activism criss-crossed Baghdad and Kurdistan.

Variously described as an autobiography or a novel, *Dreaming of Baghdad* redraws the borders of a genre that has long been debated in autobiographical scholarship. In his Foreword to *Dreaming of Baghdad*, Hamid Dabashi calls it a 'revelatory testimonial' (2009: vii), a record of Baghdad, Iraq, and the Iraqis before the devastation wrought by Saddam Hussein and George W. Bush, and reads the publication of the memoir against a plethora of Iranian memoirs produced in American culture. Zangana has by turns called *Dreaming of Baghdad* a novel and an autobiographical novel. In the prologue, her admission of the history of writing *Dreaming of Baghdad* draws an autobiographical pact:

> I wrote this book in tiny installments over eight years, when I had persistent nightmares about my past. I was writing about my life as a radical activist in Iraq in the 1970s. I wrote it at a time when I didn't want or wasn't able to deal with memories of what had happened to me in prison. I wrote it while I was living in exile, missing my family terribly, believing I would never return to live in Baghdad again. I wrote it during the Iraq–Iran war, at the height of Saddam Hussein's popularity in Iraq, Arab countries, and the West. I wrote it in first person, as a record of my memories, and in third person, as I often saw myself, as if I were standing outside of my own life, trying to remember things and events as correctly and completely as possible. (3)

Zangana's prologue–pact in English also focuses on her anxiety about the betrayal of the memory of her co-workers and co-prisoners. By offering the reader a history of *Dreaming of Baghdad*, Zangana highlights the role of memory in the representation of experience, her anxiety about truth and betrayal, and the split between the narrator and the survivor of torture. She goes on to describe her book as the first published record of 'the experience of imprisonment and struggle against the Baath regime' (1968–2003) (*DB*, 3). She wrote *Dreaming of Baghdad* to document the revolutionary struggle, to recount her torture, to heal her body of her sickness, and to overcome her repulsion, the precariousness of memory, and oblivion – for self-liberation, relief, and renewal (*AD* 82; *DB*, 101). In one of her recurrent dreams, the narrator writes in a notebook: 'She wanted above all to complete the last chapter of the autobiography she had started over three years ago' (*AD*, 129; *DB*, 129). The word used in Arabic is 'mudhakkirāt' (memoirs), a term that appears to comment on the autobiographical status of *Dreaming of Baghdad*. In her dreams, the narrator wishes to complete the memoir she has started and, in the epilogue, Zangana writes that she laboured to produce a record of her experience in *Dreaming of Baghdad* (*AD* 131; *DB*, 152). She writes, 'writing memoirs is an elusive process' (*AD*, 131); the word in English is 'memories' (*DB*, 153), although the Arabic again is explicitly 'mudhakkirāt'. In an interview, Zangana concedes that *Dreaming of Baghdad* is 'autobiographical' (Ouyang 2007: 451). She admits: 'When I was writing it I was trying to force myself to deal with a very painful episode in my past in order to move on. The detachment of reporting, the distance of third-person narrative, helped ease the pain of looking at what I had gone through in Iraq when I was imprisoned and tortured' (ibid.). She further obfuscates the genre of *Dreaming of Baghdad* by concluding: 'The novel, with its capacity for multiple perspectives, freed me to do this' (ibid.).

A recent testimony by Zangana echoes some of the scenes of *Dreaming of Baghdad*. In her testimony, Zangana alludes to *Dreaming of Baghdad* as a novel in which she wrote about the complexity of recalling memory (2015: 253). She recalls her visits to her father's ancestral Kurdish village, Zino, and her mother's visits to the prison in which she was held for her clandestine political activity in the 1970s.

Dreaming of Baghdad, partly written in the form of letters addressed to Haifa, an Iraqi exile in London in the 1980s, part prison diary in al-Za'faraniya (from 20 August to 17 December 1972), and also a series of dreams blurs the borders of genre. The narrator's memory moves between her father's Kurdish village on the Iraq–Iran border, the labyrinthine palace Qasr al-Nihaya in Baghdad, where she is tortured, and her exile in London.

Zangana writes of her Kurdish father and Arab mother in a memoir that ties her ancestry to her dreams for Iraq. *Dreaming of Baghdad* and her recent testimony dwell on language: Kurdish, the language spoken by her father, and

Arabic, her mother tongue. This is not a separation from language, but Arabic conferred on her freedom for the kind of confessional writing and literary self-expression inherent in self-representation, the exploration of memory, and the narration of torture; her father's encouragement of her fluency in Arabic enabled her to express herself in her mother tongue. She did not learn Kurdish, but wrote in Arabic. In a testimony, Zangana recalls her father's Kurdish-inflected Arabic and the sense that not speaking Kurdish distances her father from her because he is not able to fully express his love, joy, or anger in Arabic (2015: 255). She asserts that her identity is 'Iraqi-Kurdish-Arab' (261): she feels Kurdish during the atrocity enacted upon the Kurdish population of Halabja by Saddam Hussein's regime in 1988 and feels Arab during the US occupation of Iraq (Ouyang 2007: 450). Although she writes in Arabic for an Arab readership, invoking Arabic and Kurdish in her writing revisits the multilingualism of Iraq, a struggle symbolically represented by the location of the headquarters of her revolutionary group in the Kurdish mountains. Her father, who settled in Baghdad with an Arab wife, and spoke Kurdish, Turkish, and Arabic, epitomises that historical multi-ethnic Iraq.

Dreaming of Baghdad is steeped in the narrator's nostalgia for her father's ancestral Kurdish village and her comrades at the group's headquarters in the northern village of Nawchilican. The title in English, *Dreaming of Baghdad*, is the unequivocal reminder of her nostalgia for Iraq in exile. Early in *Dreaming of Baghdad*, her father takes her to his home-village, Zino, hemmed in by mountains, on the Iraq–Iran border, in Kurdistan in the late 1950s to visit his Kurdish relatives in a scene that recalls Djebar's father who takes her to the French lycée. In her father's home-village, the narrator recalls the smell of Persian carpets in her uncle's shop and her father's conversations with his family. The base at Nawchilican to which she relocated stands for her Kurdish ancestry and dreams of revolution that she shared with her group. In her testimony, she recalls the city of Kirkuk, home to Arabs, Kurds, Turks, Syrians, Assyrians, and Armenians and the inspiration for Assyrian poet Sargon Boulus (Zangana 2015: 253).

The narrator's dreams morph into a nightmare of interlopers that recalls Darwish who dreams of interrogators, torturers, and wardens in *Mural*. In one dream, while writing in her notebook, she is plagued by fear and surveillance: she wonders whether the man who appears in her dream has read her manuscript, whether she has disclosed the names of her comrades, and whether she has written notes against the regime. Like al-Zayyat in her real ward search, she is about to gather her stacks of papers and contemplates her fate, but unlike *The Search*, where the inspector wreaks havoc on the ward, Zangana's narrator fears torture.

Tortured Memory

Zangana reconfigures the genre of memoir to recall a memory that she has elided and that recurs in her dreams. She interrogates the truth of memory and the notion that trauma can be 'worked through' by narrativisation. *Dreaming of Baghdad* represents an effort to plumb the depths of the memory of prison and torture. More important, Zangana does not offer writing as a process of working through trauma by revisiting memory;[9] it took her eight years to write *Dreaming of Baghdad.* Zangana notes in the prologue: 'I also wrote this book to tell of my experience with torture. To break the silence . . . How do you talk about humiliation? . . . About being reduced to an animal sleeping with urine and feces? Thirty years later I still often wake at two a.m., the time when they used to lead me out of my cell for interrogation' (*DB*, 5). She also notes that torture has left a 'deep scar' on cultural memory and was the fate of subversive Iraqi activists (*DB*, 5).

Dreaming of Baghdad investigates the ethical challenges that the narration of torture poses to the genre of memoir. Zangana was interrogated and tortured in Qasr al-Nihaya, a torture centre run by the regime. She recalls details of her torture, the screams of her companions, the odours of the cell, and her daily physical needs. During repeated torture sessions, she would hear her comrades being tortured and a former comrade, who had been tortured, was brought in to identify her. She revisits the terror of incarceration and torture through scenes of interrogation and her body's responses. One of the recurrent dreams described by the author of the letters is of torture: 'Here is my body recognizing fear before fear reaches my brain, recognizing images of torture, not in memory but in my body's cells . . . How can I hide the trembling of my body and the pallor of my face? . . . A man approaches me, and then another, and another . . . The interrogation starts . . . Horror!' (*AD,* 15–16; *DB*, 12–13) She then notes: 'And the self splits forever' (*AD*, 16). The narrator names her comrade Fouad, whose body, disfigured by torture and dragged into the interrogation room, is a faded reminder of the youthful, revolutionary dreamer she once knew. Other comrades are arrested and executed in prison. Another comrade, Saad, was transferred to a mental hospital and made to collaborate with the secret police to identify and arrest his comrades. She revisits the day of her arrest at Bab Al-Mu'atham district in Baghdad. The narrator evokes the terror and loss of sense of self, her face covered in sores and her hair falling out by the time she is moved to Abu Ghraib. When she chances upon a mirror in the prostitutes' prison, she breaks down in an encounter that closely mirrors her split into the narrator and the narrated. The narration of torture elides the anonymity and invisibility imposed by the regime on political prisoners: when her mother visits Qasr al-Nihaya, the prison claims that she is not on the prisoner list and, when Abu Ghraib is visited by a group from a socialist country to inspect the women's prison, she is summoned to an office to cover up the incarceration of political prisoners. Instead, the memoir confers upon the narrator and each of her named co-prisoners the particularity that the regime has obliterated.

Zangana writes that she sought to evade a representation of subjectivity 'as the center of events or history' (*DB*, 3). She splits the narration into the first person and the third person: her dreams are described in the third person; her torture in Abu Ghraib and experience in the prostitutes' prison in the first person (Ghazoul 2009: 159). The third person offers a reprieve from the discomfort inherent in representations of prison and torture (Ouyang 2007: 451).

The narrator's literary testimony can be read against her forced confession in prison: she is forced to sign a statement that she was a member of the Communist Party and was arrested for possession of hand grenades, explosives, and pamphlets; that she joined the party to have sex with men, and that she was not a virgin when she entered Qasr al-Nihaya and was well treated by the security forces (*AD*, 82; *DB*, 100). While she narrates her memory, rather than her anxiety about confession and the betrayal of her comrades under torture, she tells the story of prisoners who are debilitated and dehumanised by terror and torture. To translate memory into testimony, the memoir draws the reader into the interrogation room, the halls of prison, memory, dreams, where there are moments in which she alludes to the disappearance and execution of comrades, and others in which her dreams become what

Gilmore has described as 'the unconscious language of repetition through which trauma initially speaks' (2001: 7).

The narrator sheds light on the world of the women's prison, hitherto unexplored in Iraqi literature. [10] In Abu Ghraib, the general prison, to which she is transferred after two weeks in Qasr al-Nihaya, she meets women whose oppression by men led them to murder their husbands in a patriarchal culture: Um Wahid, Um Jassim, and Um Ali. Although each of her co-prisoners is named after her eldest male son, each has a story that underscores her particularity and humanity.

The narrator, whom sleep has eluded and whose solitude debilitates her in exile in London, dreams of her torturers and hears the screams of the tortured. She lives in a perpetual state of debilitation, unable to remake her life in London. The narrator, absorbed in remembering her group, details her state. Nightmares torment her years after the event; she longs for 'solitude' in London, but fears it, too (*AD*, 32; *DB*, 35). She recalls her arrest in the environs of Qasr al-Nihaya prison, 'In August, the hottest month of the year, I felt cold' (*DB*, 42). This echoes Darwish's August lament in *Memory for Forgetfulness*. In exile, she dreams of her father, desolate and detached: 'He did not see her in his solitude' (*AD*, 124; *DB*, 144).

Although the memoir circles around dreams and fragments of memory to narrate the torture to which she was subjected, it problematises the representation of torture through the elusiveness and precariousness of memory. When the narrator chances upon an old issue of *Al-Thawrah*, the Iraqi national newspaper, in Tunis in 1999 and a missing persons ad about the disappearance of Haidar, a former prisoner and suspected infiltrator who arrived at Nawchilican, the Communist Party's central leadership base, on 1 May 1998, she wonders how she has forgotten to write about him, or whether it was her effort to suppress the memory of the tragedy of his execution. She describes the omission from her memoir as 'a lapse in memory' (*DB*, 153). She does not recall whether she was present at his execution or had learned of it from other comrades. It is implied that Haidar was executed by his comrades and she is implicated in the violence of the group. The narrator confesses her guilt and complicity in her struggle to recall whether she witnessed the execution. *Dreaming of Baghdad* restores the memory of Haidar, a survivor of prison, her guilt, and complicity. In *Dreaming of Baghdad*, the narrator concedes the elusiveness of memory and the confusion between the truth and her dreams; these are some of the effects of her trauma, the survivor's anxiety about the representation of torture, and the limits of the form.

Writing about her imprisonment and working through her memory, the narrator dreams of revolution and freedom in Iraq. In Nawchilican – where Arabic, Kurdish, Turkish, and Persian pamphlets were peddled – there is a room or library where 'a group of dreaming fighters' (*DB*, 94) met to deliberate the fate of Iraq. The memoir focuses on the subjectivity of the narrator who concedes that in the early 1970s ideology and the struggle were the raison d'être of the group. In London, she revisits moments at the base in the mountains of Kurdistan that emblematise her dreams of Iraq.

Dreaming of Baghdad rethinks the conventions of the genre and extends Arabic prison literature to lift taboos on the representation of violence. The narration of torture tests the limits of the form and subjectivity in a memoir that examines memory, testimony, and self-representation. Memory is reworked in a form that challenges the limits of autobiography and the representation of prison, contravenes the borders of the genre, and poses questions about the ethics of representation (Gilmore 2001: 43; 47). In the end, the narrator notes in a clear echo of Darwish, 'Memory is multilayered . . . It is the unwritten record of the past. Its only partner is forgetting' (*AD*, 135; *DB*, 156). Memory is inscribed on the body and in the dreams of survivors who suffer in exile from the effects of cruelty perpetrated by the state. The memoir represents a new exploration of the dehumanisation of prisoners and the suppression of dissidence. It advances new representations of the subjectivity of Iraqi revolutionary women, documents a period of postcolonial national struggle, and interrogates the practices of the state. Further, it poses questions about the future production of memoir, self-representation, and the ethical demands of the genre.

Foreign Fiction

Alia Mamdouh rose to prominence on the contemporary Arabic literary scene with the publication of her novel *Ḥabbāt al-Naftālīn* (1986) (*Naphtalene: A Novel of Baghdad*, 2005) and has reached a non-Arabic readership through translation into Western languages.[11] She left Iraq in 1982 and lived in Morocco, Lebanon, and England before settling in Paris. *The Foreigner* represents the continuity and extension of contemporary Iraqi memoirs, more specifically the experience Zangana narrates in *Dreaming of Baghdad.* Set in Paris from the mid-1990s during the sanctions on Iraq through the 2003 US invasion to the eve of the Arab revolutions in 2010, *The Foreigner* recapitulates and synthesises the story of Iraqis in the diaspora. Like Zangana in London, Mamdouh extends, in Paris, the autobiographical Iraqi history beyond the Iran-Iraq war to the violence and devastation of the twenty-first century.

Naphtalene: A Novel of Baghdad recounts the story of young Huda, whose father is a police governor at the prison in Karbala and Syrian mother is afflicted with tuberculosis, during the 1940s and '50s in al-A'dhamiyya quarter of Baghdad. An autobiographical novel and *Bildungsroman* of Huda, *Naphtalene* centers on Huda's observations of her family and culture of Baghdad. The novel captures the forgotten world of mid-century Baghdad. Hélène Cixous describes *Naphtalene* as a 'Bildungsroman of Baghdad (a narrative which assembles all the fragments of a prophetic childhood, and which, in remembering the primary elements of subjective life, proposes a vision of the world and an art form). The expression 'Bildung', which speaks of genesis, of formation, and of education, is not, however, sufficient for *Naphtalene* – for here *genesis* is also *chaos*, and *apprenticeship* is constantly turned upside down' (Cixous 2005: vi; emphasis in original). *Naphtalene* introduces and nurtures the central themes of recalcitrance and nonconformity to which Mamdouh returns *in The Foreigner* by focusing on her challenge of authority and the dictates of convention: 'In appearance, a girl. In action, *a boy*. In poetic truth, a *fiery daughter*' (Cixous 2005: vi; emphasis in original). At the same time, *Naphtalene* is a novel of the nation on the eve of the 1958 revolution against the monarchy and British control in Iraq (Ghazoul 2007: 315). As such, the novel is evocative of al-Zayyat's *The Open Door* and Djebar's *Children of the New World* as it focuses on the world of women and the rise of the national struggle.

In *The Foreigner*, Mamdouh turns to self-scrutiny in the diaspora during the mid-1990s through 2010, illuminating a world of migration and repression. Set in Paris, where the narrator has resided for a decade, *The Foreigner* commences with the memory of the fear and terror that being summoned to the Iraqi embassy evokes, alternating between the diaspora and the Baghdad of her youth amid the precariousness of the situation in Iraq. *The Foreigner*, written in the form of a fictionalised autobiography (*sīra riwā'iyya*) and a diary (*yawmiyyāt),* does not state the name of its author. Indeed, Mamdouh writes that she is not inclined towards the word autobiography (*sīra*) and that she enfolds autobiography in the world of her novels. In her words, she 'violates' (*Aa*, 20) the principles of autobiography, pointing to the intransigence characteristic of her youth and which she upholds in *The Foreigner.* In a testimony, she writes about the suppression of the individual in her youth in the discourses of mid-century national struggles; the individual was consigned to absence, oblivion or death and was not conventionally cast in the role of hero (Mamdouh 2002: 203). As Sabry Hafez notes, the result of *The Foreigner*'s open scrutiny and attention to events is a unique autobiographical work that defies categorisation and has no precedent in Arabic literature (Hafez 2015). In spite of Mamdouh's reservations about autobiography, *The Foreigner* abounds with allusions to the novels she has authored – *Al-Wala*ʿ (*The Passion*, 1995) and *Al-Ghulāma* (*The Tomboy*, 2000), a literary history that offers a testimony to the identification of the author with the narrator. Further, her novels offer forms of documentation and identification to substitute for the documents in her husband's possession; they are sources of her history, so that her autobiography coalesces with her literary works. She writes, for example, about her preservation of memory and history in her novels, but her novels in *The Foreigner* provide other forms of documentation for the Iraqi writer who has to apply for asylum in France or pass through entry ports in the US: 'In [my novels] I documented Iraq of the 1960s in *Naphtalene*; the ruling Baath party and the marriage between Baathists and Communists during the 1970s in *The Tomboy*; migration and dispossession in *The Passion* – this trilogy set my trajectory between the alleys and the quarters of Aʿdhamiyya, al-Mansūr, ḥayy al-Jāmiʿa, Palestine Street, and the University of Mustansariyya?' (*Aa*, 121). Fellow writers also appear in *The Foreigner* where the narrator alludes to her friendship with French feminist critic Hélène Cixous, Lebanese writer Hanan al-Shaykh (Ḥanān al-Shaykh), and Iraqi writers Iqbal al-Qazwini (Iqbāl al-Qazwīnī) and Inaam Kachachi (Inʿām Kachāchī). In Beirut, flanked by Nizar Qabbani (Nizār Qabbānī) and Mahmoud Darwish, at a dinner party, the writer-narrator writes of the publication and reception of a new book.

In Paris the narrator is both a foreigner and a refugee. Plagued by the terror of being kidnapped by the Iraqi Ministry of Justice, she fears persecution and writes, 'for I know the general stories about torture and what happens in secret chambers' (*Aa*, 63). The state of her marriage and her status as a wife who has deserted her husband are in turn symptomatic of the fractures in Iraq during the US occupation. *The Foreigner* is rooted in the precariousness wrought by dictatorship and war: persecution by Saddam Hussein's regime and the unremitting violence of the US occupation. *The Foreigner* is organised around a multitude of houses –literal and metaphorical – which either challenge or reinforce the narrator's diasporic status; the implications of the houses are multifarious: *bayt al- ṭā'ah* (literally, house of obedience), the husband's house to which a woman, in case of unlawful desertion, must return in Islamic law; the inferno (*bayt al-jaḥīm*); the house of French law; the house of language; the teachers' dorms; her father's house; the public bath, a center where intelligence is collected about the street, prison, hospitals, and intimate private lives (Haidar 2005: 203); and the houses of friends in Paris, Beirut, and Baghdad. On her regular visits to friends in Paris, she enters houses and meets with fellow writers in the diaspora – Berlin-based Iqbal al-Qazwini and Paris-based Inaam Kachachi. The narrator takes us into the privacy of houses and shows how the trajectories of radically different Iraqis intersect in the diaspora. Her interactions underscore the community and reciprocity in the diaspora where her circle covers a broad spectrum of Iraqis – ideological, religious, and ethnic – and contrasts with the dismemberment of Iraq.

Fear and terror dominate Mamdouh's autobiography, contributing to a literature that documents a history of violence and devastation in Iraq. The narrator writes, 'I am from an Iraqi generation whom fear hasn't left and who has not parted from fear' (*Aa*, 192). This is a sustained study of the nature and characteristics of fear that seeps into the narrator, and the continual resistance to it, in ways that have never been addressed in Arabic literature (Hafez 2015). Although fear from persecution and deportation result in her debilitation and sickness, the prevalence of fear serves a role in Mamdouh's writing; she writes, 'It [fear] runs through families, clans and perhaps even nations . . . It resides in our walls and our foundations, in our vaults and our domes' (Mamdouh 1998: 69); it is 'as if my books came out of the world to defy torture' (Faqir 1996: vii).[12] The writer-narrator returns to her solitude (*'uzla*) (*Aa*, 191) in Paris where her foreignness extends to estrangement from her country.

When the narrator-writer goes on to apply for asylum in France, she has to prepare documents and proof of her identity, but her husband has the originals in Iraq and, under the occupation, her efforts to obtain copies are unsuccessful; her friends step in to offer testimony to prove her case to a judge. In the absence of documentation – her Iraqi nationality civil status and marriage certificate – her autobiography offers a document that serves to identify the narrator and counter erasure. While the writer is identified as the author of her novels at embassies and ports of entry, these do not provide sufficient official identification. *The Foreigner* is 'documentary' (Hafez 2015) in the sense that the narrator's memory, literary history, and friends accumulate other documents and evidence. The narrator must prove that she is an Iraqi national to apply for asylum; consequently, the renewal of her passport, signatures, fingerprints, and the testimonies of fellow writers represent other forms of identification, so that the narrator feels she is 'reborn' and has been 'naturalized' as an Iraqi citizen in Paris (*Aa*, 190). The contemplation of subjectivity – its difference, otherness, distinction, and foreignness – is implied in the title (Hafez 2015).

The Foreigner circles around the theme of language and relates the writer-narrator's anxiety to dispossession. The narrator expresses a fear of the French language, which she has not mastered in Paris, where she resides, and feels that Arabic is her defence against her husband, the institution of marriage, the Ministry of Justice, the Iraqi state, and all the world's languages. She has to learn the language to be acclimatised to her milieu: 'I try, but I fail because of my solitude. Who will I speak French with, I wonder?' (*Aa*, 64) Hélène Cixous, the French critic and playwright who has dedicated her books to Mamdouh, exhorts her to learn French to read them and consequently the writer-narrator feels that everyone has conspired to expel her from the paradise of Paris because of her failure to learn the language. She remarks upon her attachment to Arabic: 'I feared that my Arabic language would appear feeble after all the atrocity and calamity that have passed through it, so I sought to record our decline in it' (*Aa*, 65). Her attachment to Arabic compensates for her separation from Iraq and her characteristic poetic prose is akin to her residence in language for a writer who fears deportation and repatriation to her country.

In 2004, the judges' citations for the Naguib Mahfouz Medal for Literature awarded to Mamdouh's novel *Al-Maḥbūbāt* (*The Loved Ones*) drew attention to her creation of a language in response to a particular historical precariousness: 'Written in exile, it [*The Loved Ones*] invents a language of exile with which to resist dispossession. It is a story about memory and history, a story against forgetting, a desperate attempt to defy obliteration through narrative, even if in fragments, even if discontinuous.'[13] Similarly, in *The Foreigner*, Mamdouh creates polyphony that centres on language and space rather than voices.

Circling back to *Naphtalene*, *The Foreigner* transposes the early novel's characters from the 1950s to the twenty-first century and reverts to the story of her father and her aunt from the world of her youth. Upon the appearance of Mamdouh's autobiography, the effects of the occupation were more reified and *The Foreigner* culminates in the writer-narrator's dispossession and fear in the present. Mamdouh reflects on Iraqi diasporic futures, creating an autobiography in the twenty-first century, as Sabry Hafez puts it, the 'century of fragmentation and fracture' (2015).

Both Zangana and Mamdouh rethink the conventions of autobiographical literary practices in the longer arc of a history of violence and atrocity. Moreover, both writers offer contemporary forms of narration and representation that are immured in the precariousness of memory and forms of testimony. Zangana, a Kurdish revolutionary, persecuted and imprisoned by the regime, lifts taboos on the writing of torture. In *Dreaming of Baghdad*, her frankness is unique for Arab autobiography. Similarly, *The Foreigner* aspires to transgress taboos and purge the fear of persecution at a moment when the strictures on Iraqi literary production are upheld. Each circles back to the fictiveness of the form; 'autofiction' and the uneasy relationship with memoir for Zangana and Mamdouh are increasingly an effect of the complexity of memory and the persecution of the writers in Iraq. While Zangana remembers the ideals of a revolutionary group during the 1970s, Mamdouh interacts with a community in the diaspora that recalls the religio-ethnic plurality of mid-century Baghdad. Both end with the solitary fate of the Iraqi writer in the diaspora. Evoking memory and writing testimony, whether against violence and atrocity in Iraq or the terror and incoherence in the diaspora, they aspire to emancipation and enfranchisement for women and minorities.

Taken together, *Dreaming of Baghdad* and *The Foreigner* devote attention to the singularity of the individual, even while embedding experience within communal events, and moments of solitude in postcolonial and post-2003 Iraq.

6

Tahrir Memoirs: Radwa Ashour and Mona Prince

On 25 January 2011, Egyptian writer Radwa Ashour (1946–2014) surveyed the scene in Egypt weeks before her surgery at the George Washington University Hospital. Her surgery was set for 11 February 2011. She would go on to recount the months spent in surgery and recovery in the United States during the 2011 Egyptian revolution and her return to take part in the events in Tahrir Square near her home in Cairo.

The result was a set of memoirs that would come to capture the political mood and recreate the form: *Athqal min Radwā: Maqāṭiʿ min Sīra Dhātīyya* (*Heavier than Radwa: Fragments of an Autobiography*, 2013), and *Al-Ṣarkhah: Maqāṭiʿ min Sīra Dhātiyya* (*The Scream: Fragments of an Autobiography*, 2015). The Tahrir memoir is a form written within the Arab revolutions, characterised by simultaneity, association, and introspection. Its forms are multifarious – journal, fragments, or diary amid waves of revolution in Egypt since 2011. The effects of the form capture the 'diary' poems of Neruda's *Isla Negra: A Notebook* where critics have observed that the poet sheds 'the rhetoric of autobiography for the present meditation of the still-changing poet': 'Unlike the prose memoir, the "notes" were intended much less as a factual autobiography than as an informal notebook in which the narrative of past events would mingle with the record of present experience. The memoirs come from retrospection, the notes from introspection' (Santí 1982: 410). The Tahrir memoir preserves autobiographical sequence along with the introspection characteristic of the form in the midst of the revolution.

The form of the diary appeared in Arabic literature as a literary device in novels such as Tawfik al-Hakim's *Yawmiyyāt Nāʾib fī al-Aryāf* (*Diary of a Country Prosecutor*, 1937) and as an autobiographical form reworked in Mahmoud Darwish's *Journal of an Ordinary Grief* (examined in Chapter 3),

Sonallah Ibrahim's belatedly published *Notes from Prison* (2013), Latifa al-Zayyat's *The Search* (examined in Chapter 2), and Mohamad Malas's *Madhāq al-Balaḥ: Yawmiyyāt* (*The Flavor of Dates: Diaries*, 2011).[1] These diaries contain some of the features of Arab memoirs, namely prison, study exchanges, and Arab nationalism, and offer a private form or day-to-day record of events prepared for publication.

In the twenty-first century, the Tahrir memoir followed more than half a century of memoirs by Egyptian women. Al-Zayyat's *The Search* is an antecedent of Ashour's memoirs in which the history of her nationalism and activism is a corollary to that of al-Zayyat in the 1940s and 1980s. In fact, Ashour works her affiliation with her lifelong friend through portraits of al-Zayyat and intertextual allusions to *The Search*.

In the Egyptian revolution, new forms burgeoned such as Egyptian writer Ahdaf Soueif's *My City, Our Revolution* (2012).[2] Soueif (b. 1950) elaborates a new form that offers her the means to 'act the revolution' and write it at the same time (2012: xiii): it is 'an intervention rather than a record' and 'a story about me, my family, and my city – told to a reader, a friend, out of a particular moment, a particular emotion' (xiii–xiv). Revisiting her Tahrir diary, written in the summer of 2011 and resumed from October 2011 to 2013, she notes that her account surveys 'the altered forms of the revolution' (xv) and the city, making it a memoir of Cairo that chronicles the magical eighteen days and the extension of the revolution. The form of the diary, retained in Soueif's *Cairo: Memoir of a City Transformed* (2014), replicates a revolution in the making, so that it does not simply record the remaking of the city, but forms part of the events.

In post-2011 Egypt, Radwa Ashour and Mona Prince also created a form inspired by the Egyptian revolution that chronicles the revolutionary moment and recasts subjectivity in the ensuing events. Ashour, writer and professor, has authored an autobiographical corpus: *al-Riḥlah: Ayyām Ṭāliba Miṣriyya fī Amrīka* (*The Journey: An Egyptian Student's Days in America*, 1983), *Aṭyāf* (*Specters*), *Heavier than Radwa*, and *The Scream*. Prince, writer and professor at Suez Canal University, is the author of a Tahrir memoir, *Revolution Is My Name*. Retracing Ashour's autobiographical corpus and Prince's memoir, this chapter focuses on the Tahrir memoir from 2012 to the present. It surveys Ashour's two-volume chronicle, *Heavier than Radwa* and *The Scream*, and

Prince's memoir to reassess a form in which the revolution has played a central role in the exploration of subjectivity.

From *Specters* to *The Scream*

In the 1980s, Ashour began an autobiographical project that spans more than a quarter-century from the 1980s to the twenty-first century. Her autobiographical oeuvre extends from *The Journey: An Egyptian Student's Days in America* (henceforth *The Journey*) to *The Scream*, chronicling stages of her life, including her activism and her career. *The Journey*, her study abroad memoir, inaugurates her autobiographical corpus. Ashour was in her mid-twenties, a young woman abroad, away from her husband Mourid Barghouti, family, and friends. She had come on a scholarship to study African American literature in the department founded by W. E. B. Du Bois at the University of Massachusetts Amherst.

The Journey self-consciously reworks the genre popularised by Egyptian men of letters such as Rifa'a al-Tahtawi, Taha Hussein, and Tawfik al-Hakim who travelled to the West to study and contributed to cultural exchange (Ashour 1993: 173). Nonetheless, unlike al-Tahtawi, Ashour was not setting out with neutrality and would not return, like subsequent generations of scholars, besotted with the 'lights of imperialism' (*R*, 6).[3] Indeed, as Rasheed El-Enany notes, the word '*Ayyām*' in the title of her memoir forms intertextual ties with Taha Hussein whose *al-Ayyām* (volume III) recounts his study in France (2006: 179). Ashour alludes to al-Tahtawi and encounters with the West in her description of the young Egyptian woman en route to the United States. By contrast, her cultural encounter with the United States laments imperialism; it evokes her relationship to the 'imperial other' (Ashour 1994: 9) and is deeply critical of US foreign policy in Vietnam and Palestine. *The Journey* belongs to Ashour's corpus of campus memoirs that commence with the University of Massachusetts Amherst (1973–5) in the United States and return to Ain Shams University in Egypt. As such, her memoir also returns to the topoi of the campus, education, and study abroad characteristic of Hussein's inaugural autobiography.

Ashour chronicles her journey to study African American literature in the United States in the 1970s against the backdrop of the 1973 Arab–Israeli War (El-Enany 2006: 180), and framed within her Third Worldism.[4] In her memoir, Ashour draws her life in 222 Prince House, the student dormitory of the University of Massachusetts Amherst. When she arrives at the student dormitory, she is alone. *The Journey* evokes her sense of 'otherness' (ibid.) on campus and fellowship with Third World students; for instance, she recalls her American roommate's fear of her nationality and religion and her circle of friends – African Americans, Puerto Ricans, and Iranians. The 1970s American student scene is characterised by a profusion of ethnicities: African American student-activists, Puerto Ricans of Palestinian descent, American roommates. In the memoir, the 1970s is a clear projection of the Egyptian student's understanding of African American history, Third world movements, and US imperialism. The 1970s abound with central events – the belatedly known 1973 War, and Pinochet's US-backed coup against the democratically elected president Salvador Allende in Chile in 1973. When Radwa learns of the 1973 War, she wonders if her fear and anxiety are because of 'the solitude of the stranger' (*'uzlat al-gharība*) abroad (*R*, 28).

In addition to the affinities with African Americans that *The Journey* holds forth, the memoir posits other affiliations within the frame of Third World concerns:[5] Radwa frequently invokes Pinochet's massacre of 5,000 people in Chile's national stadium in Santiago and the Vietnamese War. The pan-Africanism of 1960s Egypt, waning in the 1970s with Sadat's rapprochement with the West, pervades the memoir. Ashour foregrounds her encounters with multi-ethnic students: African Americans, Latinos, Puerto Ricans, and West Indians. Radwa's involvement in the university organisation of students is an extension of her Third World concerns; she and fellow students form a committee for the defence of Palestine made up of Communists, Trotskyists, leftists, African Americans, Puerto Ricans, Africans, and Latin Americans whose activities encompass the interests of Third World students on campus. While on a tour of Boston with university friends, Radwa wonders how the American Revolution never stirred her interest or imagination like the French Revolution. Passing through the landmarks of the 1770 Boston massacre and the 1773 Boston Tea Party, she recalls another event, the fresh 1973 massacre of 5,000 people in Chile's stadium after Pinochet's coup, and wonders when tourists would visit the scene of the massacre of thousands in Santiago, where Chilean songwriter and political activist Victor Jara was tortured and murdered. She learns some of the details of the massacre from Mrs

Allende in a little church at Yale University in New Haven and cheers for the Government of Popular Unity: 'I cheer like one of the people of the Southern Cone pursued in the streets with batons and tear gas bombs' (*R*, 110). Her reference to the poem that Victor Jara wrote about 5,000 detainees in the stadium before they cut off his hands and killed him puts forth another set of affiliations. Here, she foregrounds African, Arab, and Third World affiliations to frame her presence in the United States. Her Arabic memoir makes visible African Americans in the United States and increasingly the visibility of African Americans to an Egyptian student in the waning days of pan-Africanism and Third World movements. The 1970s marked the end of the Third World revolutionary dreams of the 1950s and 1960s. Yet *The Journey* is steeped in her Third Worldism through her commentary on Frederick Douglass's '4 July' speech, Chinua Achebe's lecture, and Langston Hugh's poetry.

Upon her return to Cairo, Radwa resumes her post at Ain Shams University and her husband Mourid (Barghouti) travels to Beirut to work in the Palestinian resistance radio because the Cairo offices were closed down. By the mid-1970s, Beirut was under constant bombardment. The Palestinian radio Cairo branch was reopened and shut down again in November 1977 on the eve of Sadat's trip to Jerusalem. On 19 November 1977, Radwa and Mourid were stunned by the image of Sadat shaking hands with Begin and Golda Meir. On the next day, she writes (and Barghouti recounts the story in his memoirs, examined in Chapter 3): 'five plainclothes policemen knocked on our door. They came to arrest Mourid and deport him from Egypt. I said goodbye while holding our little baby Tamim. He was five months old. If not for Tamim and the two guava trees Mourid planted in our garden – we marveled at the speed at which they grew and came to full bloom – I would not have had what would become a fervent conviction that things would not continue the way they were, but, in spite of my confidence, I knew that the days to come were the most difficult' (*R*, 176).

Ashour's autobiographical corpus chronicles her life from the young girl in the house on Manial El-Rawdah, overlooking the Abbas Bridge, the site of the massacre of Cairo University students demonstrating against the British occupation, revisited in al-Zayyat's memoir, to the university professor in the twenty-first century. Her project takes off from and extends al-Zayyat's memoir to the twenty-first century. Ashour remarks that her novels have been a way to work through defeat and a half-century of historical ruptures (Ashour 2000: 88): the founding of Israel in 1948, the 1956 Tripartite Aggression, the 1967 War, and the 1982 Israeli invasion of Lebanon. Ashour's autobiographical works trace another historical moment: the 1970s student movement, especially the 1972 student demonstrations at Cairo University. Yet *Specters* recalls the features of al-Zayyat's memoir: campus activism, government repression, security forces, and political imprisonment.[6]

Although national history has haunted her fiction, her memoirs make visible the solitude of the writer in many ways. For Ashour, the writer is both storyteller and scribe (2000: 85), but her memoirs further evoke the solitude of the writer, her independence and activism in the crises that have punctuated her career: the solitude of the professor amid the decline of the university; activism for the autonomy of the university and academic freedom (a struggle that dates back to the expulsion of Taha Hussein from the university in 1932 for his political writings); the writer and the state; state governance and the university; and the effects of illness.

Specters is both novel and memoir that explores the fates of two characters in 1970s and 1980s Egypt. Ashour metafictionally crafts her novel, intertwining the trajectory of her fictional protagonist, Shagar Abdel Ghafar, a professor of history, and autobiographical narrator, Radwa Ashour, writer and professor of English literature at Ain Shams University.[7] Clearly, Shagar is Radwa's alter ego whose fate is intertwined with and informed by Radwa's history. Radwa, the author in *Specters*, muses on ancient Egyptian conceptions of a character, including the name and shadow: 'Some of the ancient reliefs represent one Pharaoh or another with an analogous figure behind him. Perhaps these reliefs are what account for the translation of *ka*, in early studies, with the Arabic word for "double," *qarin*' (*Ab*, 151; *Sa*, 193).[8] Radwa's ruminations call attention to the metafictional framework of the 'novel' (*Ab*, 152; *Sa*, 194). Translations of the double hold forth an abundance of meanings: Radwa translates *Ka* into *qarin*, where *qarn* means 'cord that binds' or 'alike in age'; 'the *qarin* is your companion, who is one with you . . . And the *qirn*, your equal in courage and in battle'; and the *qarin* or *qarina* is the soul. In *Lisan al-Arab*, the word '*atyaaf*' (spectres), shared with Shagar's book on Deir Yassin, *Al-Atyaaf: The Story of Deir Yassin*, has a richly evocative etymology: '*taafa*' to move around and among people, to hover around; '*taif*', 'the shadow of something that has possessed you'; '*taif*' means 'anger' and 'madness'; '*taafa*' means 'to make a circuit or tour'; '*taawafa*' means 'to go or travel in it'; '*taa'if*' is 'the servant who waits on you with gentle solicitude'; '*taa'if*' is 'a part of something'; '*taif*' is 'an apparition that comes in sleep'; '*'aTaafa*', in language, is to be comprehensive; and 'taif' is 'the imagination itself' (*Ab*, 153–5; *Sa*, 196–7). In sum, Shagar is companion, equal, and the double of Radwa: her story both hovers around Radwa's; she has possessed the author; travels through her story; she is solicitous of her, forms part of her, encircles her, and is an emblem of her imagination. *Specters* encompasses the meanings of the word '*aṭyāf*' through the testimonies of the survivors of the Deir Yassin massacre – Aziza, Naziha, and Basma Zahran – who hover around Shagar's story and haunt Radwa's novel.

The narrative framework draws attention to the artifice of *Specters*: Radwa intersects with Shagar; she ruminates on the composition of the novel; and writes her own story directly: 'Should I keep her [Shagar] and interweave our stories, or drop her and content myself with telling about Radwa? But then, why did Shagar come to me when I started out writing about myself? Who is Shagar?' (*Ab*, 13; *Sa*, 17). *Specters*, designed to alternate chapters on Shagar and Radwa, both born on 26 May 1946 and professors, fuses the characters. Although strands are crafted in parallel, Radwa writes by 'a process of association' and, as she becomes better acquainted with Shagar, 'The threads have become entwined' (*Ab*, 53; *Sa*, 68) by the 1970s and 1980s (Morsy 2009: 149). *Specters* features experimental devices – double narrators, Palestinian testimonies, memoir-within-a-novel, interlaced plotlines, and a book-within-a-book. Nonetheless, Radwa's history is clearly visible: *Specters* recounts Radwa and her husband Mourid's displacements from the 1970s to the 1990s and Mourid's deportation from Egypt in 1977 (the focus of Mourid Barghouti's memoirs, examined in Chapter 3). There is symmetry, followed by convergence. In 1977, Shagar researches the 1948 Deir Yassin massacre to examine and reassess an Arab interpretation for a book, *al-Aṭyāf* (the spectres), an echo of Ashour's *Specters.*[9] Radwa is deeply marked by the 1982 Sabra and Shatila massacre. Halfway through *Specters*, the characters converge; Radwa sets Shagar's attack in London on the street where the Palestinian political cartoonist Naji al-'Ali lived in Wimbledon (al-'Ali was

Mourid and Radwa's friend). With Shagar sprawled on the street, Radwa interrupts: 'None of this happened, but now, as I write about Shagar, I imagine it happening because I know Widad and Usama [Naji al-'Ali's wife and son] . . . I know their house, the street, the Wimbledon train station. But why did I make this neighborhood the stage for the attack on Shagar?' (*Ab*, 178; *Sa*, 224). *Specters* now intersects the strands: 'The threads entwine, all of them are intertwined' (*Ab*, 129; *Sa*, 164).

Dovetailing Radwa and Shagar, *Specters* foregrounds Radwa's activism and ordeals at the university. *Specters* reviews parts of Radwa's life through Mourid's exile and Shagar's story, likewise, is full of incident. It explores the historical, political, and academic landscapes of the 1970s and 1980s in which corruption in the state and the decline of the university are prevalent. Although Radwa matriculated at Cairo University, she is appointed at Ain Shams University: 'Because the department chair at that time, Dr. Rashad Rushdi, said, "I don't want that girl." So the girl went to work elsewhere' (*Ab*, 102; *Sa*, 131). Summoned to the office of the president of the university, Shagar would have been dismissed in 1972 and September 1981, but later she is suspended from the university and spends months in prison during which she timorously contemplates her relationship with the university. Radwa, likewise, is dismissed from the university in the campaign of 1981 and frequently encounters the effects of the presence of security forces on campus.

Specters resumes the story of the fateful separation from her husband that dramatically closes *The Journey*: 'On the 19th of November 1977, Anwar al-Sadat traveled to Israel. The following day, the morning of Eid, five security officers came to our house and took Mourid, and deported him from Egypt' (*Ab*, 122; *Sa*, 156). The arrest follows Shagar's months in prison and her ruminations on her profession, alternating between Shagar and Radwa by association. Years of separation and travel commence after Mourid's deportation (he would be granted permission to return to Egypt in 1995). At the same time, Tamim, Radwa's Cairo-born son, is not granted an Egyptian nationality because his father is Palestinian and later ironically holds the status of a 'foreign student'.

Although the story of Shagar folds into that of Radwa and is in turn nurtured by it, another chronicle that haunts *Specters* is that of Latifa al-Zayyat. *Specters* draws on al-Zayyat's coming-of-age novel, the women's prison, and torture. Al-Zayyat's *The Open Door* is one of the novels that Ashour was careful to read upon her graduation (Morsy 2009: 151). In *Specters*, Radwa would unknowingly pass and cross Tahrir Square for years. *The Open Door* forms an intertext:

> Months after my graduation from the university I will read *The Open Door*. The first scene of the novel is set on the evening of February 21, 1946. Al-Zayyat wrote, 'The movie houses were deserted; likewise the other public places, the bus, the tram. Police cars were cruising the streets carrying soldiers armed with rifles. There were not many passersby . . . they talked amongst themselves.' (*Ab*, 39; *Sa*, 50)

Radwa recounts the 1946 events she reads in her friend's novel and relives them through the 1972 student demonstrations. On 24 January 1972 she goes to Cairo University where students who have staged a sit-in on campus are surrounded by security forces, arrested, and imprisoned. She and Mourid go down to Tahrir Square and sign a petition sponsored by the national committee of writers and artists in solidarity with the students. They collect signatures and return to the square and Radwa is one of the delegates chosen to send the petition to the president, the prime minister, and the head of parliament. She chronicles a history of the square: the 1975 workers' protests and the 1977 violent demonstrations. Radwa further embeds the ward search that al-Zayyat recounts – and the focus of her memoir – in *Specters*. In hospital in Budapest, where Mourid lives in exile, while undergoing treatment for pleural effusion in her lung, she follows reports of the campaign of September 1981 (embedded in al-Zayyat's memoir and examined in Chapter 2) on a Russian-made radio: 'My friends were in prison: Latifa, Amina, Awatif, Farida, Shahinda, and Safinaz; a number of my acquaintances and dozens of leading cultural and political personages of Egypt. The officially recognized detainees numbered 1,500' (*Ab*, 130; *Sa*, 166). Although Radwa's name is not among the detainees, she is one of the professors suspended from the university. Similarly, in Balatonföldvár in Hungary, she learns of Naji al-'Ali's assassination in London. Amid the public crises, private ones surface surreptitiously: the hospital, arrests, expulsion from the university, the invasion of Lebanon and the siege of Beirut, and the expulsion of the Palestinians. She is reinstated after Sadat's 1981 assassination. When she returns from Hungary after a surgery, she pauses at what she feels is her 'inattention' (*Ab*, 142; *Sa*, 181) to the Israeli occupation of Beirut and the ensuing massacres. Later, she draws on al-Zayyat's memoir *The Search* and her experience in prison and recounts a history of internments during which women were 'subjected to dragging and beating, or routine humiliation' (*Ab*, 193; *Sa*, 245).

Besides a history of activism, *Specters* is a chronicle of the university, obliquely through Radwa and explicitly through Shagar. Shagar encounters security forces with truncheons and tear-gas bombs. The general mood on campus is one of corruption, rampant plagiarism and cheating, impunity, and absence of academic freedom. Security forces routinely storm the campus and pelt students with tear-gas bombs, while soldiers attack dormitories and kill a student in the demonstrations against the 1991 bombardment of Iraq. Frustrated and defeated, Shagar resigns from the university. In the end, she goes on to the Suez Canal and returns to Cairo and, throughout, Shagar encircles Radwa, takes possession of her story, and conjures the spectres of Deir Yassin.

While *The Journey* explores the theme of study exchange, *Specters* is an excursion through fiction. Both employ a constellation of genres to reinvigorate the memoir: *The Journey* fuses letters, Mourid's poems, and speeches, whereas *Specters* reworks folktales, classical Arabic poems recited by her husband Mourid and her son Tamim, testimonies of the Deir Yassin massacre, and her trilogy *Granada* on Muslim Spain and the 1492 Reconquista. Shagar's research of Deir Yassin for her scholarly book *The Specters* is comparable to Radwa's research for *Granada*. Radwa notes that work on *Granada* 'restored to the woman her balance' (*Ab*, 184; *Sa*, 232) during the US invasion of Iraq. In *Specters*, she further elaborates literary ties to her friends Latifa al-Zayyat, Saadallah Wannous (Sa'd Allāh Wannūs), and Naji al-'Ali.

Ashour's *Heavier than Radwa* is a chronicle of Egypt's 2011 revolution and her medical trip to the United States. Ashour wrote *Heavier than Radwa*, her third excursion into autobiography, in the form of a diary that fluctuates between her surgery and the revolution. The central themes of her memoir, written in the form of a diary, are her illness, the university, activism, and the revolution. *Heavier than Radwa* recounts stages of her treatment in the United States from 2010 through 2013 and examines the state of the Egyptian university since the 1970s and her activism through the 9 May group in defence of the autonomy of the university. Within professional, medical, and national crises, she chronicles her own struggle. Reworking her diary during her illness, activism on campus, and the revolution, *Heavier than Radwa* belongs to a set of memoirs: Said's *Out of Place*, completed during his chemotherapy treatment, and Darwish's *Mural*, composed after his heart surgery. In her late memoir, Ashour takes off from al-Zayyat's *The Search* and rewrites the role of Arab writers at revolutionary moments.

Heavier than Radwa interweaves the strands of the campus, activism, and illness and extends the themes metafictionally explored in *Specters*. The writer-narrator, named for a mountain range that stretches into the East from a spring, with rivulets and valleys and gazelles,[10] near Medina, invoked by Arabs to pay tribute to firmness (*rusūkh*) in the saying 'heavier than Radwa [the mountain range]' (*athqal min Radwā*) (*AR*, 6) traces the history of her name. In the prologue, Radwa, aged 64, traces the memoir to her brother's illness, decline, and passing on 6 September 2010, which recalls al-Zayyat's autobiographical pact. Her memoir explores her battles on campus, her illness, the events of the Egyptian Revolution, and returns to her early youth, the story she explores in *Specters*. Early in the memoir, she enters Ain Shams University on 4 November 2010 with a court ruling that the presence of security forces on campus is unconstitutional and impinges on the sovereignty of the university and the freedom of faculty, students, and scholars. She meets colleagues in front of the Office of the President and hands a copy of the court ruling to the security forces. On tour of the university, followed by undercover security officers, she is intercepted by a thug who confiscates the papers she is carrying, proclaiming they are 'pamphlets', and means to intimidate her. The November incident introduces a number of battles with the university administration that she explores in the memoir.

Heavier than Radwa chronicles her illness from that fateful September in 1981 during the campaign of arrest of 1536 dissidents, including friends, through 2013 in Washington and intertwines her treatment with her activism in the university and battles with the administration. When Egypt seethes in 2011, she is naturally absent from Tahrir Square because she undergoes a series of surgeries in the United States from 17 December 2010 to 11 February 2011. In between surgeries, she learns of the resignation of Mubarak. On the eve of 25 January, she recalls the murder of Egyptian police forces in Ismailia at the hands of the occupying British forces on 25 January 1952, followed by demonstrations in Cairo in response to the massacre that grew into what would become known as the burning of Cairo. Ashour's opinion that the Cairo fire was not orchestrated by the British and the King but was a pre-1952 popular revolution was explored in her novel *Qiṭʿa min Urubba* (*A Part of Europe*, 2003). In Washington, she surveys and compares the violence in Tahrir Square when security forces attack with water hoses and tear gas with the burning of Cairo on 26 January 1952 and the January 1977 bread riots.

In the months of recovery in April, Radwa recalls lines from T. S. Eliot's *The Waste Land*: 'April is the cruelest month' (*AR*, 100), also mentioned in Darwish's *Memory for Forgetfulness*, but, for her, April was not the cruelest month, because spring held forth a note implicitly or explicitly: she was recovering and she was spurred on by her desire to return to Egypt because of a revolution that unfolded right near her house. Upon her return to Egypt, on the eve of 26 May (her birthday), she goes to Tahrir Square. She would return to the square for many months and to the university on 29 May 2011: she notes that she overlooks the departure of security forces from the campus. Thereafter she notes a turbulent wave of demonstrations, sit-ins, and strikes in the university amid calls for the resignation of presidents and deans during the revolution. She resumes her activism within the 9 March group and through strikes for the resignation of the president of the university. In the months after the revolution, she characterises her four-fold work: the university, writing, public work, and her family.

Although unequivocally a chronicle, more so than the assiduously crafted *Specters*, *Heavier than Radwa* muses on her novels – *Siraaj* begun in Budapest in the summer of 1989 – and the contrast between fiction and memoir: 'And because this book [*Heavier than* Radwa] is not a novel but a memoir, in which the author, narrator, and character are identical . . . I do not conjure up from I don't know where, a woman named Amna [*Siraaj*] or Mariama [*Granada*], or Nada [*Blue Lorries*] or Ruqayya [*The Woman from Tantoura*]' (*AR*, 252). In her memoir, Ashour contemplates the genres of autobiography (*sīra*) and diary (*yawmiyyāt*), fusing autobiography (*sīra dhātiyya*) and memoirs (*mudhakkirāt*): although they are two different forms, she acknowledges that they categorise, contemplate, and comment on her life history and, while they are similar, autobiography offers the sum of life at different stages, while memoirs largely focus on a particular stage or experience in an extended story. Ashour comments on the novelty of the form of *Heavier than Radwa*, the unexpected new accumulation of everyday events in a record of details and impressions. The diary, journal, or notebook, in which dates frame her days, recasts the form: 'There is no retrospection here, but, each day, a slow accompaniment' (*AR*, 271–2). The diary is widely held to be a form that the author does not seek to share with others, she notes, for she contemplates her state and the flow of her day, or returns to an event that was confused in her memory, and of which she hopes to make use afterwards, especially since she is a writer. The widely held notions of diary no longer hold; they are no longer stable or reified in forms of writing on the Internet. She feels that writing about the events is premature, impossible, and incomplete; a draft of a memoir and the diary offer her a form that resolves her uncertainty. She settles on the diary, a form that has to do with her state in many ways; in a testimony, she notes that she writes because she fears death and also in self-defence and the defence of others (Ashour 1993: 170). In *Heavier than Radwa*, she preserves the fragments without making any conclusions that bring together the parts and impose an interpretation. Ashour frequently expresses solicitude for her male and female readers and admits her guilt for the effects of her chronicle of illness. Consequently, she invites the reader to overlook particular chapters and read the conclusion to share a pleasant family reunion after her return from her medical trip.

Like *The Journey*, *Heavier than Radwa* recovers a cultural archive that spans Ashour's multiple affiliations – Third Worldism and the Arab world, including Palestine. *Heavier than Radwa* abounds with intertexts she weaves in *Specters* and elaborates further here: she comments on Mahmoud Darwish's *In the Presence of Absence*, of which a copy holds an inscription to her son, aspiring poet Tamim, on one of Darwish's visits to Cairo. Declaring his memoir a 'self-elegy', a declaration that tragically mirrors the effect of Ashour's *The Scream*, she includes his death after surgery within a litany of deaths of Syrian writer Saadallah Wannous and Palestinian political cartoonist Naji al-'Ali. In her elegy for Darwish, she declares that Palestine was Darwish's poem (*AR*, 330), and the death of Mahmoud Darwish and Frantz Fanon away from home raises the spectre of death abroad that haunts her memoir.

Amid changes in the course of the revolution, she expects the memoir, completed on 9 May 2013, to be open-ended. In the end, she returns to the hospital scenes and circles back to the violence on campus, the ubiquity of thugs and security forces at Ain Shams University, with which she commences the memoir, and the activities of the 9 March group for the autonomy of the university. The prevalence of violence culminates in the suspension of classes at the university. In the concluding chapter, Ashour compares Radwa to Job, evoking her deep endurance of her illness whose recurrence parallels the setbacks in the revolution.

The Scream, the sequel to *Heavier than Radwa* written from August 2013 to September 2014 and published posthumously in 2015, brings Ashour's autobiographical corpus to a close. The preface notes that the press published the memoir as a document without any changes except for explanatory notes for references to *Heavier than Radwa* and chapter headings. Chapter headings, followed by a blank page, are left intact. Ashour chose the title of the memoir and completed a concluding chapter, although some of the chapters within the memoir are sketchy. *The Scream* resumes the chronicle and focuses on Ashour's surgery in August 2013 in Denmark and radiation in Cairo from May to September 2014 amid events in Egypt. The history of the completion of the two volumes of the memoir is telling: Ashour completed *Heavier than Radwa* on 9 May 2013 and submitted the manuscript to her publisher Dār al-Shurūq in May and shortly thereafter the memoir was moved through production. Ashour stopped writing *The Scream* in September 2014 and passed away on 1 December 2014. Uncharacteristically, she did not allow her family and friends to see the manuscript in progress (*S*, 5).

The Scream takes off from ekphrasis, a commentary on Norwegian painter Edvard Munch's famous lithograph *The Scream* (1893). The eponymous memoir commences with Munch's diary entry about the composition of *The Scream*. Walking along with two friends while the sun was setting, a wave of sadness passes over Munch. He stops and leans against a fence overlooking the fjord and the city and, while his friends walk on, he feels a scream echo through nature (*Sc*, 7). Ashour wonders if the publisher will consent to duplicating the monochromatic lithograph (and her most prized version) on the cover of the second volume of *Heavier than Radwa*. The character, man or woman, on a bridge in the foreground with two men in the background, the face distorted in a scream, expresses the anguish of one who was near the city's slaughterhouse or the mental hospital where his sister was admitted. Ashour extends the composition to the experience of an individual who suddenly feels so fearful of existence that a scream passes through her body. The memoir opens with Ashour's commentary on the lithograph, the vagaries of memory, and the difficulty with reading and writing after her surgery and then goes on to count the number of the murdered, wounded, and arrested in Egypt from August to October 2014 and describes her hallucinations in an intensive care unit.

In the summer of 2014, Ashour undergoes surgery in Aarhus in Denmark after which she rests in a medically induced coma. Of seven days in a deep state of unconsciousness she recalls only a whiteness comparable to what Darwish evokes in *Mural*:

> Everything was white:
> the sea hanging above the roof of a white
> cloud was nothingness in the white
> sky of the absolute. I was
> and I wasn't. I was alone in the corners of this
> eternal whiteness . . .
> . . . I was alone in the whiteness,
> alone . . .[11]

Ashour contemplates the poetic lines and notes that there is no cloud, sky, or eternity and she does not feel alone because she is unaware of the presence of others in her state; only the whiteness is present. In her recovery, she experiences hallucinations, not poetic visions like Darwish, who saw his friends weeping and weaving a shroud for him and al-Ma'arri kicking his critics out of his poem, but some of her hallucinations are comparably earthly and concerned with women's chores, prosaic details, and everyday life.

The Scream circles around the date of 14 August 2013, the date of her surgery in Denmark and the Rab'a massacre in Egypt. It commences with the surgery, the aftermath, and returns to that date during which she was unconscious. At the same time, she writes of her surgery and the massacre at the Rab'a and Nahda sit-ins and the death by asphyxiation of detainees in a blue lorry.[12] The diary includes her belated knowledge of the massacre and ruminations on the asphyxiation. On 18 August, while she was unconscious in the hospital in Denmark, forty-eight handcuffed detainees from Rab'a in a blue lorry (made for twenty-four or twenty-five people) bearing them from a police station in a Cairo neighbourhood to Abu Za'bal prison, locked for nine hours, perish from heat, thirst, and tear gas. The tragedy recalls Ghassan Kanafani's famous novella, *Men in the Sun*, where three characters are smuggled into Kuwait and perish in a tanker-truck. Ashour notes that Kanafani's novel was a commentary on the Palestinian situation in the 1960s and a revolution started two years after its publication. While the event in *Men in the Sun* deals with Palestinian refugees in search of a prosperous future in another Arab country, the murder of political prisoners in the blue lorry followed a revolution.

Ashour's ekphrastic memoir encircles the agony, violence, solitude of the writer, and the political mood. Diary, portraits, photographs, and empty chapters set the stage for her introspection. 'Diaries of a death foretold' (*yawmiyyāt mawt mu'lan*) narrates student demonstrations at Cairo University and violence on campus: police tear gas, rubber bullets, and the deaths of students in the university. A photograph chosen by Dar al-Hilāl to adorn the cover of *The Search* is central to Ashour's portrait of Latifa al-Zayyat, a leader of the 1940s student movement (a tribute to a friendship from 1967 to 1996). Her ruminations on photographs and artworks are frequent and purposeful; they are meant to obscure her fear and concerns. When political and medical crises interrupt her writing, there are blank pages or notes on a chapter in progress – Tamim's battle, the start of radiation, the trip to Paris and 'chapter 23' (*Sb*, 168–9).

Even as *The Scream* bristles with ekphrasis, hallucinations, commentary, and ruminations, the memoir is incomplete: it ends with notes for entries that she meant to complete and shows that she continually contemplates writing but her state interrupts the immediacy and continuity of the memoir. By September 2014, *The Scream* would echo the murdered students and the exhausted author.

Tahrir Diary

Mona Prince (b. 1970), Egyptian writer and associate professor of English at Suez Canal University, has authored two novels, *Thalāth Ḥaqā'ib li-l-Safar* (*Three Suitcases*, 1998) and *Innī Uḥaddithūka li-Tara* (*So You May See*, 2008), short-story collections, and a memoir *Revolution Is My Name.* In 2013, following charges that she had criticised religion by one of her students, Prince was summoned by a disciplinary committee and suspended from Suez Canal University. Prince's debacle was one more example of the problems that plague the university, a theme that recurs in Ashour's memoirs.

In 2012, Prince published *Revolution Is My Name*, her Tahrir memoir of the eighteen days of Egypt's 2011 revolution. Prince's memoir, whose title joins the 'revolution' and the author whose 'name' has been eclipsed by the event she describes, explores the metaphor of revolution as woman (the title is an allusion to the centrality of the revolution to her subjectivity and plays on the feminine word for revolution in Arabic) and the role of women in revolutionary Egypt in the twenty-first century. A diary of the revolution, Prince's memoir proclaims an affiliation with the revolution through the title. The appearance of *Revolution Is My Name* reified the involvement of women in the 25 January Revolution in the same way that Shaarawi's *Harem Years* and al-Zayyat's *The Open Door* and *The Search* explored women's involvement in national movements.

Revolution Is My Name, written from March 2011 to February 2012, recounts events that convulsed Egypt from Tuesday, 25 January to Friday, 11 February 2011. The diary traces the narrator's involvement in the eighteen days in early 2011, focusing on the national events in Tahrir Square. The narrator reports political action in which she is directly involved but her diary focuses on the communal fruits of the revolution. Like Ashour's chronicle, *Heavier than Radwa* and *The Scream*, Prince's diary was animated by a nationwide movement and written to echo dreams of freedom and justice.

Upon arrival in Tahrir Square from Shubra on Tuesday, 25 January, the narrator notes that the youth have come to full bloom: veteran leftists stand at the borders of the square and look on at the young demonstrators who challenge the riot police in front of armoured vehicles and water cannons and no longer need the old Left's leadership or wisdom. The narrator's diary entry on the Friday of Rage chronicles the skirmishes on 28 January 2011 between the riot police and the demonstrators in Tahrir Square and recreates the profound effect of the violence in the Battle of Qasr al-Nil Bridge. In one scene, thousands of demonstrators flocking from Imbāba, Giza, and Warrāq charge into Tahrir Square, oblivious of tear gas, and rubber bullets, chanting, '*the people demand the overthrow of the regime*' (*IT*, 81; *RN*, 60; italics in translation).[13] The narrator, who joins marches, sit-ins, and checkpoints, observes the events in Tahrir Square and downtown Cairo. She travels freely across Tahrir Square, helped and supported by fellow activists and downtown residents; the narrator rides the metro, frequents the Merit publishing house office in downtown Cairo, and camps in Tahrir Square. Events unfold in Tahrir Square, now a new centre of national unity.

In the diary, the city of Suez seethes even before the revolution spreads to Cairo. Prince works at the Suez Canal University in a neglected city populated by a conservative immigrant community from Upper Egypt: 'most of its youth could be described as a bunch of unruly thugs' (*RN*, 41). Suez is rife with an atmosphere characterised by harassment and thuggery, now synonymous with 'popular pluck' and 'upgraded to heroism' (*RN*, 41). Marches from Midan al-Arbein to al-Gharib area and skirmishes between the riot police and the people of Suez ensue. The campus is refracted through the narrator's evocation of Suez. On 27 January 2011, when the revolution has swept through Suez, the head of the examination control administrations calls Prince to come to the university to grade exams. Although she 'hates' Suez, she feels proud when Suez becomes a free city on the eve of the Friday of Rage on 28 January 2011.

During the eighteen days in Tahrir Square, when state-sponsored violence is prevalent in the infamous Battle of the Camel, scenes of national unity abound. Significantly, *Revolution Is My Name* evokes the scene on 25 January that opens al-Zayyat's novel *The Open Door*. Events recreate *The Open Door*, which opens with the 1946 anti-British demonstrations through the Cairo fire on 26 January 1952 that consumes Egypt on the eve of the 1952 Revolution. In *Revolution Is My Name*, scenes of clashes – stones, Molotov cocktails, and swords – between peaceful demonstrators and regime thugs at the Egyptian Museum and Abdel Moneim Riyad Square culminate in the final battle in Tahrir Square.

Prince's memoir is a diary (*yawmiyyāt*) of the revolution and an archive of popular memory, street language, regime rhetoric, and revolutionary slogans in both colloquial Egyptian and standard Arabic. Focusing on the narrator's subjectivity in the revolution, the memoir highlights her concern with documentation (*tawthīq*). It encompasses all the discourses circulating in the square: revolutionary language, conversations evocative of the opening of al-Zayyat's *The Open Door*, and regime rhetoric. The narrator interweaves Tunisian-inspired slogans in standard Arabic, conversations among the revolutionaries, Mubarak's speeches, and 1960s and 1970s songs of the legendary Egyptian composer Sheikh Imam in an archive of a key historical moment. During the Week of Steadfastness, a million-person march is staged in the square, and the narrator, along with many other demonstrators, celebrates the fall of the regime. The Egyptian poet 'Abd al Raḥman al-Abnūdī's poem, 'The Square' (al-Mīdān), broadcast in Tahrir square, infuses the popular celebrations on 11 February 2011: 'the poem he had written for us, for the people of the square' (*IT*, 223).

Revolution Is My Name builds on a tradition of Arab women's memoirs that have captured national struggles such as the autobiographical writing of Djebar and al-Zayyat. Rather than explore the tension between solitude and revolutionary ferment that al-Zayyat so explicitly chronicles, she focuses on unity in the square against the authority of the state and the recent history of the Tahrir revolution. While al-Zayyat alternates defeat and unity, Prince rediscovers unity in Tahrir Square. The new genre of Tahrir memoir contrasts with Djebar and al-Zayyat's revolutionary autobiography, which focuses on colonialism and patriarchy in the twentieth century, and represents a communal chronicle of revolution in the twenty-first century.

These memoirs set new standards for the form in the twenty-first century. Other memoirs from the Arab revolutions open up the genre to new political imperatives. Libyan writer Hisham Matar's *The Return: Fathers, Sons and the Land in Between* (2016), a memoir of his return to post-Gaddafi Libya after the revolution to rescue the story of his father, a political prisoner in Abu Salim prison (1990–6), both refashions a form that records events into one that revisits the devastation and, like Soueif, re-forms the local into the global.

Epilogue
Arab Literature, World Literature

> Think of the modern novel: certainly a wave (and I've actually called it a wave a few times) – but a wave that runs into the branches of local traditions, and is always significantly transformed by them.
>
> Franco Moretti, *Distant Reading*

Literary Autobiography and Arab National Struggles has attended to solitude in the autobiographical production of writers who focused on or played a revolutionary role in Arab culture or national movements. It has attempted to trace the rise of autobiography in anticolonial and ant-imperialist movements that sought simultaneously to proclaim the autonomy of Arab writers at a time when they were committed to the sovereignty of the nation-state. Novelists, poets, and critics, many involved in contemporary cultural and national movements, placed a premium on solitude in autobiography. Adaptations of autobiography examined in this study show the role of national struggles in the creation of new literary forms and conceptions of subjectivity.

Franco Moretti's theory of the inequality, asymmetry, and hierarchy of the world literary system accounts for the traffic and networks of influence that are prevalent in global literary study. Examining patterns of influence and 'mobility of world literature', he deploys the model of the world literary system partitioned into core and periphery (Moretti 2013: 115). His observation of the direction of the movement of different forms focuses on the constraints of movement: movement between peripheral cultures is rare; movement from the periphery to the centre is unusual; while the flow of literary influence from the centre to the periphery is much more common (112). He advocates 'distant reading' rather than close reading for its examination of world literature beyond the canon rather than dependence on a 'small canon'

(48): 'Distant reading: where distance . . . *is a condition of knowledge*: it allows you to focus on units that are much smaller or much larger than the text: devices, themes, tropes – or genres and systems' (48–9; italics in original). To use his examination of the interrelationship of distant reading and world literature, whereby 'in cultures that belong to the periphery of the literary system (which means: almost all cultures, inside and outside Europe), the modern novel first arises not as an autonomous development but as a compromise between a western formal influence (usually French or English) and local materials' (50), the exchange may be extended to other literary forms in other cultures such as Arab culture.[1] In a sense, he notes the synthesis, interaction, or 'compromise' of 'foreign form and local materials' (52). His world-systems theory has much to do with imported literary forms and the direction of exchange in global circuits.[2]

Moretti advances a critical practice that depends on a literary world-system made up of 'powerful' and 'peripheral' literatures (2005: 221). He reads world literature through a system that 'is simultaneously *one*, and *unequal*: with a core, and a periphery (and a semi-periphery) that are bound together in a relationship of growing inequality' (2013: 46; emphasis in original). In other words, he argues that world literature may be rethought through 'one world literary system (of inter-related literatures)', although one that is 'profoundly unequal' (ibid.). Moretti's conjectures on world literature have important implications for the study of other literatures: Moretti rethinks the canon through a world literary system that incorporates the cultural production of other cultures and broadens comparative networks. These conjectures both unsettle and confirm the inequality of the world literary system by pointing to some movement of literatures (largely from centre to periphery), specifying the forms in which it may occur (113) even while acknowledging inequality. In *Modern Epic: The World-System from Goethe to Garcia Marquez* (1996), Moretti traces 'world texts' from the 1920s to the 1960s and discovers that in this new world literary system practitioners of the modern genre are what he calls 'writers from the semiperiphery' (217) – German, American, Irish, Latin American – in comparison to a canon of French and English works. For Moretti, the second *Weltliteratur* that follows the eighteenth century is what he terms 'the world literary system', 'which produces new forms by convergence' as a possible approach for '*Weltliteratur* in the twenty-first century' (228). In my view, Moretti's conjectures may be adopted to productively examine Arab literature within world literary frameworks. Although the literary world-system opens up literary exchanges, as some critics have noted (Moretti 2013: 107), the asymmetry and inequality inherent in the structure of the literary system also constrain the direction of that exchange. The travel of literature in all directions is certainly the direction to which critical practice looks but Moretti argues that the movement between peripheral literatures that do not belong to the same region (from Latin America to the Arab world by way of an example of some of the sources I note in the study of Arab autobiography) are almost rare. Such movements that occur are important areas for comparative study. Moretti's world-system explains inequality but also offers a way to think of the movement of literatures. Such literary systems may contribute to the study of comparative literature and the global reading of national and regional literatures.

Moretti's theory of world literature helps us to look at cultural cross-fertilisation in a global form and examine Arab autobiography in comparative literature. It relates to new literary approaches that reexamine the importance of other literatures to Arabic literature and changes in the direction of comparative study from East–West to South–South. In other words, it offers ways to examine contemporary Arab autobiography through new modes of inquiry into its affinities with other literatures in the global South and open up new networks for comparative study.

To Moretti's literary system can be added Aboul-Ela's 'Mariátegui tradition' by which he accounts for the migration of influences in cultures that have been subjected to colonialism and imperialism, or non-European networks overlooked by conventional criticism (Aboul-Ela 2007: 2). Aboul-Ela proposes a model of the global South that calls attention to and circumvents the practice of 'knowledge production' based on colonial models to extend beyond the Eurocentrism of comparative literary studies: 'comparative literary studies in the United States often takes primary texts – novels, poems, plays, and films – from the Global South and then processes them via Western theoretical models, especially continental theory' (11). He redresses the balance with readings of the production of culture through the unequal development he examines in cultures of the global South.

The enduring problem of Palestine and new developments such as the recent Gaza war have inspired a spate of Palestine-themed memoirs ranging from single-authored memoirs to edited volumes featuring recollections and testimonies of dispossession, occupation, and refugee camps.[3] These have given rise to the journal, diary, letters, testimony, autobiographical poetry, and eco-critical memoir. The production, development, languages, and circulation of further forms of autobiography devoted to Palestine and the experiences of Palestinians in the diaspora merit scholarly attention.

Waves of migration from the Arab world to Latin America that go back to the eighteenth century have created a large Arab diaspora in Latin America – Chile, Argentina, and Brazil – and Latin American writers of Arab descent have begun to explore migration and diaspora in memoirs. Arab autobiographical production in other languages such as Spanish and Portuguese that points to a history of Latin American Arab cultural exchange deserves future study. These have only recently been produced and have contributed to a growing body of Arab Latin American literary filiations.[4]

A comparative study of Arab autobiography and other autobiographical production in the global South, such as Latin America, South Asia, and Africa, reworks South–South comparatism in productive ways. Another way is to examine the largely overlooked comparability, translation, and circulation of memoirs from one region to another.[5] Future scholarship can trace new routes of comparison and old networks of translation in world literary study. It can lay the foundation for comparative work on the practices of autobiographical adaptation in regional literatures that expand on new comparatism devoted to fiction, poetry, and popular culture in, for example, Latin America and the Arab world.

Contemporary Arab autobiography is a growing field that has crossed into other languages and has been shaped by encounters with global literature. This study has sought to offer a comparative study of contemporary Arab autobiography that considers its affinities with other literatures in the global South. It has sought to open up new networks of comparison for the study of literary forms beyond the Eurocentrism that has largely dominated the study of autobiography through South–South comparisons. Focusing on Arab autobiography, I have attempted to show the effects of national struggles on the development of contemporary literary forms to offer new readings of Arab adaptations of the genre and new points of comparison. At the same time, the book has sought to explore the role of the writer and iterations of solitude in moments of deep public involvement. The entry of Arab autobiography into new literary and cultural networks through translation, migration, and circulation enriches the study of comparative literature and may influence the global reading of Arab literature. Autobiographical production in other languages and translation no doubt has a reach that extends to the globality of national literatures and world literary study.

Notes

Introduction

1. The first volume of *al-Ayyām* was serialised in the Egyptian newspaper *al-Hilāl* in 1926–7 (Kilpatrick 1992: 226; Malti-Douglas 1988: 3). On the completion of the autobiography, see the memoirs of Taha Hussein's wife, Suzanne Taha Hussein, *Avec Toi: De la France à l'Égypte* (Hussein 2011: 99–100). Suzanne Taha Hussein recounts: 'Pour que Taha pût surmonter son amertume et rétablir une santé compromisée, je l'avais emmené en France, dans un petit village de Haute-Savoie. Il y écrivit en neuf jours ce qui devait devenir *Al-Ayyam, Le Livre des jours*' (100) (For Taha to overcome his bitterness and restore his compromised health, I took him to France, to a small village in Haute-Savoie. There he wrote what would become *Al-Ayyam, The Days*, over nine days). See Hafez (2002).
2. For an examination of the controversy related to *On Pre-Islamic Poetry*, see Chapter 1.
3. See Hafez (2002).
4. For example, the violence of the 'Black Night of Aracataca' is revisited as 'a legendary slaughter with such uncertain traces in popular memory that there is no certain evidence it ever really happened' (García Márquez 2003: 42). By restoring the account of the massacre of the banana workers (62–3), García Márquez sought to demystify a forgotten history.
5. Philippe Lejeune offers a standard definition of autobiography that has set some of the literary conventions of the genre: 'a retrospective prose narrative written by a real person concerning his own existence, where the focus is his individual life, in particular the story of his personality' (1989: 4). Paul John Eakin notes Lejeune's admission of the limitations of his definition for 'its failure to identify a clear line of demarcation between autobiography and the autobiographical

novel' (1989: ix). Lejeune distinguished between these two genres with the autobiographical pact, a literary contract between the author and the reader that the work is devoted to the life of the author, where 'the *author*, the *narrator*, and the *protagonist* must be identical' (1989: 4–5; italics in original). However, Lejeune's definition focuses on the prose form, imposing generic limitations by excluding memoirs, autobiographical poems, and the journal or diary while privileging 'autobiographical narration' and a retrospective point of view (1989: 4).

6. On the abundance of Arab memoirs in contrast to autobiographies, see Philipp (1993: 579).
7. See Reynolds (2001).
8. See Badawi (1993) and Allen (1995).
9. For an examination of the rise of autobiography, see Misch (1973); Goodwin (1993); Weintraub (1978); Gusdorf (1972); Olney (1980).
10. For early twentieth-century Arabic scholarship that refutes Rosenthal's assumptions about the Arabic autobiographical tradition, see Reynolds (2001). On the balance between autobiography, biography, and history in Muslim theologians' classical Arabic autobiography and the medieval Islamic biographical dictionary, see Kilpatrick (1991). For examples of early Arab autobiography, see *al-Munqidh min al-Ḍalāl* (*The Deliverer from Error*), a spiritual autobiography, by the theologian and mystic al-Ghazālī (b. 450/1058, d. 505/1111); *Kitāb al-I'tibār* (*The Book of Contemplation*), a political memoir, by Syrian poet Usāma ibn Munqidh (b. 488/1095, d. 573/ 1188); *Ṭawq al-Ḥamāmah fī al-Ulfa wa-l-Ullāf* (*The Ring of the Dove*), a love treatise, by Ibn Ḥazm of Andalusia (b. 384/994, d. 456/1064); and *Al-Ta'rif bi-Ibn Khaldūn wa Riḥlatihi Gharban wa-Sharqan* (*An Account of Ibn Khaldun and His Travels West and East*), an apology, by the social historian Ibn Khaldūn (b. 732/ 1332, d. 808/ 1406). For Arabic scholarship on classical Arabic autobiography by al-Ghazālī and the philosopher Ibn Sīna (b. 370/980, d. 428/1036), who were traditionally not considered autobiographical because they focused on the individual's spirituality, see Ḍayf (1979: 77). For evidence of a classical autobiographical tradition that contests Eurocentric assumptions of the practice of autobiography, see the consideration of medieval autobiography by al-Ghazālī, Usāmah ibn Munqidh, and Ibn Khaldūn in 'Abbās (1956), 'Abd al-Dāyim (1975), and Ḍayf (1979). On journals, confessions, and anecdotes (*akhbār*) in dictionaries, chronicles, and compilations, see Ostle (1998).
11. On Ibn Jubayr, see Pellat (2012).
12. More recently, Sabry Hafez has traced modern Arabic autobiography to the

appearance of *al-Sāq 'alā al-Sāq, fī mā huwa al-Fāriyāq, aw Ayyām wa Shuhūr wa A'wām fī 'ujm al-'Arab wa-l-A'jam* (*Leg over Leg on the Question of Who Am I*) (1855) by the nineteenth-century writer and lexicologist Ahmad Faris al-Shidyaq (Aḥmad Fāris ibn Yūsuf al-Shidyāq) (Hafez 2002: 18). Hafez reads *Leg over Leg* as an Arab autobiography, with its 'variegated' elusive self, one that rests between the traditional collective self and the one in search of its individuality, tradition, and modernity (2002: 18–19). As the title suggests, *Leg over Leg* challenges tradition, with the narrator crossing leg over leg, an act that Hafez reads as an expression of social distinction and the self's differentiation of itself from others (20). Abdelfattah Kilito observes that al-Shidyaq's *Leg over Leg* is hard to classify. Part 'journey, novel, or autobiography in the third person', where a character crosses his legs and contemplates 'the two worlds, the two epochs' – East and West, tradition and modernity – it offers 'comparisons between the two legs' (Kilito 2008: 84–5). For further examination of the modern literary form of al-Shidyaq's *Leg over Leg*, see Ashour (2009). Another possible antecedent of modern Arabic autobiography is Jurjī Zaydān's 1908 *Memoirs of Jurjī Zaydān* (*Mudhakkirāt Jurjī Zaydān)*, although the publication of the memoir in full in 1966 precludes its influence on the rise of the form. See Philipp (1993); Reynolds (2001); Shuiskii (1982). On Zaydān's memoir, see also Sheehi (2004). On literature of the Nahda, see Tageldin (2012).

13. Reynolds' examination of premodern Arabic autobiography concludes with the publication of the first volume of Taha Hussein's autobiography in 1926–7 rather than at the turn of the twentieth century. Reynolds alludes to the ways in which anticolonial nationalism and independence struggles created a context that dramatically changed the literary form of Arabic autobiography (2001: 11).
14. For an examination of autobiography and colonialism, see Smith and Watson (1998); for a feminist reading of postcolonial women's autobiography, see Lionnet (1989); for an examination of colonial and postcolonial women's autobiography, see Whitlock (2007); for postcolonial autobiography, see Moore-Gilbert (2009).
15. In *Imagined Communities*, Benedict Anderson defines the nation as a discursive political formation and interprets the history of nationalism through print capitalism, the spread of literacy in the West, and the Third World's experience of colonialism. Anderson defines the nation as 'an imagined political community' and distinguishes between 'imagination' and 'creation' (1983: 6) as opposed to 'invention', 'fabrication', and 'falsity'. Timothy Brennan concedes that the novel was central to the imagination of the nation. Brennan defines the

nation not only as the modern nation-state but also as a 'condition of belonging' (1990: 45). He reinforces the centrality of literature to the formation of nations: 'Nations, then, are imaginary constructs that depend for their existence on an apparatus of cultural fictions in which imaginative literature plays a decisive role' (49). Using the historical relation between nationalism and the novel, Brennan argues that literature provided the form in which the nation was imagined. He also refers to the uses of literature in Third World nationalist movements, evoking the conditions of national belonging and commitment (47).

16. In *The Nation and its Fragments: Colonial and Postcolonial Histories*, Partha Chatterjee contested Anderson's theory because it perpetuated a misinterpretation of the rise of anticolonial nationalism through its similarity to Western nationalisms. Chatterjee disputes Anderson's interpretation that the postcolonial world draws its 'anticolonial nationalism' from the forms supplied by the West because nationalisms in Asia and Africa rest on difference from Western nationalisms. Chatterjee resists 'nationalism's autobiography', its 'flawed history', by offering his reading of the key features of anticolonial nationalisms in Asia and Africa (1993: 6).
17. See, for example, the testimonial aspects of Spanish American autobiography in Molloy (1991), especially the Introduction.
18. In *The Labyrinth of Solitude*, Octavio Paz concedes that modern man is condemned to live in solitude, which he must overcome (1985: 195). Modern man suffers from 'the illness of solitude' (204): 'a period of withdrawal and solitude – almost always during early youth – preceding a return to the world and to action' (205). For Paz, the individual lives in solitude and retirement and then returns to the world.
19. See the key works of anticolonial literature: Aimé Césaire, *Discours sur le colonialism* (*Discourse on Colonialism*) (1950), a Third World anticolonial polemic; Frantz Fanon, *Les damnés de la terre* (*The Wretched of the Earth*) (1961); and Albert Memmi, *Portrait du colonisé, précédé de portrait du colonisateur* (*The Colonizer and the Colonized*) (1957). Césaire sets out to prove that colonisation dehumanises the coloniser – to study 'how colonization works to *decivilize* the colonizer, to *brutalize* him' (Césaire 1972a: 35; italics in original) and Europe's slow but sure descent into 'savagery'. Interestingly, Césaire and Memmi wrote autobiographical works. In an interview conducted at the Cultural Congress of Havana in 1967, Césaire admits that *Cahier d'un retour au pays natal* (*Notebook of a Return to the Native Land*) (1939), written on his return from France to Martinique after an absence of ten years, is an autobiographical book 'in

which I tried to gain an understanding of myself' (Césaire 1972a: 81). *Return to My Native Land* deals with his Martinican youth and race in the Antilles. Césaire maintains that, while French literature influenced him, he sought to create a new language to communicate the African heritage: 'I wanted to create an Antillean French, a black French that, while still being French, had a black character' (Césaire 1972b: 83). Interestingly also, Albert Memmi wrote an autobiographical novel, *La Statue de sel* (*The Pillar of Salt*) (1953), about his early years in Tunisia, which preceded *The Colonizer and The Colonized.*

20. See also the second volume of Tuqan's autobiography, *al-Riḥlah al-Aṣ'ab: Sīra Dhātiyya* (*The More Difficult Journey: An Autobiography*) (1993).
21. Abdelkebir Khatibi describes the relationship between the languages of the coloniser and the colonised as an 'amour bilingue' (love in two languages). See Khatibi (1990).
22. In interviews, Darwish alluded to his reading of the Old Testament in Hebrew – also part of the school curriculum in occupied Palestine – to rework sources and motifs in *Mural* as well as the classical Arabic dictionary *Lisān al-'Arab* (the tongue of the Arabs) (Darwish 2006b: 94, 88).
23. For Anglophone autobiography by Arab-American immigrants, see Hassan (2011).
24. In *Memories of a Meltdown*, Makhzangi describes his reflections on the Chernobyl explosion in the Soviet Union: 'These are thus anti-memoirs: moments I collected while traveling through the depths of an irradiated season. Moments of spring' (2006: 22). In the preface, he also describes his memoir as a 'kind of investigative literary reportage', a 'form used by prominent authors under the urgent pressure of events that will simply not wait for the pure fermentation process of the creative spirit' (83). This can be compared to García Márquez's reportage in *Relato de un naufrago* (*The Story of a Shipwrecked Sailor*) (1970) or *Miguel Littín clandestine en Chile* (*Clandestine in Chile: The Adventures of Miguel Littín*) (1986) – a comparison that Makhzangi himself makes (Makhzangi 2006: 83).

Chapter 1

1. The publication of Taha Hussein's book *On Pre-Islamic Poetry* in 1926 provoked a controversy with the Azhar institution because his theory that Jāhilī (pre-Islamic) poetry was forged after Islam introduced a method of historical reading of Arabic poetry that challenged the veracity of Qur'anic stories. Pierre Cachia attributes the 'violent' reception of the book to 'its religious implications' (1956: 59).

2. Because of his criticism of the government, Taha Hussein was removed from his post at the Egyptian University in 1932 (Cachia 1997: 7).
3. Fedwa Malti-Douglas remarks, 'Taha Husayn's outlook was often more revolutionary and rebellious than that of most of his contemporaries' (Malti-Douglas 1988: 6).
4. Generations of Arab writers, thinkers, and intellectuals revered Taha Hussein. On the Arab reception of Hussein's heroism, see Malti-Douglas (1988: 14). In her memoir *The Search: Personal Papers*, the Egyptian writer Latifa al-Zayyat describes him as 'the father of modern secular intellectuals' at his 1973 funeral (*HT*, 95; *SP*, 68).
5. See Pascal (1960).
6. See al-'Īd (1998).
7. For fuller examination of the literary debates on 'autofiction', see Bacar (2014).
8. See Hussein (1938); for Hussein's revolutionary thought, see El-Enany (2006: 55–6).
9. For early autobiographical production in Egypt and the dominance of European influence, see Enderwitz (1998: 76).
10. On the classical Arabic autobiographical tradition, see Reynolds (2001).
11. I quote from E. H. Paxton's translation of *An Egyptian Childhood* (*EC*); Hilary Wayment's translation of *The Stream of Days* (*SD*); and Kenneth Cragg's translation of *A Passage to France* (*PF*). All references are to the Arabic edition (marked *A1*, *A2*, and *A3* for each of the volumes), followed by the English translation.
12. For further examination of the delayed autobiographical contract in *An Egyptian Childhood*, see Malti-Douglas's reading of doubling in the narration in Chapter 6 of *Blindness and Autobiography*. In the final chapter of *An Egyptian Childhood*, daughter and reader understand the implicit pact. In this way, the autobiography commences with novelistic features and concludes with the delayed autobiographical pact.
13. This is a modification of Kenneth Cragg's translation of the third volume of *The Days*, *A Passage to France*, to adhere to the original and retain Taha Hussein's use of the third person.
14. For an examination of a history of Ibrahim's political activity and arrest, see Starkey (2016: 19–23, 40).
15. For further discussion of Ibrahim's novels from *That Smell* to *al-Qanūn al-Faransī* (French Law) (2008), see Elsadda (2012), especially Chapter 6, and Starkey (2016).
16. An English translation, *The Smell of It*, was published in 1971 and, more recently,

another translation, *That Smell*, appeared. All references are to the Arabic edition (*TR*), followed by Robyn Creswell's 2013 English translation *That Smell* (*TS*).

17. For the history of the publication of *That Smell*, see Mehrez (1994: 41).
18. *That Smell*, published and censored in 1966, appeared in a complete edition in 1986. The statement is included in the 1986 edition. For the history of the novel's publication, see Sonallah Ibrahim's introduction to the 1986 edition of *That Smell* (2013); Mehrez (1994, 2008); Elsadda (2012: 120); and Starkey (2016: Chapter 3).
19. More recently, Ibrahim has published two novels, *Ice* (*al-Jalīd*) (2011) and *Berlin 69* (2014), inspired by his experiences in Moscow to which he travelled to study film directing in 1971–4 and Berlin where he worked as a journalist in 1968–71, respectively.
20. See Mehrez's references to Sonallah Ibrahim's unpublished George Antonius Memorial Lecture at St Antony's College, Oxford, in which he alludes to his literary formation in prison (2008: 75).
21. In an interview, Ibrahim remarks that the situation in Egypt in 2007 was identical to the situation in 1948: 'the Palestine question, military law, corruption, war'. See Rakha (2007).
22. On the implications of Ibrahim's rejection of the Arab Novel Award, see Ghazoul (2003) by one of the judges on the panel and Mehrez (2008).
23. For an examination of Ibrahim's status in the literary field, see Mehrez (2008), in particular, Chapters 1, 2, and 4.
24. For Sonallah Ibrahim's speech, see Ibrahim (2003: 2–3). For further discussion of Sonallah Ibrahim and the Arabic Novel Award, see Mehrez (1994: Chapter 4, 'The Value of Freedom') and (2008). Mehrez details the scene of Ibrahim's rejection speech in which he offers 'an elegy of the Arab world' that 'once upon a time was Arab' and denounces 'in public, not in fiction' Egypt's foreign policy, normalisation with Israel, corruption, human rights violations, the absence of civil rights, and the impoverishment of culture; the US occupation of Iraq; and the 'genocide against the Palestinian people' (Mehrez 2008: 73–4). Ibrahim asserted that he could not accept a literary prize from a government that lacked the credibility to award it. See Mehrez's examination of Ibrahim's stature on the Egyptian literary scene through her reading of Gamal al-Ghitani's *Akhbār al-Adab* editorial, 'Sharaf Sonallah Ibrahim' ('The Honor of Sonallah Ibrahim') on the publication of his novel *Sharaf* (Honor), *Egypt's Culture Wars*, Chapter 1.
25. *Amrikanli* appeared before the Arabic Novel Award ceremony (Mehrez 2008: 82).

26. Subsequent parenthetical references are to the Arabic edition (*T*), followed by the English translation (*S*).
27. When pressed about the cover of *Stealth*, Ibrahim demurred (Rakha 2007). In interviews, however, he notes that he was able to write *Stealth* when he had reached the age of his father in the autobiographical novel.
28. See Robyn Creswell's introduction to his translation of *That Smell and Notes from Prison* in which he comments on Ibrahim's quotation from an Arabic translation of a book on Hemingway. Ibrahim cites a statement made by Hemingway: 'But you ought to always write it to try to get it stated' (Creswell 2013: 11–12). I quote from the Arabic edition (*YW*) and Robyn Creswell's 2013 English translation (*NP*).
29. Interestingly, the French translation by Richard Jacquemond of *Stealth*, *Le petit voyeur* (2008), alludes to the action of the narrator who observes others. In interviews, Ibrahim has expressed a preference for the title in English to be able to carry over the sense of a 'little voyeur' though the English 'stealth' is a literal translation of the Arabic 'al-talaṣṣuṣ' (Ibrahim 2013b).
30. Citations from the Arabic edition (*T*) are followed by Hosam Aboul-Ela's English translation (*S*).
31. On the perspective of the child-narrator, see Mostafa (2011).
32. In his memoir *Boyhood*, J. M. Coetzee, writing of the young boy John Coetzee in the third person and the present tense, conjures similar actions. The young boy and his brother scuttle out of the house in Worcester and 'then sneak back to lurk behind doors and eavesdrop' (Coetzee 1997: 78). He writes: 'They have also pierced spy-holes in the ceiling, so that they can climb into the roof-space and peer into the living-room from above' (ibid.). On the family farm, Voëlfontein, the young boy, displays a curiosity and relief at the harmony between his family and the help: 'if he stands at the kitchen door he can hear [passing between his aunt and the two women] a low stream of talk that he loves to eavesdrop on: the soft, comforting gossip of women, stories passed from ear to ear to ear, till not only the farm but the village at Fraserburg Road and the location outside the village are covered by the stories, and all the other farms of the district too' (85).

Chapter 2

1. See Shaarawi (1981, 1986).
2. The Palestinian poet Fadwa Tuqan (1917–2003), likewise, writes of her seclusion during her formative years in Nablus in British Mandate Palestine in

her autobiography *A Mountainous Journey: An Autobiography* (1990) and the hardships endured in a patriarchal culture.

3. See Sharawi Lanfranchi (2012).
4. Fanon notes the revolutionary activity of the Algerian woman, especially her entry into the revolution by 1956 (1965: 53–4).
5. For further examination of Egyptian womanhood in the new nation-state, see Bier (2011).
6. For a comparison of Assia Djebar, Latifa al-Zayyat, and Fadwa Tuqan, see al-Nowaihi (2001), the only critical study that brings Djebar and al-Zayyat into conversation to focus on women writers' self-empowerment through autobiography. This chapter reads the commonalities between the trajectories and literary production of Djebar and al-Zayyat.
7. For a contrapuntal reading of the trajectories of Said and Djebar, see Mortimer (2005). For a reading of the metaphor of counterpoint in the work of Djebar where counterpoint is interplay, not synthesis, see Lachman (2010: 164).
8. On Algerian women writers and the production of war literature, see Tahon (1992). For the status of Algerian women's writing, see Roche (1992).
9. For her choice of silence during the October 1988 street riots in Algiers, see Zimra (1993). On the proliferation of Francophone Algerian novels in the wake of the Algerian War of Liberation, see Bouzar (1992: 51).
10. The name 'Djebar' means 'she who consoles' in the Amazigh language (Moore-Gilbert 2009: 94) and 'omnipotent' in Arabic.
11. See Marx-Scouras (1993).
12. In *A Dying Colonialism*, Fanon outlines that the comparison of territory to woman is based on the image of the Algerian veiled woman (Faulkner 1996: 847). Fanon draws attention to the use of the veil during the colonisation of Algeria by women assigned by the National Liberation Front to transport grenades to the *fidaïs* (1965: 57), the removal of the veil to participate in the revolution, and its readoption in response to Westernisation (63). Fanon describes the conquest of Algeria as a colonial unveiling of Algerian women (42).
13. Algerian conservative critics have levelled criticism at Djebar for her treatment of sexuality (Marx-Scouras 1993: 172).
14. For the politics of Maghrebian multilingualism, see Donadey (2000).
15. See Donadey (2000).
16. See Geesey (1996).
17. On the status of women's autobiography in Islamic culture, see Mortimer (2013).

18. Djebar undertakes a similar historical reconstruction in *Loin de Médine: Filles d'Ismaël* (1991) (*Far From Medina: Daughters of Ismael*), rewriting the history of the origins of Muslim civilisation from the perspective of women. The novel contains extracts culled from Muslim historians' interpretations of women from the first centuries of Islam. The third part of *Fantasia* records the testimonies of traditional Algerian women from Mount Chenoua from interviews conducted by Djebar with her maternal ancestors after the Algerian War of Independence.
19. On Djebar's musical fantasia, see al-Nakib (2005).
20. In *Fantasia*, women are present in the Algerian cavalcade (Murdoch 1993: 76), featuring the *tzarl-rit*, an expression of joy or vociferation upon misfortune.
21. See Mortimer (2013).
22. Unless otherwise noted, all translations are my own. See Djebar, *Nulle part dans la maison de mon père* (*NP*).
23. On the mother–daughter relationship in *Nowhere*, see Hiddleston (2011).
24. This is a slight modification of Mildred Mortimer's translation (2013: 125).
25. For a reading of the novel as reflective of 'the revolutionary fervor' of the 1950s, see Elsadda (2012: xl, 99).
26. For the context of *The Search*, see al-Zayyat (1994b) and Mehrez (1996).
27. For a reading of *The Open Door* within the frame of 'revolutionary womanhood' or the women's rights movement in Egypt under Nasser, see Bier (2011: 23).
28. Bier observes, 'Al-Zayyat's novel is the product of a historical moment when many doors appeared to be opening for Egyptian women' (Bier 2011: 24).
29. Elsadda cites al-Zayyat's allusion to a self-imposed 'political censorship' and attributes her silence to her disaffection with the status of women in the nation (Elsadda 2012: xl).
30. In her memoir, al-Zayyat offers insight into her ideological differences with her husband Rashad Rushdi, the conservative professor at Cairo University, and her marriage, which distanced her from her political activism.
31. See Ghazoul (1993).
32. See Kaplan (1992). On Third World prison memoirs as 'resistance literature', see Harlow (1987).
33. On the 'power of writing' in prison and the methods used by the state to control prisoners, see Harlow (1987: 125).
34. On the different national contexts of her novel and memoirs, see al-Zayyat (1994b). For a reading of *The Open Door* and a landscape of defeat (1967), death (1973), and prison (1981), see Mehrez (1996).

Chapter 3

1. Darwish asserts: 'All that concerns the reader of my biography (*sīra*) is written in the poems' (2006b: 114). He goes on to add: 'I wrote features of my autobiography in prose works such as *Journal of an Ordinary Grief* and *Memory for Forgetfulness*, in particular childhood and the Nakba' (115).
2. There are ample allusions to Federico García Lorca and Pablo Neruda in Darwish's poetry. Like Neruda, Darwish wrote a sequence of memoirs. In 1962, Neruda retreated to his hometown Isla Negra and wrote *Memorial de Isla Negra* (*Isla Negra: A Notebook*), a collection of autobiographical poems. Like Neruda, whose *Memorias* (*Memoirs*) and *Memorial* offer the sum of a life devoted to poetry and politics, Darwish experimented with the genre in *Memory* and *Mural*. Darwish's poem 'In Pablo Neruda's Home, on the Pacific', invokes the Chilean poet. The poem begins: 'In Pablo Neruda's home, on the Pacific / coast, I remembered Yannis Ritsos / at his house' (*Fī dār Bāblū Nirūdā, 'ala shāṭi' / al-Bāsifik, tadhakkartu Yānnis Ritsos / fī baytihi*). When Darwish visited Neruda's house in Isla Negra on the Pacific Coast of Chile (where Neruda wrote *Memorial de Isla Negra*), he remembered his poetic comrade Yannis Ritsos who had welcomed him in Athens and generously introduced him in an amphitheatre with a victory sign for 'brother' and Palestine. Neruda's lavish house in his home-village is the occasion for Darwish's memory of his fellow poet's 'ascetic home' overlooking the sea in ancient Athens; both Ritsos and Darwish suffered exile, displacement, imprisonment, and poverty. Ritsos, his 'brother in poem', exchanges affection for ancient Athens and Yabous, old Jerusalem, fusing memory and the future. The speaker remembers his fellow poet's welcome in Athens and an exchange of reminiscences of home. Ritsos reassures him that his Odysseus will return, and finally, if there must be a journey, the poet must wish for 'an eternal one'. See 'In Pablo Neruda's Home, on the Pacific' ('*Fī dār Bāblū Nirūdā, 'ala shāṭi' / al-Bāsifik*') in *The Butterfly's Burden*. Critics have also invoked allusions and comparisons: Munir Akash and Carolyn Forché note, 'With Nerudian transparency, his poems of the sixties and early seventies reflected his pain over the occupation of his homeland and his lingering hopes for its liberation' (xv). Denys Johnson-Davies notes: 'Darwish's reputation is that of a Lorca of the Palestinian resistance movement' (1980: xvii). Further, Darwish spoke of Borges's interest in Arab culture and his own admiration for Pablo Neruda in a conversation with Alberto Manguel (Darwish 2009a: 31). In her tribute, Judith Kazantzis compares Darwish to Neruda: 'But we all have seen

that here was a poet who, as Neruda spoke for Chile, could and did speak for his people. But rather different from Neruda, Darwish suffered oppression, prison and exile several times over' (Kazantzis 2008: 43). In his tribute to Darwish, Antoon compares the poet to Pablo Neruda who wrote of poetry's evocation of 'solitude and solidarity' (2008a: 4) – an allusion to Neruda's Nobel Prize speech, 'Towards the Splendid City', where he proclaims, 'And I believe that poetry is an action, ephemeral or solemn, in which there enter as equal partners solitude and solidarity' (Neruda 1971). For comparisons of Darwish to Tagore, Hikmet, and Pablo Neruda, see Mattawa (2014: 169).

3. For an examination of Darwish's *Memory* and Barghouti's *I Saw Ramallah*, see Reigeluth (2008).
4. Dwight Reynolds has surveyed the early development of Arabic autobiography and noted the creation of a literary tradition extending from premodern literature to the turn of the twentieth century in the Arab world. See Chapter 1.
5. On the autobiography of the poet, see Pascal (1960), especially Chapter 9.
6. For an examination of solitude, estrangement, exile, and loss, see Said, *Reflections on Exile*. See also the encounters between politics and poetry in Barghouti's poem *Midnight*. Barghouti's poem, written about Palestine while living between Cairo and Ramallah, persists as both a meditation on exile from Palestine and an elegy for its loss. Barghouti's *Midnight* is a poem on exile that becomes elegy: a communal loss mediated through the poetic speaker's sorrow. Edward Said observes that while 'literature and history contain heroic, romantic, glorious, even triumphant episodes in an exile's life, these are no more than efforts meant to overcome the crippling sorrow of estrangement' (2000d: 173). In his criticism and memoir, Said treats exile, focusing on the sorrow and loss that characterise that condition, sentiments that pervade Barghouti's *Midnight* and memoirs. Said's observations on 'exile as a condition of terminal loss' (ibid.) recall a powerful motif in Barghouti's poetry, especially *Midnight*, a poem on the desolation of exile and occupation, whose production synthesises elegy in between Palestinian and Egyptian contexts. While Said focuses on the production of modern Western culture by 'exiles, émigrés, refugees', Barghouti's poetry expresses the tragedy of exile in the Arab world. As Said observes, 'exiles are aware of at least two [cultures, settings], and this plurality of vision gives rise to an awareness of simultaneous dimensions, an awareness that – to borrow a phrase from music – is contrapuntal': 'For an exile, habits of life, expression, or activity in the new environment inevitably occur against the memory of these things in another

environment. Thus both the new and old environments are vivid, actual, occurring together contrapuntally' (186).

7. For the effect of the loss of Palestine on post-1948 Arabic prose, see Said (2000d), especially 'Arabic Prose and Prose Fiction after 1948'.
8. In *Journal of an Ordinary Grief*, Darwish (2010) reconstructs the massacre of Kufr Qasem from Palestinian testimonies.
9. Ibrahim Muhawi notes that Darwish wrote a 'trilogy' of prose works: *Journal of an Ordinary Grief*; *Memory for Forgetfulness*; and *In the Presence of Absence* (2010: ix).
10. For the tension between the poetic and the political in Darwish's poetry, see Said (1994); Wazen (2006); Ghazoul (2012). Jihan Ramazani reads Said's fascination for 'Darwish the vexed and introspective poet' (2010: 159). For an examination of the relationship of the personal to the political in *Limādhā Tarakta al-Ḥiṣāna Waḥidan*? (*Why Have You Left the Horse Alone?*), see Antoon (2002). Jeffrey Sacks notes the relation of the political and the aesthetic, and writes, 'To linger in this way is not to leave behind the political engagements of Darwish's early poetry and prose, and "resistance literature," but to read the political in Darwish anew' (2015: 31). For the examination of love poetry in *State of Siege*, a poem written during the 2002 Israeli occupation of the West Bank, as a political act, see Langley (2012).
11. In Ramallah, under occupation, siege, and the isolation imposed by Israel (Darwish 2006b: 125), Darwish notes: 'When I want to write, I go out of Ramallah to make use of my solitude in Amman' (148).
12. Of *Memory*, Darwish notes: 'The purpose of this prose book is liberation from the effect of Beirut, and in it I described a day of siege' (Darwish 2006b: 147).
13. For a 'misreading' of *Memory for Forgetfulness* through a human rights report of the Israeli 'three-week siege' of Gaza in 2008–9, see Harlow (2012). This 'misreading' attends to 'the geography and the event' rather than the historical context examined by *Memory*'s translator Ibrahim Muhawi.
14. *Memory* first appeared in *Al-Karmel*, a literary quarterly edited by Darwish from 1981.
15. I quote from Ibrahim Muhawi's translation of *Memory for Forgetfulness*. Subsequent parenthetical references are to the original (*DN*), followed by the English translation (*MF*).
16. In 1973, Darwish became a member of the executive council in the Palestinian Liberation Organization (PLO) from which he resigned after the Oslo treaty on 13 September 1993 (Muhawi 1995: xiv).

17. In his testimony, 'Portable Absence: My Camp Re-membered' in *Seeking Palestine*, Palestinian poet Sharif Elmusa evokes a comparable moment in which he conjures up his younger self in the refugee camp and dwells on how he would observe his blue-eyed children accompanying him on his visit to the site of the camp many years later.
18. In a conversation with Muhawi, Darwish described the text as 'nervous, tense' ('*mutawattir*'), which sought to capture the madness (*junūn*), or possession by Beirut (Muhawi 1995: xx–xxi).
19. See Darwish's *Olive Leaves* (*Awrāq al-Zaytūn*) (1969). See also Darwish (1980).
20. In 1995, Darwish spoke of a state of separation or rupture by which the 'poet goes out of the self' and looks upon it (Darwish 1995b: 205): 'in the past I was both the individual and the community . . . In Beirut the collective voice became stronger (this is by the way my worst poetic stage) . . . In the present stage, there is a going back to the self. Yet the paradox is that the self has a communal memory. The most prominent voice becomes that of the "I"' (206).
21. On self-elegy, see Fuss (2013). Another poetic autobiography written as a final work in 2006 is *In the Presence of Absence*. Antoon describes *In the Presence of Absence* as a 'self-elegy' in which the poet envisions his death: 'The book's cover itself mimics a tombstone, if we read the author's name and the title as one sentence: "Mahmoud Darwish, in the presence of absence"' (2011: 6).
22. The relationship of epic to elegy is suggested by Akash and Forché, who observe, 'Darwish's poetic fraternity includes Federico García Lorca's canto hondo (deep song), Pablo Neruda's bardic epic range, [and] Osip Mandelstam's elegiac poignancy' (2003: xviii).
23. Ghazoul examines the genres of epic and lyric in *Mural* and the creation of a hybrid genre she calls an 'epic hymn' (2012: 39).
24. There are three translations of *Mural*: Munir Akash and Carolyn Forché (2003); Fady Joudah (2009); and Rema Hammami and John Berger (Darwish 2009e). I quote from the original (*J*) and Joudah's translation (*M*).
25. The word in the original in this stanza is 'woman'.
26. For a quarter of a century, Darwish observes, he returned to the land 'by way of the Arabic sentence' (*JO*, 139).
27. On Darwish's adaptation of Imru' al-Qays in his poetry, see Antoon (2002).
28. Similarly, in *Journal of an Ordinary Grief*, Darwish repossesses dates, borders, and events: 'Dates, South: May 15, 1948; East: November 1956; West: June 5, 1967; North: September 1970. These are the borders of my body' (*JO*, 145).

The poet-narrator lays emphasis upon the body, fusing the poet with land and history.

29. As Darwish notes, *Mural* is an epic without 'community, nation, geographical exile or map but an estranged self in a strange world and an individual "I" suffering from solitude' (2006: 53).
30. For an examination of Barghouti's memoirs, see Abdel Nasser (2014).
31. Subsequent references are to the Arabic edition (*RR*), followed by the English translation (*SR*).
32. This is an experience shared by poet Sharif Elmusa: 'studying in Cairo in 1967' and barred from entry to the 'territory that became Palestine in 1948', the West Bank and his camp, Al-Nuwayma, he became 'a refugee from a refugee camp' (2013: 30).
33. The word in the original is '*ghurba*' (*RR,* 8) of which a more literal translation would be 'estrangement'.
34. For an eco-critical reading of *I Saw Ramallah* through the politics of water in occupied Palestine that joins a growing Palestinian autobiographical literature such as Raja Shehadeh's *Palestinian Walks*, see Farrier (2012).
35. In *I Was Born There, I Was Born Here*, the poet invokes Latin American poets further: 'I'd wonder at the "blooming good health" of Pablo Neruda, because he looked like a bank director – as though a poet had to look wasted, half dead, and pale, like someone who's fallen into a chasm or just been pulled out of one!' (*WH*, 27; *BT*, 15).

Chapter 4.

1. In an interesting parallel, García Márquez and Said whose memoirs chronicle their formation and youth, allude to *The Thousand and One Nights* in a manner that prefigures their future work: García Márquez's fiction and Said's scholarship. In *Living to Tell the Tale*, García Márquez notes the effects of his discovery of *The Thousand and One Nights* on his fiction (2002: 265; 2003: 219–20). In *Out of Place*, Said revisits his sources of stories and films such as *The Arabian Nights* adventures whose embeddedness in Orientalist practices eluded him: 'It was very odd, but it did not occur to me that the cinematic Aladdin, Ali Baba, and Sinbad, whose genies, Baghdad cronies, and sultans I completely possessed in the fantasies I counterpointed with my lessons, all had American accents, spoke no Arabic, and ate mysterious foods' (*OP*, 34). Besides these fantasies, he is repeatedly accused of 'fibbing' (*OP*, 37), and García Márquez's father would accuse him of lying. Interestingly, Taha Hussein in *The Days* recounts that 'the

youth' had stories from the *Arabian Nights* read to him: 'Among the stories brought by the book-peddlers, which were often in the hands of the lads, was one which was an excerpt from *The Arabian Nights*, and known as the story of Hassan of Basra . . . Now among these adventures there was something that filled the lad with admiration, and that was the account of the rod given to this Hassan on one of his journeys, one of the special properties of which was that, if you struck the ground with it, the earth split open and there came forth nine persons to carry out the behests of the possessor of the rod' (*EC*, 59).

2. Andrew F. Rubin notes the points of comparison between Conrad and Said in his Foreword to *Joseph Conrad and the Fiction of Autobiography*: 'Both were born and lived under the dictates of foreign or colonial rule. Driven out of their native homelands, the two wrote in a language that was not their native tongue. They shared the unsettling experiences of dislocation, exile, and marginalization. Caught in the disjuncture between two worlds (the disappearing *anciens régimes* or colonial worlds from which they would arrive and would ultimately remain), their cultural and political uprooting demanded, to echo Said, adjustments and "certain arrangements and accommodations"' (Rubin 2008: ix).
3. In the last quarter-century, the list of Palestinian memoirs in English has increased. For other Arab American Anglophone memoirs, see Aboul-Ela (2006: 30) and Hassan (2011). Hassan (2011: 113) examines Palestinian Anglophone memoirs by Fawaz Turki: *The Disinherited: Journal of a Palestinian Exile* (1972); *Soul in Exile: Lives of a Palestinian Revolutionary* (1988); and *Exile's Return: The Making of a Palestinian American* (1994). Other Anglophone Palestinian memoirs include Bassam Abu-Sharif's *Tried by Fire* (1995); Sari Nusseibeh's *Once Upon a Country: A Palestinian Life* (2007); Ibtisam Barakat's *Tasting the Sky: A Palestinian Childhood* (2007); Ghada Karmi's *In Search of Fatima: A Palestinian Story* (2002) (Hassan 2011: 231) and *Return: A Palestinian Memoir* (2015). See also Jean Said Makdisi's *Beirut Fragments: A War Memoir* (1990) and *Teta, Mother and Me: Three Generations of Arab Women* (2006); Raja Shehadeh's *Palestinian Walks: Notes on a Vanishing Landscape* (2008); *Stranger in the House* (2009); *A Rift in Time: Travels with my Ottoman Uncle* (2010); and *The Third Way: A Journal of Life in the West Bank* (1982). For a comparison between Said's memoir and Raja Shehadeh's Anglophone memoirs, which draw upon the Palestinian landscape, see also Moore (2013). For new Anglophone Palestinian memoirs on exile by Sharif Elmusa, Jean Said Makdisi, Raja Shehadeh and others, see Penny Johnson and Raja Shehadeh, *Seeking Palestine* (2013). Poet Sharif Elmusa, in prose and poetry, reflects on Palestine and his subjectivity

through reflections on expulsion and his return to the ruins of his 'refugee camp – Al-Nuwayma in Jericho, still in historic Palestine' (2013: 23). Elmusa attends to a question that troubles Arab writers who write in a non-native language: 'I began to pour my Palestinian feelings into the English I penned. I had to mother my tongue . . . Writing in English brought me into a more intimate relationship with American culture and, at the same time, heightened my sense of exile. It relieved me of the burden of being a spokesman for the nation – perhaps an unavoidable tendency among Palestinian poets' (24–5).

4. For the underdevelopment of the study of Palestinian life-writing, see Moore-Gilbert (2009: 112–13).
5. Interestingly, *A Portrait of the Artist as a Young Man* is the source of the epigraph of Sonallah Ibrahim's pseudo-autobiographical *That Smell*. See Chapter 1.
6. Bayoumi and Rubin note 'undertones of Proust' in *Out of Place* (Bayoumi and Rubin 2000: 399). For Proustian influences on *Out of Place*, see also Gindi (2000).
7. For a reading of Said's memoir as an immigrant narrative, see Hassan (2011). For a reading of Arab-American cultural production as American literature in the US from the 1940s to the 1960s, see Fadda-Conrey (2014: 18).
8. On Said's *Out of Place* as a transnational understanding of US citizenship and the self-formation of Arab immigrants to the US, see Fadda-Conrey (2014: Chapter 3).
9. See also *After the Last Sky: Palestinian Lives* (1999a), an autobiographical collection featuring photographs of Palestine.
10. On Said's appropriation of the genre and its relation to his postcolonial criticism, see Luca (2006: 127).
11. Tellingly, Andrew F. Rubin notes in his Foreword to *Joseph Conrad and the Fiction of Autobiography*: '*Orientalism* is informed by Said's engagement with Conrad's radical view of language: "The Orient was a word," Said writes, "which later accrued to it a wide field of meanings, associations, and connotations" . . . These did not necessarily refer to the real Orient but to the field surrounding the word (*Orientalism* 203)' (Rubin 2008: xv).
12. For the 'documentary authority' of portraits in *Out of Place*, see Moore-Gilbert (2009: 120–1). Michael Wood describes Edward Said's pictures in *Out of Place* as 'solitary' (2007: 12).
13. For a tribute to her father, see Said (2007).

Chapter 5

1. There is an early English translation, *Through the Vast Halls of Memory* (1990) by Paul Hammond, and *Dreaming of Baghdad* (2009), co-translated by Haifa Zangana and Paul Hammond. The Arabic edition appeared in 1995. I quote from *Dreaming of Baghdad* (*DB*) and *Fī Arwiqat al-Dhākirah* (*AD*). The epilogue in *Dreaming of Baghdad* was published in the journal *al-Kātibah* (The Writer) in London.
2. Zangana has written extensively about torture, the occupation of Iraq, the role of women, and revolution. Since 2003, she has commented on the fate of political prisoners, the rights of women, and freedom in the Arab world in the London-based newspaper *al-Quds* and in *The Guardian*.
3. On the persistence of the importance of literature and the arts in Iraqi culture in decades of war and occupation, see Ghazoul (2009a). On the forms of cultural resistance to the occupation of Iraq, see Zangana (2009). Elsewhere Zangana has written about the torture of Iraqi prisoners in US detention centres. See Zangana, Clark, and Reifer (2010).
4. For notes on a lecture Zangana gave at the University of London in 1998, see Haidar (2005: 193).
5. The description is an excerpt from Jean Genet's report from the camps of Sabra and Shatila a day after the massacre in 1982 (Antoon 2011: 166).
6. Zangana is known for her activism for Palestine and Iraq, for human rights, and now in the anti-war movement. She is the co-founder of Tadamun: Iraqi Women Solidarity.
7. I quote from Galway Kinnell's translation of Pablo Neruda's 'I Explain a Few Things' (Neruda 2007: 33).
8. Personal communication with Haifa Zangana on 13 June 2015.
9. For an interview with Zangana, see Grace (2007: 195).
10. For an examination of the historical and national specificity of Third World women's prison memoirs – Palestinian, Egyptian, South African, and Latin American – see Harlow (1987).
11. Alia Mamdouh's novels, *Naphtalene* and *The Loved Ones*, awarded the 2004 Naguib Mahfouz Medal for Literature, have been translated into English.
12. Fakir cites Mamdouh in her introduction to Peter Theroux's translation, *Mothballs: A Story of Baghdad*.
13. See the citation quoted by Ferial Ghazoul, Chair of the 2004 Naguib Mahfouz Medal for Literature (Ghazoul 2007: 320).

Chapter 6

1. For an introduction and translation of an excerpt from Malas's memoir by Margaret Litvin, see Malas (2016).
2. Soueif published *Cairo: My City, Our Revolution* in London in January 2012. An American edition includes *Cairo: My City, Our Revolution*, from January to October 2011, and resumes the memoir from October 2011 in *Cairo: Memoir of a City Transformed* (2014). I quote from the expanded edition.
3. Ashour (1983). Hereafter cited by page number. All unattributed translations are my own.
4. For fuller examination of the East–West encounter in Ashour's *The Journey*, see Rasheed El-Enany (2006) and Hartman (2004). For an examination of Ashour's *The Journey* that explores affiliations between Arabs and African Americans in the United States, see Hartman (2005).
5. On Third World solidarity in *The Journey*, see Hartman (2005: 399).
6. For a comparison of al-Zayyat and Ashour, more specifically representations of the Egyptian university in *The Open Door* and *Specters*, see Morsy (2009). Morsy focuses on Ashour's 'campus novel' in which she traces its discontents over time and al-Zayyat interweaves the university in her examination of Professor Ramzy's hypocrisy, while here I focus on the commonalities between al-Zayyat and Ashour as well as the resonances of al-Zayyat's *The Search* in *Specters*. Moreover, Morsy alludes to autobiographical literature that centres on academics or writers and includes criticism or satire of the institution of the university such as *The Days* – one of the works under study here (140).
7. Throughout the chapter, I refer to the author as Ashour and the characters in her memoirs, *Specters* (*S*), *Heavier Than Radwa* (*HR*), and *The Scream* (*S*), as Radwa.
8. Hereafter cited by page number.
9. For further examination of the chronology and narration of *Specters*, see Andrea (2014).
10. Elsewhere, Ashour notes that she has exhausted (*ajhadtu*) and overextended (*athqaltu*) the reader with her chronicle of her medical crises (*AR*, 83) in an interlude in which she toys with the idea of providing comic relief in the form of lighthearted scenes from the hospital.
11. Ashour quotes from Darwish's *Mural*. I quote from Fady Joudah's English translation (*M*, 101).

12. *Blue Lorries* is the title of the English translation of one of her novels (the title in Arabic is *Faraj*).
13. Prince (2012, 2014). Hereafter cited by page number.

Epilogue

1. Moretti quotes from Matti Moosa's *The Origins of Modern Arabic Fiction*, Edward Said's *Beginnings*, and Roger Allen's *The Arabic Novel* on the influence of European literature on the appearance and development of the Arabic novel in the nineteenth century (2013: 51).
2. Moretti concludes: 'This, then, is the basis for the division of labour between national and world literature: national literature, for people who see trees; world literature, for people who see waves' (2013: 61).
3. For some of these Palestine-themed memoirs and volumes, see Shehadeh (2007, 2002, 2003) and Johnson and Shehadeh (2013).
4. See, for example, the memoir *Volverse Palestina* (*Becoming Palestine*) (2013) by Lina Meruane, a Chilean writer of Palestinian descent, who chronicles her return to Palestine in an effort to trace the origins of her surname.
5. See, for example, the Colombian writer Héctor Abad Faciolince's memoir *El olvido que seremos* (*Oblivion*) (2006) and the 2014 Arabic translation *al-Nisyān*. A conversation with Héctor Abad, 25 June 2014.

Bibliography

Abad Faciolince, Héctor (2006), *El Olvido que seremos*, Bogotá: Planeta.

_____ (2013), *Oblivion: A Memoir*, trans Anne McLean and Rosalind Harvey, Tiverton: Old Street Publishing.

_____ (2014), *Al-Nisyān*, trans. Mark Jamāl, Cairo: al-ʻArabī Publishing.

"Abbās, Iḥsān (1956), *Fann al-sīrah*, Beirut: Dār al-Thaqāfah.

ʻAbd al-Dāyim, Yaḥyā Ibrāhīm (1975), *Al-Tarjamah al-Dhātiyya fī al-Adab al-ʻArabī al-Ḥadīth* (Autobiography in Modern Arabic Literature), Beirut: Dār Iḥyā' al-Turāth al-ʻArabī.

Abdalla, Ahmed (1985), *The Student Movement and National Politics in Egypt 1923–1973*, London: Saqi Books.

Abdel Nasser, Tahia (2002), 'African Autobiography: The Contribution of Women', *Alif: Journal of Comparative Poetics*, 22, 58–75.

_____ (2014), 'Between Exile and Elegy, Palestine and Egypt: Mourid Barghouti's Poetry and Memoirs', *Journal of Arabic Literature*, 45, 244–64.

al-Abnūdī, ʻAbd al-Raḥmān (2012), 'Al-Mīdān', *Alif: Journal of Comparative Poetics*, 32, 322–5.

Aboul-Ela, Hosam (2006), 'Edward Said's "Out of Place": Criticism, Polemic, and Arab American Identity', *MELUS*, 31, no. 4, 15–32.

_____ (2007), *Other South: Faulkner, Coloniality, and the Mariátegui Tradition*, Pittsburgh: University of Pittsburgh Press.

_____ (2010), 'Is There an Arab (Yet) in This Field?: Postcolonialism, Comparative Literature, and the Middle Eastern Horizon of Said's Discourse Analysis', *Modern Fiction Studies*, 56, no. 4, 729–50.

Ahmad, Aijaz (1987), 'Jameson's Rhetoric of Otherness and the "National Allegory"', *Social Text*, 17, 3–25.

_____ (1992), *In Theory: Classes, Nations, Literatures*, London: Verso.

Akash, Munir (2000), 'Introduction', in *Mahmoud Darwish: The Adam of Two Edens*, Syracuse: Syracuse University Press, pp. 19–46.

Akash, Munir and Carolyn Forché (2003), 'Introduction', in *Mahmoud Darwish: Unfortunately, It Was Paradise*, Berkeley: University of California Press, pp. xv–xix.

Allen, Roger (1982), 'Review of *An Egyptian Childhood: An Autobiography of Taha Hussein* by Taha Hussein', trans. E. H. Paxton, *World Literature Today*, 56, no. 3, 566.

_____ (1995), *The Arabic Novel: An Historical and Critical Introduction*, 2nd edn, Syracuse: Syracuse University Press.

Alloula, Malek (1986), *The Colonial Harem*, trans Myrna Godzich and Wlad Godzich, with an introduction by Barbara Harlow, Minneapolis: University of Minnesota Press.

Amireh, Amal (1995), 'Rev. of *Memory for Forgetfulness: August, Beirut, 1982*, by Mahmoud Darwish', *World Literature Today*, 69, no. 4, 859.

Anderson, Benedict, R (1983), *Imagined Communities: Reflections on the Origins and Spread of Nationalism*, London: Verso.

_____ (1998), *The Spectre of Comparisons: Nationalism, Southeast Asia, and the World*, New York: Verso.

Andrea, Bernadette (2014), '"Habituation Devours Things": Radwa Ashour's *Specters* and the E(n)strangement of Life-Writing', *Journal of Women of the Middle East and the Islamic World*, 12, 169–94.

Anishchenkova, Valerie (2014), *Autobiographical Identities in Contemporary Arab Culture*, Edinburgh: Edinburgh University Press.

Antoon, Sinan (2002), 'Mahmoud Darwish's Allegorical Critique of Oslo', *Journal of Palestine Studies*, 31, no. 2, 66–77.

_____ (2008a), 'An Entourage of Violins and Clouds', *Banipal*, 33, 4–5.

_____ (2008b), 'Returning to the Wind: On Darwish's *La Taʿtadhir ʿAmma Faʿalta*', in Hala Nassar and Najat Rahman (eds), *Mahmoud Darwish: Exile's Poet*, Northampton, MA: Interlink Books, pp. 215–38.

_____ (2009), 'In Memoriam: Mahmoud Darwish (1941–2008)', *The Arab Studies Journal*, 17, no. 1, 98–9.

_____ (2011), 'Translator's Preface', in *In the Presence of Absence*, Mahmoud Darwish, trans. Sinan Antoon, New York: Archipelago, pp. 5–9.

Ashcroft, Bill, Gareth Griffiths and Helen Tiffin (eds) (1989), *The Empire Writes Back: Theory and Practice in Post-Colonial Literatures*, London: Routledge.

Ashour, Radwa (1992), *Sirāj*, Cairo: Dār al-Hilāl.

_____ (1993), 'My Experience with Writing', trans. Rebecca Porteous, *Alif: Journal of Comparative Poetics*, 13, 170–5.

_____ (1994), 'My Experience with Writing', in Ferial Ghazoul and Barbara Harlow (eds), *The View from Within: Writers and Critics on Contemporary Arabic Literature*, Cairo: The American University in Cairo Press, pp. 7–11.

_____ (1996), 'Riḥlat Laṭīfa al-Zayyāt' (The Journey of Latifa al-Zayyat), in Sayyid al-Baḥrāwī (ed.), *Laṭīfa al-Zayyāt al-Adab wa al-Waṭan*, Cairo: Nūr, Dār al-Mar'ah al-'Arabiyah li- al-Nashr wa Markaz al-Buḥūth al-'Arabiyah li al-Nashr, pp. 117–20.

_____ (2000),'Eyewitness, Scribe and Story Teller: My Experience as a Novelist', *The Massachusetts Review*, 41, no. 1, 85–92.

_____ (2003a), *Granada: A Novel*, trans. William Granara, Syracuse: Syracuse University Press.

_____ (2003b), *Qiṭ'ah min Urūbbā: Riwāyah*, Cairo: Dār al-Shurūq.

_____ (2007a), *Aṭyāf*, Cairo: Dār al-Shurūq.

_____ (2007b), *Siraaj: An Arab Tale*, trans. Barbara Romaine, Austin: Center for Middle Eastern Studies, The University of Texas at Austin.

_____ (2009), *Al-Ḥadatha al-Mumkina: Al-Shidyāk wa-l Sāq 'ala al-Sāq, al-Riwāyah al-Ūlā fī al-Adab al-'Arabī al-Ḥadīth*, Cairo: Dār al-Shurūq.

_____ (2011), *Specters*, trans. Barbara Romaine, Northampton, MA: Interlink Books.

_____ (2013), *Athqal min Radwā: Maqāṭi' min Sīra Dhātīyya*, Cairo: Dār al-Shurūq.

_____ (2014), *Blue Lorries*, trans. Barbara Romaine, Doha: Bloomsbury Qatar Foundation Publishing.

_____ (2015a), *Al-Riḥlah: Ayyām Ṭāliba Miṣriyya fī Amrīka*, Cairo: Dār al-Shurūq.

_____ (2015b), *Al-Ṣarkhah: Maqāṭi' min Sīra Dhātīyya*, Cairo: Dār al-Shurūq.

Bacar, Darouèche Hilali (2014), 'L'autofiction en question: Une relecture du roman arabe à travers les œuvres de Mohamed Choukri, Sonallah Ibrahim et Rachid El-Daïf', PhD dissertation, Université Lumière Lyon II.

Badawi, M. M. (1975), *A Critical Introduction to Modern Arabic Poetry*, New York: Cambridge University Press.

_____ (1985), *Modern Arabic Literature and the West*, New York: University of Oxford Press.

_____ (1993), *A Short History of Modern Arabic Literature*, Oxford: Clarendon Press.

_____ (ed.) (1992), *Modern Arabic Literature*, New York: Cambridge University Press.

al-Baḥrāwī, Sayyid (1996a), 'Adab Laṭīfa al-Zayyāt Yu'īd Ṭarḥ Su'āl al-Adab wa al-Waṭan', *Nūr*, 6, 31–3.

_____ (1996b), 'al-Adab wa al-Waṭan: Naḥwa Manẓūr Jadīd li al-'Ilāqah bayna al-Adab wa al-Siyāsah', in Sayyid al-Baḥrāwī (ed.), *Laṭīfa al-Zayyāt al-Adab wa al-Waṭan*, Cairo: Nūr, Dār al-Mar'ah al-'Arabiyah li-al-Nashr wa Markaz al-Buḥūth al-'Arabiyah li al-Nashr, pp. 7–11.

Bakhtin, M. M (1986), *Speech Genres and Other Late Essays*, trans Vern W. McGee, Caryl Emerson and Michael Holquist (eds), Austin: University of Texas Press.

Barghouti, Mourid (1997a), *I Saw Ramallah*, trans. Ahdaf Soueif, Cairo: American University in Cairo Press.

_____ (1997b), *Ra'aytu Rāmallāh*, Cairo: Dār al-Hilāl.

_____ (2008), *Midnight and Other Poems*, trans. Radwa Ashour, Yorkshire: Arc Publications.

_____ (2009), *Wulidtu Hunāka, Wulidtu Hunā*, Beirut: Riad El-Rayyes Books.

_____ (2011), *I Was Born There, I Was Born Here*, trans. Humphrey Davies, Cairo: The American University in Cairo Press.

Barrada, Muḥammad (1996), 'Ḥamlat taftīsh awrāq shakhṣiyyah', in Sayyid al-Baḥrāwī (ed.), *Laṭīfa al-Zayyāt al-Adab wa al-Waṭan*, Cairo: Nūr, Dār al-Mar'ah al-'Arabiyah li- al-Nashr wa Markaz al-Buḥūth al-'Arabiyah li al-Nashr, pp. 175–7.

The Battle of Algiers (1966), dir. Gillo Pontecorvo, Casbah Films.

Bayoumi, Moustafa and Andrew Rubin (2000), 'Introduction', in Moustafa Bayoumi and Andrew Rubin (eds), *The Edward Said Reader*, New York: Vintage Books, pp. xi–xxxiv.

Ben Jelloun, Tahar (1993), *Harrouda*, Reinbek bei Hamburg: Rowohlt.

Bennett, Sophie (1998), 'A Life of One's Own', in Robin Ostle, Ed de Moor and Stefan Wild (eds), *Writing the Self: Autobiographical Writing in Modern Arabic Literature*, London: Saqi Books, pp. 283–91.

Bernard, Anna (2007), '"Who Would Dare to Make It into an Abstraction": Mourid Barghouti's *I Saw Ramallah*', *Textual Practice*, 21, no. 4, 665–86.

_____ (2013), *Rhetorics of Belonging: Nation, Narration, and Israel/Palestine*, Liverpool: Liverpool University Press.

_____ and Ziad Elmarsafy (eds) (2012), 'Intimacies: In Memoriam Mahmoud Darwish' (special issue), *Interventions: International Journal of Postcolonial Studies*, 14, no. 1, 1–12.

Bhabha, Homi, K. (ed.) (1990), *Nation and Narration*, London: Routledge.

Bier, Laura (2011), *Revolutionary Womanhood: Feminisms, Modernity, and the State in Nasser's Egypt*, Stanford: Stanford University Press.

Blair, Dorothy S. (1985), 'Introduction', in *Fantasia: An Algerian Cavalcade*, Assia Djebar, trans. Dorothy S. Blair, New York: Quartet Books, pp. xv–xx.

Booth, Marilyn (2000), 'Translator's Introduction', in *The Open Door*, Latifa al-Zayyat, trans. Marilyn Booth, Cairo: American University in Cairo Press, pp. ix–xxxi.

Bouzar, Wadi (1992), 'The French-Language Algerian Novel', *Research in African Literatures*, 23, no. 2, 51–9.

Brault, Pascale-Anne and Michael Nass (2001), 'To Reckon with the Dead: Jacques Derrida's Politics of Mourning', in *The Work of Mourning*, Jacques Derrida, trans Pascale-Anne Brault and Michael Nass, Chicago: University of Chicago Press, pp. 1–30.

Brennan, Timothy (1990), 'The National Longing for Form', in Homi K. Bhabha (ed.), *Nation and Narration*, London: Routledge, pp. 44–70.

Bruss, Elizabeth (1976), *The Changing Situation of a Literary Genre*, Baltimore: Johns Hopkins University Press.

Bugeja, Norbert (2012), *Postcolonial Memoir in the Middle East: Rethinking the Liminal in Mashriqi Writing*, New York: Routledge.

Butler, Judith (2012), '"What Shall We Do without Exile?": Said and Darwish Address the Future', *Alif: Journal of Comparative Poetics*, 32, 30–54.

Cachia, Pierre (1956), *Taha Husayn: His Place in the Egyptian Literary Renaissance*, London: Luzac.

_____ (1997), 'Introduction', in *An Egyptian Childhood*, trans. E. H. Paxton, Cairo: The American University in Cairo Press, pp. 3–7.

_____ (2012), 'Ṭaha Ḥusayn', in P. J. Bearman, Th. Banquis, C. E. Bosworth, E. van Donzel, and W. P. Heinrichs (eds), *Encyclopaedia of Islam*, 2nd edn, Brill Online, http://referenceworks.brillonline.com/entries/encyclopaedia-of-islam-2/taha-husayn-COM_1148?s.num=111&s.start=100 (accessed 21 December 2016).

Césaire, Aimé (1972a [1950]), *Discourse on Colonialism*, trans. Joan Pinkham, New York: Monthly Review Press.

_____ (1972a), 'An Interview with Aimé Césaire', René Depestre, trans. Maro

Riofrancos, in *Discourse on Colonialism*, trans. Joan Pinkham, New York: Monthly Review Press, pp. 81–94. Chatterjee, Partha (1993), *The Nation and its Fragments: Colonial and Postcolonial Histories*, Princeton: Princeton University Press.

Choukri, Mohammed (1980), *Le Pain nu: récit autobiographique*, trans. Tahar Ben Jelloun, Paris: F. Maspero.

_____ (1993), *For Bread Alone*, trans. Paul Bowles, London: Saqi Books.

_____ (1996), *Al-Khubz al-Ḥāfī: Sīra Dhātiyya Riwā'iyya*, Beirut: Dār al-Sāqī.

Cixous, Hélène (2005), 'Foreword', trans. Judith Miller, in *Naphtalene: A Novel of Baghdad*, trans. Peter Theroux, New York: The Feminist Press, pp. v–vii.

Coetzee, J. M. (1997), *Boyhood*, London: Vintage Books.

Cragg, Kenneth (1997), 'Introduction', in *A Passage to France: The Third Volume of the Autobiography*, Taha Hussein, trans. Kenneth Cragg, Cairo: American University in Cairo Press, pp. 237–43.

Creswell, Robyn (2013), 'Translator's Introduction', in *That Smell and Notes from Prison*, Sonallah Ibrahim, trans. Robyn Creswell (ed.), New York: New Directions, pp. 1–16.

Dabashi, Hamid (2009), 'Foreword', in *Dreaming of Solitude*, Haifa Zangana, trans Haifa Zangana and Paul Hammond, New York: The Feminist Press, pp. vii–xi.

D'Afflitto, Isabella Camera (1998), 'Prison Narratives: Autobiography and Fiction', in Robin Ostle, Ed de Moor and Stefan Wild (eds), *Writing the Self: Autobiographical Writing in Modern Arabic Literature*, London: Saqi Books, pp. 148–56.

Darwish, Mahmoud (1969), 'Biṭāqat hawīyah', in *Awrāq al-Zaytūn*, Beirut: Dār al-'Awdah, pp. 9–16.

_____ (1973), *Yawmiyyāt al-Ḥuzn al-'Ādī*, Beirut: Markaz al-Abḥāth, al-Mu'assassah al- 'Arabīyah lil-Dirasāt wa al-Nashr.

_____ (1980), 'Identity Card', trans. Denys Johnson-Davies, in *The Music of Human Flesh*, London: Heinemann, pp. 10–12.

_____ (1995a), *Memory for Forgetfulness: August, Beirut, 1982*, trans. Ibrahim Muhawi, Berkeley: University of California Press.

_____ (1995b), 'Personal Interview with Mahmoud Darwish, Interview by Randa Abou-bakr', in *The Conflict of Voices in the Poetry of Dennis Brutus and Mahmūd Darwīsh*, Randa Abou-Bakr, Wiesbaden: Reichert Verlag, pp. 205–7.

_____ (1999), 'Poetry and Palestine', *Boundary* 2, 26, 81–3.

_____ (2000a), *In the Presence of Absence*, trans. Sinan Antoon, New York: Archipelago.

_____ (2000b), *Jidārīyya*, 2nd edn, Beirut: Riad El-Rayyes.

_____ (2002), *Ḥālat Ḥiṣār*, Beirut: Riad El-Rayyes.

_____ (2003), 'Mural', trans Munir Akash and Carolyn Forché, in *Unfortunately, It Was Paradise*, trans Munir Akash and Carolyn Forché (eds) with Sinan Antoon and Amira El-Zein, Berkeley: University of California Press, pp. 119–62.

_____ (2004a), 'Edward Said: A Contrapuntal Reading', trans. Mona Anis, *Al-Ahram Weekly*, 30 September–6 October.

_____ (2004b), 'Ṭibāq', *Al-Ḥayat*, 10 August.

_____(2006a), *Fī Ḥadrat al-Ghiyāb*, Beirut: Riad El-Rayyes.

_____(2006b), 'Ḥiwār ma' Mahmoud Darwish', interview by Abdo Wazen, in *Mahmoud Darwish: al-Gharīb Yaqa'u 'alā Nafsih*, Abdo Wazen, Beirut: Riyad al-Rayyes, pp. 57–154.

_____(2007a), *Dhākirah li-l Nisyān: al-Zamān Bayrūt, al-Makān Yawm min Ayyām Ab 1982*, Beirut: Riyad al-Rayyes.

_____(2007b), 'Fī Dār Bāblū Nirūdā, 'ala Shāṭi' al-Basifik', in *The Butterfly's Burden*, trans. Fady Joudah, Port Townsend: Copper Canyon, pp. 306–10.

_____(2007c), 'Hadhā huwa al-Nisyān', in *The Butterfly's Burden*, trans. Fady Joudah, Port Townsend: Copper Canyon, p. 232.

_____(2007d), 'In Pablo Neruda's Home, on the Pacific', in *The Butterfly's Burden*, trans. Fady Joudah, Port Townsend: Copper Canyon, pp. 307–11.

_____(2007e), 'Man anā, dūna Manfā?' in *The Butterfly's Burden*, trans. Fady Joudah, Port Townsend: Copper Canyon, pp. 88–90.

_____(2007f), 'This is Forgetfulness', in *The Butterfly's Burden*, trans. Fady Joudah, Port Townsend: Copper Canyon, p. 233.

_____(2007g), 'Who Am I, Without Exile?' in *The Butterfly's Burden*, trans. Fady Joudah, Port Townsend: Copper Canyon, pp. 89–91.

_____(2009a), *A River Dies of Thirst*, trans. Catherine Cobham, New York: Archipelago Books.

_____(2009b), *Almond Blossoms and Beyond*, trans. Mohammad Shaheen, Northampton, MA: Interlink Books.

_____(2009c), 'Counterpoint: For Edward Said', in *If I Were Another*, trans. Fady Joudah, New York: Farrar, Straus and Giroux, pp. 183–92.

_____(2009d), 'Mural', trans. Fady Joudah, in *If I Were Another*, New York: Farrar, Straus and Giroux, pp. 99–145.

_____(2009e), *Mural*, trans. Rema Hammami and John Berger, New York: Verso.

_____(2010), *Journal of an Ordinary Grief*, trans. Ibrahim Muhawi, New York: Archipelago.

Ḍayf, Shawqī (1979), *Al-Tarjamah al-shakhṣīyah*, Cairo: Dār al-Ma'ārif.

Derrida, Jacques (1980), 'The Law of Genre', trans. A. Ronell, *Critical Inquiry*, 7, 55–81.

_____(2003), *The Work of Mourning*, Pascale-Anne Brault and Michael Naas (eds), Chicago: University of Chicago Press.

Djebar, Assia (1985), *Fantasia: An Algerian Cavalcade*, trans. Dorothy S. Blair, London: Quartet Books.

Djebar, Assia (1991), *Loin de Médine: filles d'Ismaël*, Paris: A. Michel.

_____ (1992a), *L'Amour, la fantasia*, Casablanca: Éditions Eddif.

_____ (1992b), 'Forbidden Gaze, Severed Sound', *Women of Algiers in Their Apartment*, trans. Marjolijn de Jager, Charlottesville: University Press of Virginia, pp. 133–51.

_____ (1992c), *Women of Algiers in Their Apartment*, trans. Marjolijn de Jager, Charlottesville: University Press of Virginia.

_____ (1999), *Ces voix qui m' assiègent*, Paris: Éditions Albin Michel.

_____ (2007), *Nulle part dans la maison de mon père*, Paris: Albin Michel.

Donadey, Anne (1996), 'Rekindling the Vividness of the Past: Assia Djebar's Films and Fiction', *World Literature Today*, 70, no. 4, 885–92.

_____ (2000), 'The Multilingual Strategies of Postcolonial Literature: Assia Djebar's Algerian Palimpsest', *World Literature Today*, 74, no. 1, 27–36.

Döring, Tobias (2006), 'Edward Said and the Fiction of Autobiography', *Wasafiri*, 21, no. 2, 71–8.

Dyer, Rebecca (2007), 'Poetry and the Politics of Mourning: Mahmoud Darwish's Genre-Transforming Tribute to Edward W. Said', *PMLA*, 122, no. 5, 1,447–62.

Eakin, Paul John (1985), *Fictions in Autobiography: Studies in the Art of Self-Invention*, Princeton: Princeton University Press.

_____ (1989), 'Foreword', in *On Autobiography*, Philippe Lejeune, trans. Katherine Leary, Minneapolis: University of Minnesota Press, pp. vii–xxviii.

Eileraas, Karina (2007), 'Dismembering the Gaze: Speleology and Vivisection in Assia Djebar's *L'amour, la fantasia*', in Nawar Al-Hassan Golley (ed.), *Arab Women's Lives Retold: Exploring Identity through Writing*, New York: Syracuse University Press, pp. 16–34.

El-Enany, Rasheed (2006), *Arab Representations of the Occident: East-West Encounters in Arabic Fiction*, London: Routledge.

Elmusa, Sharif S. (2013), 'Portable Absence: My Camp Re-membered', in Penny Johnson and Raja Shehadeh (eds), *Seeking Palestine: New Palestinian Writing on Exile and Home*, Northampton, MA: Olive Branch Press, pp. 22–41.

Elsadda, Hoda (2012), *Gender, Nation, and the Arabic Novel*, New York: Syracuse University Press.

Enderwitz, Susanne (1998), 'Public Role and Private Self', in Robin Ostle, Ed de Moor, and Stefan Wild (eds), *Writing the Self: Autobiographical Writing in Modern Arabic Literature*, London: Saqi Books, pp. 75–81.

_____ (2002), 'Palestinian Autobiographies: A Source for Women's History', in Manuela Marín and Randi Deguilhem (eds), *Writing the Feminine: Women in Arab Sources*, London: I. B. Tauris, pp. 49–72.

Fadda-Conrey, Carol (2014), *Contemporary Arab-American Literature: Transnational Reconfigurations of Citizenship and Belonging,* New York: New York University Press.

Fanon, Frantz (1963 [1961]), *The Wretched of the Earth*, trans. Richard Philcox, London: MacGibbon and Kee.

_____ (1965), 'Algerian Unveiled', in *A Dying Colonialism*, trans. Haakon Chevalier, New York: Grove Press, pp. 35–67.

Faqir, Fadia (1996), 'Introduction', in *Mothballs: A Story of Baghdad*, trans. Peter Theroux, Reading: Garnet Publishing, pp. v–ix.

Farrier, David (2012), 'Washing Words: The Politics of Water in Mourid Barghouti's *I Saw Ramallah*', *The Journal of Commonwealth Literature*, 48, no. 2, 187–99.

Faulkner, Rita A. (1996), 'Assia Djebar, Frantz Fanon, Women, Veils, and Land', *World Literature Today*, 70, no. 4, 847–55.

Franco, Jean (2002), *The Decline and Fall of the Lettered City: Latin America in the Cold War*, Cambridge, MA: Harvard University Press.

_____ (2013), *Cruel Modernity*, Durham, NC: Duke University Press.

Furani, Khaled (2012), *Silencing the Sea: Secular Rhythms in Palestinian Poetry*, Stanford: Stanford University Press.

Fuss, Diana (2013), *Dying Modern: A Meditation on Elegy*, Durham, NC: Duke University Press.

García Márquez, Gabriel (1967), *Cien años de soledad*, Madrid: Ediciones Cátedra.

_____ (1987), *Clandestine in Chile*, trans. Asa Zatz, New York: New York Review Books.

_____ (1988), 'The Solitude of Latin America (Nobel Lecture, 1982)', trans. Marina Castañeda, in Julio Ortega (ed.) with Claudia Elliott, *Gabriel García Márquez and the Powers of Fiction*, Austin: University of Texas Press, pp. 87–91.

_____ (1989 [1970]), *The Story of a Shipwrecked Sailor*, trans. Randolph Hogan, New York: Vintage.

_____ (2002), *Vivir para contarla*, Mexico City: Diana.

_____ (2003), *Living to Tell the Tale*, trans. Edith Grossman, New York: Alfred A. Knopf.

Geesey, Patricia (1996), 'Collective Autobiography: Algerian Women and History in Assia Djebar's *L'amour, la fantasia*', *Dalhousie French Studies*, 35, 153–67.

Ghaussey, Soheila (1994), 'A Stepmother Tongue: "Feminine Writing" in Assia Djebar's *Fantasia: An Algerian Cavalcade*', *World Literature Today*, 68, no. 3, 457–62.

al-Ghazālī (2014), *al-Munqidh min al-Ḍalāl wa-al-Mūṣil ilā Dhī al-'Izzah wa-al-Jalāl*, Tunis: Dār Kīrānīs lil-Ṭibā'ah wa-al-Nashr wa-al-Tawzī'.

Ghazoul, Ferial (1993), 'Idyulujīyat Binyat al-Qaṣṣ: Laṭīfa al-Zayyāt Namūdhajan', *Fuṣūl*, 12, no. 1, 108–22.

_____ (1994), 'Awrāq Shakhṣīyah: Namūdhajan li al- Ṣayrūra al-Dhātiyya', *Adab wa Naqd*, 106, 36–48.

_____ (1996), 'al-Muqāwamah 'abra al-Mufāraqah' (Resistance through Paradox), in Sayyid al- Baḥrāwī (ed.), *Laṭīfa al-Zayyāt al-Adab wa al-Waṭan*, Cairo: Nūr, Dār al-Mar'ah al- 'Arabiyah li-al-Nashr wa Markaz al-Buḥūth al-'Arabiyah li al-Nashr, pp. 197–200.

_____ (2003), 'Ṣun'allāh Ibrahīm wa Jamālīyāt al-Irbāk' (Sonallah Ibrahim and the Poetics of Confusion), *Akhbār al-Adab*, 9 November.

_____ (2007a), 'Afterword', in *The Loved Ones*, Alia Mamdouh, trans. Marilyn L. Booth, New York: The Feminist Press, pp. 301–24.

_____ (2007b), 'Rev. of *Children of the New World: A Novel of the Algerian War*, Assia Djebar', *Journal of Middle East Women's Studies*, 3, no. 2, 120–2.

_____ (2009a), 'Afterword', in *Dreaming of Baghdad*, Haifa Zangana, trans Haifa Zangana and Paul Hammond, New York: The Feminist Press, pp. 158–68.

_____ (2009b), 'Literature and the Arts in Contemporary Iraqi Culture', *International Journal of Contemporary Iraqi Studies*, 3, no. 3, 233–6.

_____ (2012), 'Darwish's *Mural*: The Echo of an Epic Hymn', *Interventions: International Journal of Postcolonial Studies*, 14, no. 1, 37–54.

Ghazoul, Ferial and Barbara Harlow (eds) (1994), *The View from Within: Writers and Critics on Contemporary Arabic Literature*, Cairo: American University in Cairo Press.

Gilmore, Leigh (2001), *The Limits of Autobiography: Trauma and Testimony*, Ithaca: Cornell University Press.

Gindi, Nadia (2000), 'On the Margins of a Memoir: A Personal Reading of Said's *Out of Place*', *Alif: Journal of Comparative Poetics*, 20, 284–98.

Gonzales-Quijano (1998), 'The Territory of Autobiography: Maḥmūd Darwīsh's *Memory for Forgetfulness*', trans. Hannah Davis, in Robin Ostle, Ed de Moor, and Stefan Wild (eds), *Writing the Self: Autobiographical Writing in Modern Arabic Literature*, London: Saqi Books, pp. 183–91.

Goodwin, James (1993), *Autobiography: The Self Made Text,* New York: Twayne Publishers.

Grace, Daphne M. (2007), 'Arab Women Write the Trauma of Imprisonment and Exile', in Nawar Al-Hassan Golley (ed.), *Arab Women's Lives Retold: Exploring Identity through Writing*, New York: Syracuse University Press, pp. 181–200.

Gracki, Katherine (1996), 'Writing Violence and the Violence of Writing in Assia Djebar's Algerian Quartet', *World Literature Today*, 70, no. 4, 835–43.

Green, Mary Jean (2013), 'Assia Djebar in the Twenty-First Century: Rewriting Identities', *Contemporary French and Francophone Studies*, 17, no. 1, 49–57.

Gusdorf, Georges (1972), 'Conditions and Limits of Autobiography', in James Olney (ed.), *Autobiography: Essays Theoretical and Critical*, Princeton: Princeton University Press, pp. 28–48.

Guth, Stephan (1998), 'Why Novels – Not Autobiographies? An Essay in the Analysis of a Historical Development', in Robin Ostle, Ed de Moor, and Stefan Wild (eds), *Writing the Self: Autobiographical Writing in Modern Arabic Literature*, London: Saqi Books, pp. 139–47.

Hafez, Sabry (1993), *The Genesis of Arabic Narrative Discourse: A Study in the Sociology of Modern Arabic Literature*, London: Saqi Books.

_____ (2002), 'Raqsh al-Dhāt la Kitābatiha: Taḥawwulāt al-Istratijīyāt al-Naṣṣiya fī al-Sīra al- Dhātiyya' (Variegating the Self: Transformation of Textual Strategies in Autobiography), *Alif: Journal of Comparative Poetics*, 22, 7–33.

_____ (2004), 'Edward Said's Intellectual Legacy in the Arab World', *Journal of Palestine Studies*, 33, no. 3, 76–90.

_____ (2010), 'Edward Said in Contemporary Arabic Culture', in Adel Iskandar and Hakem Rustom (eds), *Edward Said: A Legacy of Emancipation and Representation*, Berkeley: University of California Press, pp. 170–90.

_____ (2015), "Aliya Mamduḥ Kitabat al-Sīrah fī *al-Ajnabiyah*' (Alia Mamdouh: Writing Autobiography in *The Foreigner*), *Nizwa*, http://www.nizwa.com (accessed 21 September 2015).

Haidar, F. A (2005), 'Afterword', in *Naphtalene: A Novel of Baghdad*, Alia Mamdouh, trans. Peter Theroux, New York: The Feminist Press, pp. 191–212.

Hallaq, Boutros (1998), 'Autobiography and Polyphony', trans. Michelle Hartman, in Robin Ostle, Ed de Moor, and Stefan Wild (eds), *Writing the Self: Autobiographical Writing in Modern Arabic Literature*, London: Saqi Books, pp. 192–206.

Harlow, Barbara (1987), *Resistance Literature*, London: Methuen.

_____ (2012), 'The Geography and the Event', *Interventions: International Journal of Postcolonial Studies*, 14, no. 1, 13–23.

Hartman, Michelle (2004), '"Besotted with the Bright Lights of Imperialism"?: Arab Subjectivity Constructed against New York's Many Faces', *Journal of Arabic Literature*, 35, no. 3, 270–96.

_____ (2005), 'Writing Arabs and Africa(ns) in America: Adonis and Radwa 'Ashour from Harlem to Lady Liberty', *International Journal of Middle East Studies*, 37, no. 3, 397–420.

Hassan, Salah D. (2013), 'Baleful Postcoloniality and Auto/Biography', *Biography*, 36, no. 1, 1–9.

Hassan, Waïl S (2002), 'Arab-American Autobiography and the Reinvention of Identity: Two Egyptian Negotiations', *Alif: Journal of Comparative Poetics*, 22, 7–35.

_____ (2008), 'Translator's Introduction', in *Thou Shalt Not Speak My Language*, Abdelfattah Kilito, trans. Waïl S. Hassan, Syracuse: Syracuse University Press, pp. vii–xxvi.

_____ (2011), *Immigrant Narratives: Orientalism and Cultural Translation in Arab American and Arab British Literature*, New York: Oxford University Press.

Hiddleston, Jane (2011), 'The Mother as Other: Intimacy and Separation in the Maternal Memories of Assia Djebar's *Nulle part dans La maison de mon père*', *Journal of Romance Studies*, 11, no. 2, 21–33.

Hussein, Suzanne Taha (2011), *Avec Toi: De la France à l'Égypte*, Paris: Les Éditions du Cerf.

Hussein, Taha (1938), *Mustaqbal al-Thaqāfah fī Miṣr*, Cairo: Maṭba'at al-Ma'ārif.

______ (1995 [1926]), *Fī al-Shi'r al-Jāhilī*, Cairo: Dār al-Nahr.

______ (1997), *The Days*, trans E. H. Paxton, Hilary Wayment, and Kenneth Cragg, Cairo: The American University in Cairo Press.

Ibn Ḥazm, 'Alī ibn Aḥmad (1930), *Ṭawq al-Ḥamāmah fī al-Ulfa wa-l-Ullāf*, Damascus: Maktabat 'Arafah.

Ibn Khaldūn (1951), *Al-Ta'rīf bi-Ibn Khaldūn wa Riḥlatihi Gharban wa-Sharqan*, Cairo: Lajnat al-Ta'līf wa-al-Tarjamah wa-al-Nashr.

Ibrahīm, Salām (2007), Rev. of *Fī Arwiqat al-Dhākirah*, Haifa Zangana, *Al-Ḥiwār al-Mutamaddin*, 1826, http://ahewar.org/debat/show.art.asp?aid=88634 (accessed 1 April 2015).

Ibrahim, Sonallah (1986), *Tilka al-Rā'iḥa*, 4th edn, Cairo: Dār Shuhdī.

_____ (1993), *Dhāt*, 2nd edn, Cairo: Dār al-Mustaqbal al-'Arabī.

_____ (2003), 'Speech', *Akhbār al-Adab*, 26 October: 2–3.

_____ (2005), *Yawmīyyāt al-Wāḥāt*, Cairo: Dār al-Mustaqbal al-'Arabī.

_____ (2007), *al-Talaṣṣuṣ*, Cairo: Dār al-Mustaqbal al-'Arabī.

_____ (2008), *Le petit voyeur*, trans. Richard Jacquemond, Paris: Actes Sud.

_____ (2009), *Stealth*, trans. Hosam M. Aboul-Ela, London: Aflame.

_____ (2011a), *al-Jalīd*, Cairo: Dār al-Thaqāfah al-Jadīdah.

_____ (2011b), 'The Imagination as Transitive Act: An Interview with Sonallah

Ibrahim', Interview by Elliot Colla, *Jadaliyya,* 12 June, http://www.jadaliyya.com/pages/index/1811/the-imagination-as-transitive-act_an-interview-wit (accessed 28 March 2015).

_____ (2013a), *That Smell and Notes from Prison,* trans. and ed. Robyn Creswell, New York: New Directions.

_____ (2013b), 'You Have to Decide What Is Valuable and Fight for It', Interview by Maria Golla, *Prague Writers' Festival,* 24 January, http://www.pwf.cz/rubriky/pwf-2013/authors/interviews/sonallah-ibrahim-you-have-to-decide-what-is-valuable-and-fight-for-it_9591.html (accessed 28 March 2015).

_____ (2014), *Bīrlīn 69,* Cairo: Dār al-Thaqāfah al-Jadīdah.

al-'Īd, Yomna (1998), 'The Autobiographical Novel and the Dual Function', in Robin Ostle, Ed de Moor, and Stefan Wild (eds), *Writing the Self: Autobiographical Writing in Modern Arabic Literature,* London: Saqi Books, pp. 157–77.

Idris, Youssef (1986), 'Introduction', in *Tilka al-Rā'iḥa,* Cairo: Dār Shuhdī, pp. 25–9.

Iskandar, Adel and Hakem Rustom (2010), 'Introduction: Emancipation and Representation', in Adel Iskandar and Hakem Rustom (eds), *Edward Said: A Legacy of Emancipation and Representation,* Berkeley: University of California Press, pp. 1–22.

Jabra, Jabra Ibrahim (1993), *Al-Bi'r al-Ūlā: Fuṣūl min Sīra Dhātiyya,* Beirut: al-Mu'assasah al- 'Arabiyah lil-Dirāsāt wa al-Nashr.

_____ (1994), *Shāri' al-Amīrāt: Fuṣūl min Sīra Dhātiyya,* Beirut: al-Mu'assasah al-'Arabiyah lil-Dirāsāt wa al-Nashr.

_____ (1995), *The First Well: A Bethlehem Boyhood,* trans. Issa J. Boullata, Fayetteville, AS: University of Arkansas Press.

_____ (2005), *Princesses' Street: Baghdad Memories,* trans. Issa J. Boullata, Fayetteville, AS: University of Arkansas Press.

Jacquemond, Richard (2008), *Conscience of the Nation: Writers, State, and Society in Modern Egypt,* trans. David Tresilian, Cairo: American University in Cairo Press.

Jameson, Fredric (1986), 'Third-World Literature in the Era of Multinational Capitalism', *Social Text,* 15, 65–88.

Jayyusi, Salma Khadra (ed.) (1992), *Anthology of Modern Palestinian Literature,* New York: Columbia University Press.

Jayyusi, Salma Khadra (2008), 'Foreword: "Mahmoud Darwish's Mission and Place in Arab Literary History"', in Hala Khamis Nassar and Najat Rahman (eds), *Mahmoud Darwish: Exile's Poet,* Northampton, MA: Interlink Books, pp. vii–xiv.

_____ (ed.) (1992), *Anthology of Modern Palestinian Literature*, New York: Columbia University Press.

Johnson, Penny and Raja Shehadeh (eds) (2013), *Seeking Palestine: New Palestinian Writing on Exile and Home*, Northampton, MA: Olive Branch Press.

Johnson-Davies, Denys (1980), 'Introduction', in *The Music of Human Flesh*, Mahmoud Darwish, London: Heinemann, pp. vii–xvii.

Joudah, Fady (2007), 'Translator's Preface', in *The Butterfly's Burden: Poems by Mahmoud Darwish*, trans. Fady Joudah, Port Townsend, WA: Copper Canyon Press, pp. xi–xvii.

_____ (2009a), 'Introduction: Mahmoud Darwish's Lyric Epic', in *If I Were Another*, trans. Fady Joudah, New York: Farrar, Straus and Giroux, pp. vii–xxviii.

_____ (2009b), 'Mahmoud Darwish's Lyrical Epic', *Human Architecture*, VII (Special Issue), 7–18.

Joyce, James (1991), *A Portrait of the Artist as a Young Man*, New York: Penguin.

Kahf, Mohja (2010), 'Packaging "Huda": Sha'rawi's Memoirs in the United States Reception Environment', in Mona Baker (ed.), *Critical Readings in Translation Studies*, London: Routledge, pp. 28–45.

Kaplan, Caren (1992), 'Resisting Autobiography: Out-law Genres and Transnational Feminist Subjects', in Sidonie Smith and Julia Watson (eds), *De/Colonizing the Subject*, Minneapolis: University of Minnesota Press, pp. 115–38.

Kassem-Draz, Céza (1982), 'Opaque and Transparent Discourse: A Contrastive Analysis of the *Star of August* and "The Man of the High Dam" by Son' Allah Ibrahim', *Alif: Journal of Comparative Poetics*, 2, 32–50.

Kazantzis, Judith (2008), 'The Great World Poet', *Banipal*, 33, 43.

Khalidi, Rashid (1997), *Palestinian Identity: The Construction of Modern National Consciousness*, New York: Columbia University Press.

_____ (2008), 'Remembering Mahmud Darwish (1941–2008)', *Journal of Palestine Studies*, 38, no. 1, 74–7.

Khatibi, Abdelkebir (1971), *La Mémoire tatouée: autobiographie d'un decolonisé*, Paris: Les Lettres nouvelles.

_____ (1990), *Love in Two Languages*, trans. Richard Howard, Minneapolis: University of Minnesota Press.

Khoury, Elias (1996a), 'Al-Shāhid al-Shahīd: Taḥīyah īla Laṭīfa al-Zayyāt', in Sayyid al- Baḥrāwī (ed.), *Laṭīfa al-Zayyāt al-Adab wa al-Waṭan*, Cairo: Nūr, Dār al-Mar'ah al- 'Arabiyah li-al-Nashr wa Markaz al-Buḥūth al-'Arabiyah li al-Nashr, pp. 111–13.

_____ (1996b), 'Narā bi 'Uyūniha', *Adab wa Naqd*, 135, 47–8.

_____ (2009), 'The Poet Is Dead: Elias Khoury Remembers His Friend Mahmoud Darwish', *The Arab Studies Journal*, 17, no. 1, 100–9.

Kilito, Abdelfattah (2008), *Thou Shalt Not Speak My Language*, trans. Waïl S. Hassan, Syracuse: Syracuse University Press.

Kilpatrick, Hilary (1991), 'Autobiography and Classical Arabic Literature', *Journal of Arabic Literature*, 22, 1–20.

Kilpatrick, Hilary (1992), 'The Egyptian Novel from *Zaynab* to 1980', in M. M. Badawi (ed.), *Modern Arabic Literature*, Cambridge: Cambridge University Press, pp. 223–69.

Lachman, Kathryn (2010), 'The Allure of Counterpoint: History and Reconciliation in the Writing of Edward Said and Assia Djebar', *Research in African Literatures*, 41, no. 4, 162–86.

Langley, Tom (2012), 'Exceptional States', *Interventions: International Journal of Postcolonial Studies*, 69–82.

Lejeune, Philippe (1975), *Le pacte autobiographique*, Paris: Éditions du Seuil.

_____ (1982), 'The Autobiographical Contract', in Tzvetan Todorov (ed.), *French Literary Theory*, Cambridge: Cambridge University Press, pp. 192–222.

_____ (1989), *On Autobiography*, trans. Katherine Leary, Minneapolis: University of Minnesota Press.

Lindsey, Ursula (2010), 'Sonallah Ibrahim: Closure by Stealth', *The National*, 25 June, http://www.thenational.ae/news/world/sonallah-ibrahim-closure-by-stealth#full (accessed 28 March 2015).

Lionnet, Françoise (1989), *Autobiographical Voices: Race, Gender, Self-Portraiture*, Ithaca: Cornell University Press.

_____ (1995), *Postcolonial Representations: Women, Literature, Identity*, Ithaca: Cornell University Press.

_____ (1998), 'The Politics and Aesthetics of Métissage', in Sidonie Smith and Julia Watson (eds), *Women, Autobiography, Theory: A Reader*, Madison: The University of Wisconsin Press, pp. 325–36.

Luca, Ioana (2006), 'Edward Said's *Lieux de Mémoire*: *Out of Place* and the Politics of Autobiography', *Social Text*, 24, no. 2, 125–44.

Makdisi, Jean Said (1990), *Beirut Fragments: A War Memoir*, New York: Pesea Books.

_____ (2005), *Teta, Mother, and Me: An Arab Woman's Memoir*, London: Saqi Books.

Makhzangi, Mohamed (2006), *Memories of a Meltdown: An Egyptian between Moscow and Chernobyl*, trans. Samah Selim, Cairo: American University in Cairo Press.

Malas, Mohamad (2016), 'Portrait of a Friend: Sonallah Ibrahim', trans. Margaret Litvin, *Alif: Journal of Comparative Poetics*, 36, 201–25.

Malti-Douglas, Fedwa (1988), *Blindness and Autobiography: Al-Ayyam of Taha Husayn*, Princeton: Princeton University Press.

Mamdouh, Alia (1986), *Ḥabbāt al-naftālīn*, Cairo: GEBO.

_____ (1998), 'Creatures of Arab Fear', in Fadia Faqir (ed.), *In the House of Silence: Autobiographical Essays by Arab Women Writers*, trans Shirley Eber and Fadia Faqir, Reading: Garnet Publishing, pp. 65–71.

_____ (2002), 'Anā: Shadharāt min Sīrat al-Shaghaf (Me: Fragments from a History of Infatuation)', *Alif: Journal of Comparative Poetics*, 22, 203–7.

_____ (2005), *Naphtalene: A Novel of Baghdad*, trans. Peter Theroux, New York: The Feminist Press.

_____ (2013), *Al-Ajnabīyah: Buyūt Riwā'iyah* (The Foreigner), Beirut: Dār al-Adāb.

Manguel, Alberto (2008), 'Mahmoud Darwish: "I don't belong to myself"', *Banipal*, 33, 30–1.

Manisty, Dinah (1998), 'Negotiating the Space between Private and Public: Women's Autobiographical Writing in Egypt', in Robin O. Ostle, Ed de Moor, and Stefan Wild (eds), *Writing the Self: Autobiographical Writing in Modern Arabic Literature*, London: Saqi Books, pp. 272–82.

Marx-Scouras, Danielle (1993), 'Muffled Screams/Stifled Voices', *Yale French Studies*, 82, 172–82.

Masmoudi, Ikram (2010), 'Portraits of Iraqi Women: Between Testimony and Fiction', *International Journal of Contemporary Iraqi Studies*, 4, nos 1 and 2, 59–77.

Matar, Hisham (2016), *The Return: Fathers, Sons and the Land in Between*, London: Viking.

Mattawa, Khaled (2014), *Mahmoud Darwish: The Poet's Art and His Nation*, New York: Syracuse University Press.

Mehrez, Samia (1992), 'Translation and the Postcolonial Experience: The Francophone North African Text', in Lawrence Venuti (ed.), *Rethinking Translation: Discourse, Subjectivity, Ideology*, London: Routledge, pp. 120–38.

_____ (1994), *Egyptian Writers between History and Fiction: Essays on Naguib Mahfouz, Sonallah Ibrahim, and Gamal al-Ghitani*, Cairo: American University in Cairo Press.

_____ (1996), 'Kitabat al-Waṭan: Laṭīfa al-Zayyāt bayna al-Bāb al-Maftūḥ wa Ḥamlat Taftīsh', in Sayyid al-Baḥrāwī (ed.), *Laṭīfa al-Zayyāt al-Adab wa al-Waṭan*, Cairo: Nūr, Dār al-Mar'ah al-'Arabiyah li-al-Nashr wa Markaz al-Buḥūth al-'Arabiyah li al-Nashr, pp. 137–41.

_____ (2002), '*Ahmed de Bourgogne*: The Impossible Autobiography of a *Clandestine*', *Alif: Journal of Comparative Poetics*, 22, 36–71.

_____ (2003), 'The Value of Freedom', *Al-Ahram Weekly Online*, 30 October–5 November.

_____ (2008), *Egypt's Culture Wars: Politics and Practice*, London: Routledge.

Memmi, Albert (1965 [1957]), *The Colonizer and the Colonized*, Boston: Beacon Press.

______ (1966), *La Statue de sel*, Paris: Gallimard.

Mernissi, Fatima (1995), *Dreams of Trespass: Tales of a Harem Girlhood*, Cambridge, MA: Perseus Books.

Meruane, Lina (2013), *Volverse Palestina*, Barcelona: Penguin Random House.

Misch, Georg (1973), *A History of Autobiography in Antiquity*, 2 vols, Westport, CT: Greenwood Press.

Molloy, Sylvia (1991), *At Face Value: Autobiographical Writing in Spanish America*, Cambridge: Cambridge University Press.

Moor, Ed de (1998), 'Autobiography, Theory and Practice: The Case of al-Ayyām', in Robin Ostle, Ed de Moor, and Stefan Wild (eds), *Writing the Self: Autobiographical Writing in Modern Arabic Literature*, London: Saqi Books, pp. 128–38.

Moore, Lindsey (2013), 'Ruins, Rifts and the Remainder: Palestinian Memoirs by Edward Said and Raja Shehadeh', *Postcolonial Studies*, 16, no. 1, 28–45.

Moore-Gilbert, Bart (2009), *Postcolonial Life-Writing: Culture, Politics and Self-Representation*, London: Routledge.

_____ (2013), '"Baleful Postcoloniality" and Palestinian Women's Life Writing', *Biography*, 36, no. 1, 51–70.

Moretti, Franco (1996), *Modern Epic: The World System from Goethe to Garcia Marquez*, trans. Quintin Hoare, New York: Verso.

_____ (2000), *The Way of the World: The Bildungsroman in European Culture*, trans. Albert Sbragia, London: Verso.

Moretti, Franco (2005), 'World-Systems Analysis, Evolutionary Theory, "Weltliterature"', *Review (Fernand Braudel Center)*, 28, no. 3, 217–28.

_____ (2013), *Distant Reading*, London: Verso.

Morsy, Faten (2009), 'The University in *The Open Door* and *Aṭyāf*', *Alif: Journal of Comparative Poetics*, 29, 139–52.

Mortimer, Mildred (1988), 'Entretien avec Assia Djebar, Écrivain Algérien', *Research in African Literatures*, 19, no. 2, 197–205.

_____ (1996), 'Reappropriating the Gaze in Assia Djebar's Fiction and Film', *World Literature Today*, 70, no. 4, 859–66.

_____ (1997), 'Assia Djebar's "*Algerian Quartet*": A Study in Fragmented Autobiography', *Research in African Literatures*, 28, no. 2, 102–17.

_____ (2005), 'Edward Said and Assia Djebar: A Contrapuntal Reading', *Research in African Literatures*, 36, no. 3, 53–67.

_____ (2013), 'Writing the Personal: The Evolution of Assia Djebar's Autobiographical Project from *L'Amour, La Fantasia* to *Nulle Part Dans La Maison de mon Père*', *Journal of Women's History*, 25, no. 2, 111–29.

Mostafa, Dalia Said (2011), 'Son'allah Ibrahim's al-Talaṣṣus: The Politics of Modernity in Egypt through the Child-Narrator's Lens', *Journal of Postcolonial Writing*, 47, no. 4, 416–27.

Muhawi, Ibrahim (1995), 'Introduction', in *Memory for Forgetfulness: August, Beirut, 1982*, Mahmoud Darwish, trans. Ibrahim Muhawi, Berkeley: University of California Press, xi–xxx.

_____ (2010), 'Foreword', in *Journal of an Ordinary Grief*, Mahmoud Darwish, trans. Ibrahim Muhawi, New York: Archipelago Books, pp. ix–xiii.

Murdoch, H. Adlai (1993), 'Rewriting Writing: Identity, Exile and Renewal in Assia Djebar's *L'amour, la fantasia*', *Yale French Studies*, 83, 71–92.

Naaman, Mara (2006), 'America Undone: Sonallah Ibrahim's Intra-Imperial Investigations', *Alif: Journal of Comparative Poetics*, 26, 71–93.

al-Nakib, Mai (2005), 'Assia Djebar's Musical Ekphrasis', *Comparative Literature Studies*, 42, no. 4, 253–76.

al-Naqqāsh, Rajā' (1972), *Mahmoud Darwish: Shā'ir al-Ard al-Muḥtallah*, Beirut: Mu'assasat al-Abḥāth al-'Arabiyah.

Neruda, Pablo (1970), *Isla Negra: A Notebook*, trans. Alastair Reid, New York: Farrar, Straus and Giroux.

_____ (1971), 'Nobel Lecture: Towards the Splendid City', 13 December, http://www.nobelprize.org/nobel_prizes/literature/laureates/1971/neruda-lecture.html (accessed 21 September 2015).

_____ (2001), *Memoirs*, trans. Hardie St. Martin, New York: Farrar, Straus and Giroux.

_____ (2007), 'Explico Algunas Cosas' ('I Explain a Few Things'), trans. Galway Kinnell, in Ilan Stavans (ed.), *I Explain a Few Things: Selected Poems*, Pablo Neruda, New York: Farrar, Straus and Giroux, pp. 29–33.

al-Nowaihi, Magda (2001), 'Resisting Silence in Arab Women's Autobiographies', *International Journal of Middle East Studies*, 33, no. 4, 477–502.

Nu ʿaymah, Mikhail (1962), *Sabʿūn. Ḥikayat ʿUmr*, vol. I, Beirut: Sadir.
Olney, James (ed.) (1980), *Autobiography: Essays Theoretical and Critical*, Princeton: Princeton University Press.
Ostle, Robin (1998), Introduction, in Robin Ostle, Ed de Moor, and Stefan Wild (eds), *Writing the Self: Autobiographical Writing in Modern Arabic Literature*, London: Saqi Books, pp. 18–23.
Ouyang, Wen-Chin (2007), 'Interview with Haifa Zangana', *Comparative Critical Studies*, 4, no. 3, 447–53.
Pascal, Roy (1960), *Design and Truth in Autobiography*, Cambridge, MA: Harvard University Press.
Paz, Octavio (1985), *The Labyrinth of Solitude*, trans Lysander Kemp, Yara Milos, and Rachel Phillips Belash, New York: Grove Press.
Pellat, Ch (2012), 'Ibn Djubayr', in P. Bearman, Th. Bianquis, C. E. Bosworth, E. van Donzel, and W. P. Heinrichs (eds), *Encyclopaedia of Islam*, 2nd edn, Brill online, http://dx.doi.org/10.1163/1573-3912_islam_SIM_3145 (accessed 14 June 2016).
Philipp, Thomas (1990), *The Autobiography of Jurji Zaidan, Including Four Letters to His Son*, Washington, DC: Three Continents Press.
_____ (1993), 'The Autobiography in Modern Arab Literature and Culture', *Poetics Today*, 14, no. 3, 573–604.
Prince, Mona (2011), *So You May See*, trans. Raphael Cohen, Cairo: American University in Cairo Press.
_____ (2012), *Ismī Thawra*, Cairo: n.p.
_____ (2014), *Revolution Is My Name: An Egyptian Woman's Diary from Eighteen Days in Tahrir*, trans. Samia Mehrez, Cairo: American University in Cairo Press.
al-Qāsim, Samīh et al. (eds) (1999), *Maḥmūd Darwīsh, al-Mukhtalif al-Ḥaqīqī: Dirasāt wa Shahadāt*, ʿAmmān: Dār al-Shurūq lil-Nashr wa al-Tawzīʿ.
Rachid, Amina (1995a), 'Al-Tārīkh wa al-Adab fī Kitabāt al-Mar'a', *Nur*, 5, 4–5.
_____ (1995b), 'Laṭīfa al-Zayyāt, Sīra Dhātiyya', *Nur*, 5, 7–9.
Rachid, Amina, Radwa Ashour, Sayyid al-Bahrawi, Itidal ʿUthman, and Farida al-Naqqash (1994), 'Dr. Laṭīfa al-Zayyāt Tuḥadithuna: al-Ibdāʿ wa al-Siyāsah Abqayānī ʿalā Qadamayy', *Adab wa Naqd*, 67–91.
Rahman, Najat (2008), 'Interview with Mahmoud Darwish: On the Possibility of Poetry at a Time of Siege', in Hala Khamis and Najat Rahman (eds), *Mahmoud Darwish: Exile's Poet*, Northampton, MA: Olive Branch Press, pp. 319–26.
Rakha, Youssef (2007), 'Sonallah Ibrahim: Imagining Stasis', *Al-Ahram Weekly Online*, 15–21 February.

Ramazani, Jahan (2010), 'Edward Said and the Poetry of Decolonization', in Adel Iskandar and Hakem Rustom (eds), *Edward Said: A Legacy of Emancipation and Representation*, Berkeley: University of California Press, pp. 159–69.

Reigeluth, Stuart (2008), 'The Art of Repetition: The Poetic Prose of Mahmoud Darwish and Mourid Barghouti', in Hala Khamis Nassar and Najat Rahman (eds), *Mahmoud Darwish, Exile's Poet: Critical Essays*, Northampton, MA: Olive Branch Press, pp. 293–318.

Reynolds, Dwight F. (ed.) (2001), *Interpreting the Self: Autobiography in the Arabic Literary Tradition*, Berkeley: University of California Press.

Roche, Anne (1992), 'Women's Literature in Algeria', *Research in African Literatures*, 23, no. 2, 209–15.

Rooke, Tetz (1997), *In My Childhood: A Study of Arabic Autobiography*, Stockholm: Stockholm University.

_____ (1998), 'The Arabic Autobiography of Childhood', in Robin Ostle, Ed de Moor, and Stefan Wild (eds), *Writing the Self: Autobiographical Writing in Modern Arabic Literature*, London: Saqi Books, pp. 100–14.

_____ (2008), '*In the Presence of Absence*: Mahmoud Darwish's Testament', *Journal of Arabic and Islamic Studies*, 8, 11–25.

Rubin, Andrew N. (2008), 'Foreword', in Edward Said, *Joseph Conrad and the Fiction of Autobiography*, New York: Columbia University Press, pp. ix–xviii.

Sacks, Jeffrey (2015), *Iterations of Loss: Mutilation and Aesthetic Form, Al-Shidyaq to Darwish*, New York: Fordham University Press.

Sa'di, Ahmad H. and Lila Abu-Lughod (eds) (2007), *Nakba: Palestine, 1948, and the Claims of Memory*, New York: Columbia University Press.

Said, Edward (1978), *Orientalism*, London: Penguin.

_____ (1979), *The Question of Palestine*, New York: Vintage.

_____ (1983), *The World, The Text, The Critic*, Cambridge, MA: Harvard University Press.

_____ (1993), *Culture and Imperialism*, New York: Vintage.

_____ (1994), 'On Mahmoud Darwish', *Grand Street*, 12, no. 4, 112–15.

_____ (1996), *Representations of the Intellectual*, New York: Vintage.

_____ (1999a), *After the Last Sky: Palestinian Lives*, New York: Columbia University Press.

_____ (1999b), *Out of Place: A Memoir*, New York: Alfred A. Knopf.

_____ (1999c), 'The Hazards of Publishing a Memoir', *Al-Ahram Weekly*, 2–9 December.

_____ (2000a), 'Foreword', in *I Saw Ramallah*, Mourid Barghouti, trans. Ahdaf Soueif, Cairo: The American University in Cairo Press, pp. vii–xi.

_____ (2000b), *The Edward Said Reader*, eds Moustafa Bayoumi and Andrew Rubin, New York: Vintage Books.

_____ (2000c), 'An Interview with Edward W. Said', in Moustafa Bayoumi and Andrew Rubin (eds), *The Edward Said Reader*, New York: Vintage Books, pp. 419–44.

_____ (2000d), *Reflections on Exile and Other Essays*, Cambridge, MA: Harvard University Press.

_____ (2001), *Power, Politics, and Culture: Interviews with Edward W. Said*, ed. Gauri Viswanathan, New York: Pantheon Books.

_____ (2004), *Humanism and Democratic Criticism*, New York: Palgrave Macmillan.

_____ (2005), 'The Public Role of Writers', in Sandra Bermann and Michael Wood (eds), *Nation, Language, and the Ethics of Translation*, Princeton: Princeton University Press, pp. 15–29.

_____ (2006), *On Late Style: Music and Literature against the Grain*, New York: Pantheon Books.

_____ (2008 [1967]), *Joseph Conrad and the Fiction of Autobiography*, New York: Columbia University Press.

Said, Najla (2007), 'Tribute to My Father', in Ferial Ghazoul (ed.), *Edward Said and Critical Decolonization*, Cairo: American University in Cairo Press, pp. 21–5.

_____ (2013), *Looking for Palestine: Growing Up Confused in an Arab-American Family*, New York: Penguin.

Sankara, Edgard (2011), *Postcolonial Francophone Autobiographies: From Africa to the Antilles*, Charlottesville: University of Virginia Press.

Santí, Enrico Mario (1982), *Pablo Neruda, the Poetics of Prophecy*, Ithaca: Cornell University Press.

Seyhan, Azade (2003), 'Enduring Grief: Autobiography as "Poetry of Witness" in the Work of Assia Djebar and Nazim Hikmet', *Comparative Literature Studies*, 40, no. 2, 159–72.

Shaarawi, Huda (1981), *Mudhakkirāt Huda Sha'rawi*, Cairo: Dār al-Hilāl.

_____ (1986), *Harem Years: The Memoirs of an Egyptian Feminist (1879–1924)*, trans and ed. Margot Badran, London: Virago Press.

Shaheen, Mohammad (2009), 'Introduction', in *Almond Blossoms and Beyond*, Mahmoud Darwish, Northampton, MA: Interlink Books, pp. vii–xi.

Sharawi Lanfranchi, Sania (2012), *Casting off the Veil: The Life of Huda Shaarawi Egypt's First Feminist*, ed. John Keith King, London: I. B. Tauris.

Sheehi, Stephen (2004), *Foundations of Modern Arab Identity*, Gainesville: University Press of Florida.

Shehadeh, Raja (2002), *Strangers in the House: Coming of Age in Occupied Palestine*, New York: Penguin.

_____ (2003), *When the Birds Stopped Singing: Life in Ramallah under Siege*, Hanover, NH: Steerforth Press.

_____ (2007), *Palestinian Walks: Forays into a Vanishing Landscape*, New York: Simon & Schuster.

Shidyāq, Aḥmad Fāris and Nasīb Wahībah Khāzin (1966), *Al-Sāq 'ala al-Sāq fī mā huwa al- Fāryāq: aw Ayyām wa-Shuhūr wa-A'wām fī 'Ajam al-'Arab wa al-A'jām*, Beirut: Dār Maktabat al-Ḥayāh.

Shuiskii, Sergei A. (1982), 'Some Observations on Modern Arabic Autobiography', *Journal of Arabic Literature*, 13, 111–23.

Siddiq, Muhammad (2010), 'Significant but Problematic Others: Negotiating "Israelis" in the Works of Mahmoud Darwish', *Comparative Literature Studies*, 47, no. 4, 487–503.

Smith, Sidonie and Julia Watson (1998), 'Introduction: Situating Subjectivity in Women's Autobiographical Practices', in Sidonie Smith and Julia Watson (eds), *Women, Autobiography, Theory: A Reader*, Madison: The University of Wisconsin Press, pp. 3–52.

Soueif, Ahdaf (2000), 'Becoming Edward Said', Rev. of *Out of Place: A Memoir*, *Journal of Palestine Studies*, 29, no. 3, 90–6.

_____ (2012), *Cairo: My City, Our Revolution*, London: Bloomsbury.

_____ (2014), *Cairo: Memoir of a City Transformed*, New York: Anchor Books.

Starkey, Paul (2006a), '"Heroes" and Characters in the Novels of Sun'allāh Ibrāhīm', *Middle Eastern Literatures*, 9, no. 2, 147–57.

_____ (2006b), *Modern Arabic Literature*, Edinburgh: Edinburgh University Press.

_____ (2016), *Sonallah Ibrahim: Rebel with a Pen*, Edinburgh: Edinburgh University Press.

Sylvain, Patrick (2009), 'Darwish's Essentialist Poetics in a State of Siege', *Human Architecture*, VII, 137–50.

Tageldin, Shaden M. (2009), 'Which *Qalam* for Algeria?: Colonialism, Liberation, and Language in Djebar's *L'Amour, la Fantasia* and Mustaghanimi's *Dhākirat al-Jasad*', *Comparative Literature Studies*, 46, no. 3, 467–97.

_____ (2012), 'Proxidistant Reading: Toward a Critical Pedagogy of the Nahdah in U.S. Comparative Literary Studies', *Journal of Arabic Literature*, 43, nos 2–3, 227–68.

Tahon, Marie-Blanche (1992), 'Women Novelists and Women in the Struggle for Algeria's National Liberation (1957–1980)', *Research in African Literatures*, 23, no. 2, 39–50.

Tuqan, Fadwa (1985), *Riḥlah Jabalīyah, Riḥlah ṣaʿbah*, ʿAmmān: Dār al-Shurūq.

_____ (1990), *A Mountainous Journey: An Autobiography*, trans Olive Kenny and Naomi Shihab Nye, St Paul, MN: Graywolf Press.

_____ (1993), *Al-Riḥlah al-Aṣʿab: Sīrah Dhātiyya*, ʿAmmān: Dār al-Shurūq.

Turki, Fawaz (1972), *The Disinherited: Journal of a Palestinian Exile*, New York: Monthly Review Press.

_____ (1988), *Soul in Exile: Lives of a Palestinian Revolutionary*, New York: Monthly Review Press.

_____ (1994), *Exile's Return: The Making of a Palestinian American*, New York: Free Press.

Turner, Bryan (2000), 'Edward Said and the Exilic Ethic: On Being Out of Place', *Theory, Culture & Society*, 17, no. 6, 125–9.

Usāmah ibn Munqidh (1930), *Kitāb al-Iʿtibār*, Princeton: Maṭbaʿat Jāmiʿat Prinstūn.

Watson, Julia (1988), 'Shadowed Presence: Modern Women Writers' Autobiographies and the Other', in James Olney (ed.), *Studies in Autobiography*, New York: Oxford University Press, pp. 180–9.

Wazen, Abdo (2006), *Mahmoud Darwish: al-Gharīb Yaqaʿu ʿalā Nafsih: Qirāʾa fī Aʿmālih al-Jadīdah*, Beirut: Riad El-Rayyes.

_____ (2008), 'The Timeless Poet Who Created his Own Modernity', trans. Elliott Colla, *Banipal*, 33, 26–8.

Weintraub, Karl (1978), *The Value of the Individual Self: Circumstance in Autobiography*, Chicago: University of Chicago Press.

Whitlock, Gillian (2007), *Soft Weapons: Autobiography in Transit*. Chicago: University of Chicago Press.

Wild, Stefan (1998), 'Searching for Beginnings in Modern Arabic Autobiography', in Robin Ostle, Ed de Moor, and Stefan Wild (eds), *Writing the Self: Autobiographical Writing in Modern Arabic Literature*, London: Saqi Books, pp. 82–99.

Wood, Michael (2007), 'Desperate Youth', in Ferial Ghazoul (ed.), *Edward Said and Critical Decolonization*, Cairo: American University in Cairo Press, pp. 12–14.

Woodhull, Winifred (1993), *Transformations of the Maghreb: Feminism, Decolonization and Literature*, Minneapolis: University of Minneapolis Press.

Zangana, Haifa (1995), *Fī Arwiqat al-Dhākirah*, London: Dār al-Ḥikmah.

_____ (2007), 'Introduction', in *Women on a Journey between Baghdad and London*, trans. Haifa Zangana, Austin: University of Texas Press, pp. ix–xvi.

_____ (2009a), *Dreaming of Baghdad*, trans Haifa Zangana and Paul Hammond, New York: The Feminist Press.

_____ (2009b), 'Iraqi Resistance Has Its Song', *International Journal of Contemporary Iraqi Studies*, 3, no. 3, 277–86.

_____ (2012), 'Solitude and Dream: Literature Post-9/11', Interview by Frances Pinter, *Open Democracy*, 19 June 2012, https://www.opendemocracy.net/frances-pinter-haifa-zanaga/solitude-and-dream-literature-post-911 (accessed 16 May 2015).

_____ (2015), 'A Non-Personal Portrait: Remembrance of a Hybrid Origin', *Alif: Journal of Comparative Poetics*, 35, 253–69.

Zaydān, Jurjī (1968), *Mudhakkirāt Jurjī Zaydān*, Beirut: Dār al-Kitāb al-Jadīd.

al-Zayyat, Latifa (1986), *Al-Shaykhūkhah wa Qiṣaṣ Ukhrā* (Old Age and Other Stories: A Short Story Collection), Cairo: Dār al-Mustaqbal al-'Arabi.

_____ (1989), *Al-Bāb al-Maftūḥ*, Cairo: General Egyptian Book Organization.

_____ (1991), 'Shihādah (Testimony)', *Fuṣūl*, 9, no. 43, 183–6.

_____ (1992a), 'Al-Kātib wa al-Ḥuriyyah' (The Writer and Freedom), *Fuṣūl*, 11, no. 3, 237–9.

_____ (1992b), *Ḥamlat Taftīsh: Awrāq Shakhṣīyyah*, Cairo: Dār al-Hilāl.

_____ (1993), 'Laṭīfa al-Zayyāt fī mir'āt Laṭīfa al-Zayyāt (Latifa al-Zayyat in the Mirror of Latifa al-Zayyat)', *'Ibdā'*, 12, 54–8.

_____ (1994a), 'Ḥawla Kitāb Ḥamlat Taftīsh', *Adab wa naqd*, 106, 32–5.

_____ (1994b), 'On Political Commitment and Feminist Writing', in Ferial Ghazoul and Barbara Harlow (eds), *The View from Within: Writers and Critics on Contemporary Arabic Literature*, Cairo: American University in Cairo Press, pp. 246–60.

_____ (1994c), *Ṣāḥib al-Bayt*, Cairo: Riwāyāt al-Hilāl.

_____ (1996a), 'Shihadāt Mubdi'ah' (Testimony of a Writer), *Adab wa Naqd*, 135, 17–20.

_____ (1996b), *The Search: Personal Papers*, trans. Sophie Bennett, London: Quartet Books.

_____ (1997a), 'My Experience of Writing', in *The Owner of the House*, trans. Sophie Bennett, London: Quartet Books.

_____ (1997b), *The Owner of the House*, trans. Sophie Bennett, London: Quartet Books.

_____ (2000), *The Open Door*, trans. Marilyn Booth, Cairo: American University in Cairo Press.

Zimra, Clarisse (1992), 'A Woman's Memory Spans Centuries', *Women of Algiers in Their Apartment*, Assia Djebar, Charlottesville, VA: University Press of Virginia, pp. 167–87.

_____ (1993), 'When the Past Answers Our Present: Assia Djebar Talks About *Loin de Médine*', *Callaloo*, 16, no. 1, 116–31.

_____ (1995), 'Disorienting the Subject in Djebar's *L'Amour, la fantasia*', *Yale French Studies*, 149–70.

_____ (2005), 'Afterword', in *Children of the New World*, Assia Djebar, trans. Marjolijn de Jager, New York: The Feminist Press, pp. 201–33.

Index

EU Authorised Representative:
Easy Access System Europe Mustamäe tee 50, 10621 Tallinn, Estonia
gpsr.requests@easproject.com

Printed and bound by CPI Group (UK) Ltd, Croydon, CR0 4YY
26/05/2025
01882820-0001